Theory-Based Assessment, Treatment, and Prevention of Sexual Aggression

Theory-Based Assessment, Treatment, and Prevention of Sexual Aggression

GORDON C. NAGAYAMA HALL

New York   Oxford
OXFORD UNIVERSITY PRESS
1996

Oxford University Press

Oxford   New York
Athens   Auckland   Bangkok   Bombay
Calcutta   Cape Town   Dar es Salaam   Delhi
Florence   Hong Kong   Istanbul   Karachi
Kuala Lumpur   Madras   Madrid   Melbourne
Mexico City   Nairobi   Paris   Singapore
Taipei   Tokyo   Toronto

and associated companies in
Berlin   Ibadan

Published by Oxford University Press, Inc.,
198 Madison Avenue, New York, New York 10016

Oxford is a registered trademark of Oxford University Press

Library of Congress Cataloging-in-Publication Data
Hall, Gordon C. Nagayama.
Theory-based assessment, treatment, and prevention of sexual
aggression / Gordon C. Nagayama Hall.
p.   cm.
Includes bibliographical references and index.
ISBN 0-19-509039-X
1. Sex crimes.   2. Sex offenders.   I. Title.
[DNLM: 1. Sex Offenses—prevention & control.   2. Aggression—
psychology.   3. Models, Psychological.   WM 611 H176t 1996]
RC560.S47H35   1996
616.85'83—dc20
DNLM/DLC   95-14353
for Library of Congress

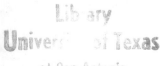
9 8 7 6 5 4 3 2 1

Printed in the United States of America
on acid-free paper

To Uni, Zomi, and Nathan

Preface

Sexual aggression is a pervasive social problem, with devastating and sometimes permanent effects on victims. Unlike other problems of aggression, however, there has been a disproportionate amount of attention paid to victim-based methods of preventing sexual aggression. Perhaps the lack of emphasis on perpetrators of sexual aggression reflects society's denial of responsibility for sexually aggressive behavior. Sexually aggressive behavior is interpreted by some perpetrators as simply an assertion of the masculine role. Thus, a societal emphasis on perpetrators would constitute an admission, particularly on the part of males, of a shared responsibility for the existence of sexually aggressive behavior.

The emphasis in this book is on perpetrators and potential perpetrators of sexually aggressive behavior. Insofar as the vast majority of sexual aggressors are male, the focus of this book is on male perpetrators. In the introduction, I make a case for an emphasis on perpetrators in addressing the problem of sexual aggression.

The literature on the assessment and treatment of sexually aggressive behavior has reached a level of development that warrants critique as well as integration. There is a relatively large body of literature on clinical interventions with sexual offenders. However, there have been few attempts to integrate this literature into a theoretical framework. Those attempts at building theoretical frameworks have tended to be too complex to guide clinical applications. The goal of this book is to develop the quadripartite model of sexual aggression (Hall & Hirschman, 1991, 1992; Hall, Shondrick, & Hirschman, 1993a) that is comprehensive, yet sufficiently parsimonious for research, clinical, and preventive applications. The quadripartite model suggests that physiological sexual arousal, cognitive distortions, affective dyscontrol, and developmentally related personality problems are motivational precursors of sexually aggressive behavior. In addition, I attempt to integrate theory and research from the developmental, sexuality, aggression, and social psychological literature that is relevant to sexual aggression.

The sexual offenders who have been studied in the clinical intervention literature constitute a minority of all sexual aggressors. Most sexual aggressors are not apprehended and convicted of their offenses and, consequently, are not seen in clinical settings. Thus, the majority of sexual aggressors do not receive any form of intervention, and preventive efforts that encompass large groups of males are needed. However, similar to most treatment interventions, most prevention programs have targeted potential victims of sexual aggression. The section in this book on prevention is an attempt to review what is known from prevention science and to apply it to the prevention of sexually aggressive behavior.

The book is divided into four parts: theories, assessment, treatment, and prevention. Chapters 2, 4, and 6 review the general literature on theories, assessment, and treatment of sexually aggressive behavior. Chapters 3, 5, and 7 review my own work in these areas in the context of the quadripartite model. Because theory development of sexually aggressive behavior has been somewhat limited, I integrate aspects of theories of nonsexual aggressive behavior, many of which are quite sophisticated and carefully articulated, in chapters 2 and 3. The material in chapters 4, 5, 6, 7, and 8 specifically focuses on the assessment and treatment of sexual aggressors. I describe specific clinical applications of the quadripartite model to assessment of sexual aggressors in chapter 5 and to treatment of sexual aggressors in chapter 7.

Given the paucity of literature on the prevention of sexually aggressive behavior among potential perpetrators, part IV on prevention is the most speculative section of the book. Potential protective factors against sexually aggressive behavior are reviewed in chapter 8, as are general programs to prevent risk factors from developing, which are covered in chapter 9. In that various disorders may share the same risk factors, most of these programs were designed to prevent antisocial behavior in general. But a few programs are reviewed that have been specifically designed to prevent sexually aggressive behavior among potential perpetrators.

I thank Temi Moffitt, Stan Sue, and Mieko Yoshihama for their feedback during the writing of the manuscript. I also thank my suitemates Mike McBeath and Aloen Townsend for their help with statistical issues. Richard Hirschman, Maria Root, and Bill George provided important input on an earlier draft of the book. Joan Bossert of Oxford University Press has been particularly encouraging about the value of writing this book.

Most of all, I thank Jeanne Nagayama Hall, who has been a constant source of encouragement and feedback throughout my career and during the writing of this book, and Jacquelyn Nozomi Nagayama Hall, whose playfulness has provided a respite from my toils. I hope that the issues I raise in this book will make the world better for them in at least a small way.

January 1995   G. C. N. H.
Kent, Ohio

Contents

Theory-Based Assessment, Treatment, and Prevention of Sexual Aggression

1

Introduction

Sexual aggression is a problem that has a broad societal impact. Although current methods of estimation do not allow us to determine if sexual aggression is occurring at epidemic rates, most prevalence studies estimate that between 1 in 10 and 1 in 4 adult women have been raped or sexually assaulted (Koss, 1992, 1993a). Prevalence figures are similar for child victims of sexual aggression (Finkelhor, 1984). Approximately 1 in 4 adult men admit to perpetrating sexual aggression (Koss, Gidycz, & Wisniewski, 1987). When sexual aggression is broadly defined as anything ranging from unwanted kissing to sexual intercourse, 77.6% of women reported having unwanted sexual experiences, and 57.3% of men report perpetrating such unwanted sexual experiences (Muehlenhard & Linton, 1987). It seems that each day the news media carry new accounts of sexual abuse involving perpetrators, victims, and survivors of all social strata and backgrounds (Daro, 1988; Peters, Wyatt, & Finkelhor, 1986). Often the perpetrators are pillars of society, including clergy, police, teachers, and physicians. Most perpetrators of sexual aggression are acquainted with the victims and include husbands and fathers (Finkelhor, 1984; Koss et al., 1994).

The fascination of the public with sexual aggression may be the perception of the fusion (or confusion) of sex and violence in sexually aggressive acts. For many laypersons, sexual aggression may be viewed as a sexual act because of the sexual contact between perpetrator and victim.

3

Unlike most other victims of assault, victims of sexual assaults are often viewed as potentially provoking sexual aggression, and the sexual history of victims of sexual assault has been introduced as evidence in court proceedings (Allison & Wrightsman, 1993; Dixon, 1991). The sexual components of sexual aggression have also been emphasized, perhaps to the point of overemphasis, by behavioral researchers who have studied the relationship of sexual arousal and sexually aggressive behavior without considering other potentially important motivational variables (Barbaree & Marshall, 1991) or other well-articulated general theories of sexual and aggressive behavior. Feminist scholars have alternatively emphasized the violent aspects of sexual aggression, and have emphasized that sexual aggression is a "pseudosexual" act of violence (Brownmiller, 1975; Clark & Lewis, 1977; Darke, 1990; Russell, 1938a). However, recent feminist scholarship has included sexual motivation as a possible factor in sexually aggressive behavior (Donat & D'Emilio, 1992; Estrich, 1987; Koss, 1993b).

Is sexual aggression a sexual or a violent act? In this book, evidence will be presented that sexually aggressive behavior may have both sexual and aggressive motivational precursors, as well as other motivational precursors that are neither sexual nor aggressive.

Societal Acceptance of Sexual Aggression

The effects of sexual abuse on victims are serious and can be lifelong (Briere, 1988; Browne & Finkelhor, 1986; Hanson, 1990; Kendall-Tackett, Williams, & Finkelhor, 1993; Koss et al., 1994; Wyatt, Newcomb, & Riederle, 1993). Senator Joseph Biden, who introduced the Violence Against Women Act in 1990, compared violence against women to other diseases: "If the leading newspapers were to announce tomorrow a new disease that, over the past year, had afflicted from 3 to 4 million citizens, few would fail to appreciate the seriousness of the illness. Yet, when it comes to the 3 to 4 million women who are victimized by violence each year, the alarms ring softly" (Biden, 1993, p. 1059).

Senator Biden is correct that most would view such a widespread illness as serious. However, the large numbers of victimized women may cause many to see such victimization as normal rather than as a result of men's pathological behavior. In a recent survey of college students, 77.6% of women and 57.3% of men had been involved in some form of sexual aggression, broadly defined as any unwanted sexual activity ranging from kissing to sexual intercourse (Muehlenhard & Linton, 1987).

Thus, sexual aggression could be considered "normal" insofar as the majority of men and women are involved as perpetrators or victims.

Former football star and sports broadcaster O. J. Simpson considered his physical abuse of his ex-wife, which included punching and kicking her so severely that she required hospitalization, to be normal. According to Simpson, these abusive experiences were "no more than every long-term relationship experiences" ("Spouse Battering," June 21, 1994). Moreover, Simpson actually viewed himself as a victim, or in his words "like a battered husband or boyfriend" ("Spouse Battering," June 21, 1994). Such battering of this former star running back seems rather implausible at the hands of his wife or anyone else, given Simpson's physical size, strength, and legendary resiliency against would-be tacklers on the football field (and in airports, as seen in television commercials).

Perhaps the perception of violence against women as normal may be in part a function of its proponents. When a disorder has proponents who argue against its seriousness, it is not viewed as seriously. Consider cigarette smoking: Although there is ample evidence of the link between cigarette smoking and lung cancer, as well as emerging evidence of the effects of secondary smoke on persons in the smoker's environment, the tobacco industry flourishes with government support. Although the approximately 1 in 4 male and female adults who are at risk for lung cancer as a result of cigarette smoking (Centers for Disease Control, 1992) is roughly twice the percentage of women who are violently victimized annually, smoking continues to have societal acceptance, albeit less than it did before the Surgeon General's report on smoking and health 30 years ago (U.S. Department of Health, 1964).

Are there societal proponents of sexual aggression as there are for smoking? The proponents of sexual aggression in society may be those who advocate or fail to oppose interpersonal violence. These proponents are primarily men. Men constitute the majority of persons in positions of power (e.g., politicians) and may not be sensitive to the effects of violence on victims.

Violence is condoned, at least tacitly, by those who oppose gun control. Strict gun control could reduce weapons-related violence to near zero, as in Japan (Keisatsucho, 1992). Perhaps the tradition of personal freedom and individual rights being valued over social responsibility in the United States, which is not a tradition in Japan, has resulted in a reluctance to restrict the availability of weapons and ammunition (Herman, 1990; Lore & Schultz, 1993). In presenting his health-care program in 1993, President Bill Clinton decried the access of adolescents to powerful weapons. Although a bill banning assault weapons has been approved, the president was unwilling to implement Senator Daniel Moynihan's proposal to tax ammunition 1000% as a method of financing the health-care program. Moreover, the assault-weapons bill has no provision to confiscate assault weapons that were acquired before the passage of the bill.

Others identified themselves as advocates of violence following the caning in Singapore of an American who had damaged property. In introducing a 1994 bill in California to paddle juveniles convicted of graffiti vandalism, Assemblyman Mickey Conroy stated, "My goal is to humble these punks early on so we don't see them later in court as murderers" (Associated Press, May 25, 1994). Moreover, in the school district in the town in which I live there are advocates of corporal punishment, although the school board recently banned corporal punishment in the school district. Apparently, these advocates of physical punishment do not recognize the irony of this "fight fire with fire" approach to stopping violence and other forms of acting out.

Although many may support gun control and the banishment of corporal punishment, other more pervasive and acceptable forms of violence, including violent sports such as football, boxing, and hockey, may be more difficult to oppose. Professional sports in particular are bastions of sexism (e.g., men are owners, coaches, and participants; women are relegated to being spectators or scantily clad cheerleaders) and racism (e.g., extremely few ethnic minorities in management or ownership; "stacking" in which the minority players on a team are forced to compete with each other for a single playing position; team names including Indians, Braves, Redskins). Professional sports are relatively insulated from change and may prolong and preserve the gender segregation that occurs among children across cultures between the ages of 3 and 11 (Maccoby, 1988). The relegation of females to a secondary status and the reward of males for a narrow physical definition of achievement that is associated with sports begin in secondary school, during which time male athletic events become the main cultural events of schools (Enke & Sudderth, 1991).

Other proponents of violence are the creators and consumers of violent media. Of the 10 top-grossing films in history (*Variety* magazine, cited in *Newsweek*, December 20, 1993, p. 116), *Jurassic Park*, *Star Wars*, *Indiana Jones and the Last Crusade*, *Terminator 2*, *Jaws*, and *Batman* contain at least a moderate amount of violence. Although the films other than *Terminator 2* may not be considered by many in the film industry and the public as violent, based on their PG ratings, this may underscore the pervasiveness and tolerance of violent acts, such as assault and murder, in media coverage as well as in society. (The other four relatively nonviolent films in the top 10 are *E.T.*, *Ghost*, *Home Alone*, and *Pretty Woman*). Moreover, *Terminator 2*, which contains gratuitous, graphic violence, has grossed the sixth largest amount of money in history and was indirectly condoned by President George Bush insofar as its star, Arnold Schwarzenegger, was appointed to head a national physical fitness campaign.

Violent themes in the media are not a recent phenomenon. Although violence has become more graphic of late, *Bonanza*, one of the most watched television programs by the baby boomer generation, who are now potential perpetrators of sexual aggression and parents of potential perpetrators, was replete with messages supportive of the macho script (Mosher & Sirkin, 1984). The familiar theme from *Bonanza*, which was sung by the Cartwrights on horseback in the program's pilot episode but was (mercifully) dropped, had the following lyrics:

> *We got a right to pick a little fight — Bonanza!*
> *If anyone fights anyone of us, he's gotta fight with me!*
> *We're not a one to saddle up and run — Bonanza!*
> *Anyone of us who starts a little fuss,*
> *Knows he can count on me!*
> *One for four! Four for one!*
> *This we guarantee!*
> *We got a right to pick a little fight — Bonanza!*
> *If anyone fights anyone of us, he's gotta fight with me!*
> (Feran, 1994)

The lyrics of this song, although viewers never heard them, accurately reflected the attitudes about violence portrayed on the program. The Cartwrights had a *right* to violent behavior, and violence was justified if any member of the Cartwright clan engaged in it. The Kennedy family's closing ranks in support of William Kennedy Smith after he had been accused of sexually aggressive behavior is reminiscent of the solidarity of the Cartwright family. Insofar as the macho script consists of viewing violence as manly, seeing danger as exciting, and displaying calloused attitudes toward women (Mosher & Sirkin, 1984), another right of the macho man is having sex with women. If sex is a right and women are considered men's property, then a woman's resistance to sex is moot.

Feminists have argued that males are socialized to be sexually aggressive against women (Herman, 1990). Sexual aggression enforces male domination and female submission and, rather than constituting deviant behavior, is relatively common among men across cultures (Rozee,

1993). Violence against women is also condoned by the film rating system, which imposes greater restrictions on films that portray nonviolent sex than on those that portray sexual violence. Similarly, television restricts sex more than sexual violence. However, the availability of pornography per se is not associated with increased societal sexual violence (Kutchinsky, 1991), and laboratory evidence suggests that sexually violent media are more harmful than sexual media, in that sexually violent films facilitate aggressive behavior among men (Donnerstein, Linz, & Penrod, 1987). Moreover, media that depict violence combined with sexual activity appear to facilitate men's aggressive behavior more than do media that depict nonsexual violence. Thus, societal support for violent behavior may reduce the perception that sexual aggression against women is as serious a problem as other disorders that affect millions of people.

Even when men desire to reduce sexually aggressive behavior, skepticism regarding such efforts is understandable. Any fox guarding the chicken coop should be mistrusted. Because most men are not sexually victimized during adulthood, issues of sexual victimization may be less salient to them than they are to women. It is hoped that men can become sensitized by women to sexual victimization issues. For preventive efforts to become effective, both men and women need to be involved. Sexual aggression is not strictly a women's or children's issue—the impact of sexual aggression affects all of society. Analogous to ethnic minorities in the United States who have been attempting to sensitize the majority to issues of discrimination, prevention of sexual aggression is for everyone's benefit—not just for the victims' benefit. The pervasiveness of sexual aggression means that most persons during their lifetime will be affected by sexual aggression, either directly as a victim or perpetrator, or indirectly by having a relative or friend who is a victim or perpetrator. Many persons may not know of the involvement of their relatives or friends as victims or perpetrators because of the stigma associated with acknowledging such involvement or the difficulties of both victims and perpetrators in defining sexually aggressive experiences as coercive (Kahn, Mathie, & Torgler, 1994; Scully & Marolla, 1984).

A Focus on Perpetrators

Senator Biden's illness analogy for violence against women is useful in examining how sexual aggression is treated and prevented. Two methods of combating disease are: (1) terminating it at its source by destroying virulent agents and (2) helping at-risk individuals develop defenses against the disease via medical (e.g., antibody-inducing agents) or behavioral (e.g., changing behaviors to reduce risk) means. In community psychology, these two approaches are known as systems-centered prevention, which intervenes in high-risk situations (e.g., reducing access to weapons), and person-centered prevention, which involves interventions with persons at high-risk (e.g., persons living in high-violence communities; Cowen, 1983).

Societal response to sexual aggression is clearly weighted toward person-centered — specifically, victim-centered — prevention. For example, Senator Biden's 1990 Violence Against Women Act includes a provision for service to survivors of violence, but interventions with potential or actual perpetrators of violence against women are missing. Sexual-assault-prevention programs typically involve women (e.g., Hanson & Gidycz, 1993; Schewe & O'Donohue, 1993a) or children (Daro, 1991; Kaufman & Zigler, 1992; Melton, 1992; Reppucci & Haugaard, 1989; Swift, 1979; Tutty, 1992). Such an emphasis on reducing the effects of a disease by intervening with potential victims is warranted in situations in which the source or cause of an illness is unknown or when the virulent agent is particularly resistant to interventions. Although the source of sexually aggressive behavior is clearly known, perhaps the emphasis on its effects has been a function of the resistance to change among perpetrators and potential perpetrators. Victim responsibility for prevention of sexual aggression seems unique when compared to prevention programs for other types of crimes, such as child physical abuse (Melton, 1992).

The emphasis of sexual-assault-prevention programs on victims and survivors rather than on perpetrators seems analogous to traditional expectations that it is the woman's responsibility in sexual situations to arrange for birth control or to protect against sexually transmitted diseases (Oliver & Hyde, 1993). This overemphasis on victims and survivors may be related to society's negative judgments of persons who assume the role of receptive or passive partner in relationships, who traditionally have been females (Wyatt, 1994). However, people do not want to be sexually assaulted any more than they want to be assaulted in any other manner, whether they are actively attempting to prevent the assault or not. Neither the woman who goes to a bar for a drink, nor the woman who wears "revealing" clothing, nor the woman who sunbathes nude at a nude beach is asking to be raped, nor is the woman who unsuccessfully attempts to resist a rapist's advances. To argue that any of these women wants to be raped is to accept the rape myth that some women enjoy being raped or have a secret desire to be raped (Koss et al., 1994). Male victims of nonsexual forms of assault are rarely held responsible for the assault, yet the potential responsibility of female victims of assault, particularly sexual assault, is often considered in court proceedings as well as by the public (Allison & Wrightsman, 1993; Dixon, 1991; Donat & D'Emilio, 1992; Goldberg-Ambrose, 1992).

Shared responsibility for an interpersonal outcome is plausible when two parties consent to an interpersonal relationship. For example, consenting sexual partners should both bear responsibility for avoiding sexually transmitted diseases. However, in coercive behavior, such as sexual aggression, the responsibility squarely lies with one party—the perpetrator (Hall, Shondrick, et al., 1993a; Margolin & Burman, 1993; Shotland, 1992). Even in situations in which a victim may be perceived as contributing to the coercive behavior (e.g., "codependent"), there may be issues of power disparity between the perpetrator and the victim (e.g., dependence on perpetrator for family financial support) that make it difficult, if not undesirable, for the victim to take protective action (Wyatt, 1994).

Unlike physical aggression against women that might be justified by some men in some situations as a form of self-defense, it is difficult to construe sexual aggression as having a defensive function. Also, unlike verbal or physical violence against partners, women cannot retaliate in a reciprocal manner when it comes to sexual aggression. Sexual aggression is a disproportionate response to *any* form of perceived provocation. Thus, an overemphasis on treating survivors of sexual aggression may cater to blaming the victim, in that the survivor is made responsible for preventing sexual aggression. This emphasis on victims may divert attention from critical issues involving perpetrators (American Psychological Association Commission on Violence and Youth, 1993; Browne, 1993; Gilbert, Heesacker, & Gannon, 1991; Hall & Hirschman, 1991; Kaufman & Zigler, 1992; Margolin & Burman, 1993; Melton, 1992; Schewe & O'Donohue, 1993a).

Women younger than 35 years of age who live in cities fear rape more than murder, and over half restrict their activities as a result of this fear (Warr, 1985). Such fear is based in reality, in that the male peers of these young women have the greatest potential for committing sexually aggressive acts (see chapter 4 and G. Hall, 1988). Thus, interventions with survivors are an extremely important approach to empowerment (Hall & Hirschman, 1991; Margolin & Burman, 1993). However, the mere fact that women live in fear and that rape survivors need to be empowered suggests that women's existence continues to be dictated by the men who have made it necessary to be empowered against being sexually abused. Thus, traditionally masculine methods of empowerment, such as physical aggression, are used with survivors, whereas perpetrators are typically not expected to adopt traditionally feminine characteristics of empowerment, such as cooperation (cf. Riger, 1993). Perhaps a disproportionately greater amount of attention should be directed toward perpetrators that would more accurately reflect their level of responsibility in sexually aggressive behavior. Increased targeting of perpetrators may reduce the necessity of survivors' adopting male tactics and continuing to have their lives dictated by perpetrators. The emphasis in this book on males is not intended to ignore or devalue the experiences of females, as has been typical of much of the psychological literature, but to focus on the source of the problem of sexually aggressive behavior.

When perpetrators of sexual aggression are given attention by the media or by clinicians and researchers, they tend to be perpetrators that have been apprehended and convicted for sexual offenses. However, perpetrators who have been apprehended and convicted constitute a small minority of all sexual aggressors (Koss, Gldycz, & Wisniewsky, 1987), in that the vast majority of sexual aggressors are not apprehended or convicted because their crimes are not viewed as serious by society and the court system. Nevertheless, the sexual aggressors who are apprehended and convicted are a convenient target for blame. A disproportionate focus on sexual offenders as perpetrators makes sexual aggression an extreme act committed only by a few "abnormal" individuals who are unlucky enough to be caught for it. However, feminists have argued that sexual aggression is a result of normal male socialization, and a broader emphasis on the many men who are sexually aggressive but do not get caught underscores men's corporate responsibility for sexual aggression, as well as for reducing and preventing it. Thus, societal emphases on victims or on extreme groups of sexual aggressors may divert blame for sexual aggression from most men.

Males (perpetrators in this book will be referred to as male) constitute the vast majority of perpetrators of sexual aggression (Koss et al., 1994). Unlike physical aggression that is perpetrated by both males and females (Eagly & Steffen, 1986; Hyde, 1984; Straus & Gelles, 1986), males are far more likely than females to perpetrate sexual aggression. For example, in the Epidemiological Catchment Area studies in Los Angeles, 93% of the perpetrators of child sexual abuse were male (Siegel, Sorenson, Golding, Burnam, & Stein, 1987), as well as at least 75% of perpetrators of sexual abuse against adults (Sorenson, Stein, Siegel, Golding, & Burnam, 1987). McConaghy (1993) has suggested that the relatively high percentage of female perpetrators against adults in the Sorenson et al. (1987) study may have been a function of men's viewing excessive pressure for sexual activity as sexual assault.

As with the focus on female survivors of sexual aggression, an emphasis on female perpetrators of sexual aggression may serve to divert attention from critical issues involving the men who are most commonly perpetrators. The publicity surrounding cases of female perpetrators of sexual aggression is usually disproportionate to the percentage of women who are sexually aggressive (Driver, 1989). Perhaps the implied political message in such selective publicity is that sexual aggression perpetrated by males is sufficiently "normal" so that it is not newsworthy, whereas the same behavior perpetrated by females is deviant and heinous.

A "males as victims" mentality also focuses on the perpetrators of sexual aggression who themselves have been sexually victimized. However, being sexually abused does not inevitably lead to becoming sexually abusive. Few females who are sexually abused become sexually abusive (Herman, 1990; Kendall-Tackett, Williams, & Finkelhor, 1993), and many sexually aggressive men have not been sexually abused, particularly men who are sexually aggressive against women (Prentky & Knight, 1993). Moreover, unwanted sexual contact may have somewhat different consequences for males than for females and may be less traumatic for many males (Condy, Templer, Brown, & Veaco, 1987). This is not to discount the seriousness of sexual aggression perpetrated by females. However, male-initiated sexual aggression is a far more pervasive societal problem than that which is perpetrated by females, with male perpetrators outnumbering female perpetrators by at least 3 to 1 in sexual aggression against adults (Sorenson et al., 1987) and 9 to 1 in sexual aggression against children (Siegel et al., 1987).

Perhaps the emphasis on perpetrators as victims is in part an effort to generate public sympathy and attention to the psychological problems of perpetrators. Public sympathy is reserved for victims: Victims deserve help; perpetrators deserve punishment. Many view the millions of dollars spent on prison facilities as more than adequate attention to perpetrators. Hence, mental health agencies and institutes that deal with sexual abuse typically emphasize interventions and prevention for victims. Perpetrators are viewed as the purview of the correctional system, in which punishment can be meted out, rather than of the mental health system, in which the emphasis is on rehabilitation. However, sympathy for victims can motivate efforts to prevent sexual aggression among potential perpetrators. Effective prevention of sexual aggression among potential perpetrators may save multiple persons from becoming victims, in that sexual aggressors tend to commit multiple acts of sexual aggression with multiple victims (Abel et al., 1987).

Research Approaches

How should sexual aggression be studied? I and others have proposed that models of sexual aggression be developed that will guide research and clinical work (G. Hall, 1990a; Hall & Hirschman, 1991; Quinsey & Marshall, 1983). From a methodological perspective, the purposes of such models are *predictive* or *explanatory* (Cohen & Cohen, 1983). Predictive models are empirically based and are evaluated by how accurate they are at predicting behavior, whereas explanatory models are theoretically based and identify causal variables. Theories of behavior are often irrelevant in the development of predictive models, and predictive models are often necessarily complex. In contrast, the most useful explanatory models are parsimonious, which allows hypothesis testing and replication (Carver & Scheier, 1992; Morgan, 1894). Prediction is important in the explanatory approach to the extent that the predicted criterion is a relatively accurate measure of a theoretical construct, although there are seldom any extremely accurate measures of such constructs (Howard, 1990). For example, official arrest records, self-report, and laboratory behavior have all been used as criteria to measure sexual aggression, but each method has its limitations. Official records may underestimate actual sexually aggressive behavior. Self-report of sexually aggressive behavior may be subject to social desirability influences (Walker, Rowe, & Quinsey, 1993), and is not *in vivo* sexual aggression (Hall & Hirschman, 1993, 1994). Laboratory behavior is *in vivo*, but may not accurately represent the most severe forms of sexual aggression.

Predictive and explanatory modeling are analogous to *criterion-related validity* and *construct validity* in the test-construction field (Campbell, 1960; Cronbach & Meehl, 1955). The Minnesota Multiphasic Personality Inventory (MMPI; Hathaway & McKinley, 1940) is an example of an instrument based on the predictive, criterion-related approach. Individual items were included on the test's scales if they were correlated with criterion variables (i.e., diagnosis) and not included if they did not correlate with the criterion variables. The State-Trait Anxiety Inventory (Spielberger, Gorsuch, & Lushene, 1970) is an example of the explanatory, construct approach in that the test was designed to measure the constructs of situational (state) and chronic (trait) anxiety. The test is internally valid in that items were retained in the test if they could be categorized, via factor analysis, into factors that corresponded with state and trait anxiety. External (i.e., criterion-related) validity was less critical in the initial development of the test than was internal (i.e., construct) validity.

Predictive models of sexual aggression are judged on their accuracy in predicting sexually aggressive behavior. Univariate models tend to have less predictive utility than multivariate models (G. Hall, 1990a). However, theory and parsimony may guide predictive models to the extent that theory may inform the initial selection of predictive variables (Popper, 1972), and extremely complex predictive models may be difficult to implement. Despite the recent development of complex predictive models, the most single powerful predictor of future sexually aggressive behavior remains past sexually aggressive behavior (G. Hall, 1990a).

Explanatory models of sexual aggression are useful to the extent that they are: (1) sufficiently comprehensive to accommodate the heterogeneity of sexual aggressors; (2) sufficiently parsimonious to allow hypothesis testing and replication across settings; and (3) applicable in clinical contexts (Hall & Hirschman, 1991, 1993). Sexual aggressors are a heterogeneous population, and attempting to identify a single etiological variable that explains all sexually aggressive behavior is to oversimplify a complex behavioral problem. Current theories of sexual aggression have undergone a transformation toward multivariate models, and it has become generally accepted that sexually aggressive behavior is not caused by any single variable (Hall, Hirschman, & Beutler, 1991). However, a by-product of the quest to develop multivariate models is a complexity and specificity of setting or population that has prevented replication across settings. There are extremely few instances of models being validated by researchers other than by the models' originators, quite possibly because of this complexity. Moreover, complex constructs (e.g., three-way interactions among variables) may be of limited relevance in clinical settings because such complex constructs are difficult for clinicians and clients to use in any practical sense. Thus, parsimony is imperative if models of sexual aggression are to be useful.

The Importance of Parsimony

One of my early experiences that taught me the necessity of parsimony was with Leon, who had been my friend since early childhood. Leon was not what you would call a baseball fan. However, he did go to a Seattle Pilots–Washington Senators game with me in 1969 at Sick's Stadium when we were both 13 years old. Leon was not particularly interested in all the statistics and trivia that I knew about the Pilots. In fact, Leon was more interested in boldly waving the Washington Senators' pennant that I had bought to raise the ire of the Pilots fans in the first-base bleachers from where we were watching the game.

I, on the other hand, was an avid fan of baseball and baseball statistics. In fact, I copiously scored each play of the game on the scorecard that I had bought. Near the middle of the game, I wanted to go to the concession stand to buy drinks for Leon and me. In order to avoid missing the game in the rush to the concession stands between innings, I decided to hurry out to the concession stand while the game was being played. Because I wanted a complete scoring of every play of the game, I asked Leon if he would score the next play of the game while I went to the concession stand. Since I was going to buy him a drink, he agreed to do so. I painstakingly explained the baseball scoring system, in which each defensive player is numbered (pitcher = 1, catcher = 2, first base = 3, etc.), and provided examples (e.g., if a ground ball was hit to the shortstop and the shortstop threw to the first baseman to get the batter out, the play would be scored 6–3). I also explained that a strikeout is scored "K" and he already knew the difference between a single, double, triple, and home run, having played baseball. When I left for the concession stand, there were no men on base, so Leon's scoring task would be fairly easy.

I hurriedly bought the two drinks and returned to see that I had missed only one batter. I gave Leon his drink and looked at the scorecard, where Leon had recorded "OUT." I asked Leon what had happened during the play and he said that the batter was out. However, he could not recall exactly how the runner had got out, other than that the batter had not struck out.

What Leon had done was capture, in a very parsimonious fashion, the essence of the event. In the grand scheme of the game (and of history), it did not matter how the out was made. The important consequence was that the batter was out, as Leon had indicated on the scorecard.

My obsession with baseball detail is analogous to the theoretical and clinical obsession with complexity that I have described in this chapter. In my clinical work with sexual aggressors, the importance of parsimonious explanations has also been underscored. Sexual aggressors have told me that their urges to be sexually aggressive are extremely compelling. Thus, interventions to prevent sexually aggressive behavior must be both powerful and easy to implement. Abstract concepts may be of limited use in changing a sexual aggressor's behavior. For example, when asked what he had learned in a prison treatment program, a client in one of my outpatient treatment programs reported that he learned that he had come from a "dysfunctional family," but that no one ever told him what a dysfunctional family was. Thanks to Leon and my clients, I appreciate the elegance and importance of parsimony.

A recent example suggests that the media are also resistant to viewing sexually aggressive behavior as parsimonious. About two years ago, I was asked by a television network to contribute to a documentary on sex offenders. I agreed to participate because some of this network's other programming on scientific topics that I had seen had appeared quite responsible. The network provided me with a thick file on a child-molester case and asked me to comment. The file revealed that the child molester had been arrested for a series of child molestations, but had been released into the community each time after a relatively brief period of incarceration or counseling. He also had been in treatment with therapists. In that there exists relatively definitive evidence that past sexual aggression is the best predictor of future sexual aggression (G. Hall, 1990a and chapter 4, this book), I suggested to the telephone interviewer from the network that this child molester's multiple molestations could have been predicted from his past behavior, but that the agencies and individuals involved in the case did not consider the past offense data as seriously as they should have. Although the interviewer mentioned that the network wanted to schedule a filming session with me, they did not subsequently contact me. When the documentary was finally aired, it featured a psychologist, who had treated the child molester after the child molester had been arrested multiple times, enumerating the vagaries of the case and concluding that the case was an enigma. This interview, replete with the therapist's speculations about the case, constituted the major portion of the documentary, whereas my interview was not aired. Thus, the producer apparently believed that the mysterious clinical judgment approach would make better TV than my parsimonious actuarial approach. Perhaps the producer could not believe that crimes so heinous could be explained in such a straightforward and brief (possibly too brief for the documentary) manner.

The production of this television documentary illustrates the need for the media, and perhaps the public, to view sexual aggression as a complex behavior that requires complex explanations. This may also be the motivation for the media's emphasis on atypical sexual aggression perpetrated by strangers, when the preponderance of sexually aggressive acts are perpetrated by persons who are acquainted with victims (Daro, 1988; Kendall-Tackett & Simon, 1987; Koss, 1993a). Nevertheless, complex explanations do little to advance clinical interventions to prevent sexual aggression, which may be the most critical reason for developing explanations of sexual aggression (chapter 6).

Despite the necessity of parsimonious theoretical models for clinical applications, clinicians may also be reciprocally responsible for excessively complex approaches to clinical problems. Martin Seligman, whose commitment to parsimony has been laudable in his development of the theory of learned helplessness and, more recently, learned optimism, described clinicians' penchant for complexity as follows:

> I think the world can be divided into complophiles and simplophiles. I think most clinical psychologists are complophiles, who believe in how complicated people are and how important it is to have very rich and

widespread clinical experience. I am an unabashed simplophile. I believe that the richness of clinical experience is something to be fought against. One should always be looking for the simples that pervade it. (Cloitre, 1993, p. 261)

Clinically developed approaches are often highly dependent on individual clinicians' skills, and are often not replicable by researchers or clinicians in other settings. Clinicians also may have difficulty in adequately articulating their approaches for use in standardized treatment manuals that can be used in settings other than the one in which the treatment was originated (Beutler, 1993; Cohen, Sargent, & Sechrest, 1986). Approaching each sexual aggressor on an idiographic basis, or with an overemphasis on heterogeneity, may produce an infinite number of hypotheses to explore to find "what works." Although behavior therapists including myself, who are well established in treating sexual aggressors, have emphasized parsimonious approaches to clinical problems, the theoretical nihilism of behavior therapy may propagate such idiographic, and often idiosyncratic, approaches to problems. However, such idiographic clinical approaches that are devoid of a conceptual framework overlook important nomothetic communalities among sexual aggressors that may be useful in treatment and prevention.

In this book, I will attempt to present a comprehensive, yet parsimonious, approach to sexual aggression. Rather than presenting an approach that is intended to compete with other approaches, my goal in this book is to integrate the strengths of various approaches, as I have discussed elsewhere (G. Hall, 1980; Hall, Hirschman, et al., 1993). I have attempted to integrate various approaches in the quadripartite model of sexual aggression (Hall & Hirschman, 1991, 1992), which will provide a framework for this book.

The quadripartite model of sexual aggression (Hall & Hirschman, 1991, 1992) integrates elements of existing theoretical models of sexual aggression. The heterogeneity of sexual aggressors is accounted for by positing physiological sexual arousal, cognitions that justify sexual aggression, affective dyscontrol, and personality problems as etiological factors. These four factors function as motivational precursors that increase the probability of sexually aggressive behavior. The relative prominence of these precursors within different sexually aggressive populations corresponds with major subtypes of sexual aggressors.

Various types of sexual aggressors, including adolescents and adults in clinical and nonclinical settings, and sexually aggressive behavior, including that directed against children and adults, are discussed in this book. The emphasis on hands-on sexual aggression perpetrated by males against women and children reflects the amount of attention to these issues in the psychological literature. This is not to discount the seriousness of "hands-off" sexual aggression, including sexual harassment, voyeurism, and exhibitionism (Charney & Russell, 1994; Fitzgerald, 1993; Freund, 1990). My hope is that the approach in this book is sufficiently parsimonious to be applicable by other theorists and researchers, and my 13 years of clinical work with sexual aggressors compels me to make this book clinically relevant.

I

TOWARD A THEORY OF SEXUAL AGGRESSION

2

Theories of Sexual Aggression

What causes males to rape women and molest children? Sexual aggression involves sexual behavior that is aggressive. In that there are both sexual and aggressive components to sexual aggression, consideration of both sexual and aggressive behavior are important. Sexual behavior is often motivated by physiological sexual arousal and aggressive behavior is often motivated by affective states, including anger and depression. In addition to physiological sexual arousal and affective motivation, Hall and Hirschman (1991, 1992) have proposed that sexually aggressive behavior is motivated by cognitive distortions and by developmentally related personality problems. In this chapter, recent theoretical formulations of sexual behavior, aggressive behavior, and sexually aggressive behavior will be reviewed within the framework of each of these four motivational variables. Theories of sexual aggression are categorized on the basis of either their major emphasis (e.g., physiological; Barbaree & Marshall, 1991) or, when theories include more than one of the four motivational variables, their unique emphasis (e.g., affective dyscontrol; Finkelhor, 1984).

Physiological Models of Sexual Aggression

Most heterosexual males are sexually aroused by consenting sexual activity between men and women. Atypical conditions, such as negative affect or nonconsenting sexual activity, reduce sexual arousal in normal males (Barlow, 1986; Bozman & Beck, 1991; Keating & Over, 1990). Thus, persons who are sexually aroused under such atypical conditions, including many sexual aggressors, are considered deviant (American Psychiatric Association, 1994).

It appears more intuitive that sexually aggressive behavior should be motivated by sexual arousal than by many other variables. Although some forms of sexual aggression do not require the perpetrator to become sexually aroused (e.g., sexual fondling) and many sexual aggressors experience sexual dysfunction (Marshall & Barbaree, 1990b), many types of sexual aggression do involve sexual arousal during sexually aggressive behavior. Many rapists and child molesters exhibit high levels of sexual arousal to rape and pedophilic stimuli, respectively, relative to consenting-adult sexual stimuli (Barbaree & Marshall, 1989, 1991; Hall, Shondrick, & Hirschman, 1993b; Harris, Rice, Quinsey, Chaplin, & Earls, 1992; Lalumiere & Quinsey, 1994). Many rapists and child molesters also exhibit greater arousal to deviant stimuli than do men who have not been sexually aggressive (Barbaree & Marshall, 1989, 1991; Hall, Shondrick, et al., 1993b; Harris et al., 1992; Lalumiere & Quinsey, 1994).

Physiological Sexual Arousal

Physiological sexual arousal has been emphasized in various theoretical models of sexual aggression. In some theories, sexual arousal in response to deviant stimuli has a biological or neurohormonal basis (Hucker & Bain, 1990) and in others it is based on learning, such as classical conditioning via masturbation to pornography (Laws & Marshall, 1990; Marshall & Barbaree, 1984; Quinsey, 1984). The Diagnostic and Statistical Manual of Mental Disorders (DSM-IV-R) of the American Psychiatric Association (1994), the most widely utilized diagnostic system of mental health professionals, has also implemented this sexual-arousal approach to classify different sexually deviant behaviors. The DSM definition of paraphilias emphasizes sexual arousal to deviant stimuli, such as children, clothing, or violence (Hall & Andersen, 1993).

For most sexually aggressive and nonaggressive men, their sexual arousal to stimuli depicting consenting sexual acts is greater than their sexual arousal to stimuli depicting rape or nonsexual violence (Baxter,

Barbaree, & Marshall, 1986; Blader & Marshall, 1989; G. Hall, 1989b; Hall, Proctor, & Nelson, 1988). Although it has been argued that the sexual-arousal patterns of less pathological sexual aggressors (e.g., acquaintance rapists) are qualitatively different from the sexual-arousal patterns of more pathological sexual aggressors (e.g., incarcerated sexual offenders; Barbaree, Seto, Serin, Amos, & Preston, 1994), a recent meta-analysis suggests that these patterns are not (Hall, Shondrick, et al., 1993b). Among child molesters and normals, stimuli that depict "consenting" sex with a child elicit greater sexual arousal than stimuli that depict sex with a child as nonconsenting, and nonconsenting pedophilic stimuli elicit greater sexual arousal than stimuli that depict nonsexual violence against children (Hall et al., 1988; Hall, Hirschman, & Oliver, in press). Although many child molesters do exhibit disproportionately high sexual arousal in response to pedophilic stimuli, it appears that sadistic sexual arousal is not a primary motivational component for most child molesters (Hall et al., 1988).

Physiological sexual arousal appears to be a more prominent motivational variable among child molesters than among rapists of women, but many child molesters and rapists do not exhibit sexual arousal in response to pedophilic or rape stimuli (Barbaree & Marshall, 1989, 1991; Hall, Shondrick, et al., 1993b). Moreover, many men who do not exhibit *trait* sexual arousal to deviant stimuli (e.g., rape) will exhibit sexual arousal to deviant stimuli under certain *state* conditions. Barbaree and Marshall (1991) described several studies with college students in which sexual arousal in response to rape stimuli approximated sexual arousal in response to consenting sexual stimuli when state variables were introduced, including alcohol intoxication, excuses for a rapist's behavior (i.e., being provoked to anger by a woman, being intoxicated, being in a long-term relationship with the victim), and exposure to pornography with rape themes. These subjects exhibited sexual arousal to consenting stimuli that exceeded their sexual arousal to rape stimuli in the absence of these disinhibitors. Barbaree and Marshall (1991) described the process by which sexual arousal to rape stimuli as *disinhibition* insofar as such sexual arousal typically is inhibited, but is disinhibited by state variables.

It was suggested that such disinhibition may be applicable to acquaintance or date rape (Barbaree & Marshall, 1991). However, none of the college subjects described by Barbaree and Marshall (1991) was identified as sexually aggressive. Thus, it appears that state disinhibition of sexual arousal to deviant stimuli is not sufficient to produce sexually aggressive behavior, in that most of the subjects described by Barbaree and Marshall (1991) presumably had actually experienced the state variables (e.g., being provoked by a woman, alcohol intoxication, being in a long-term relationship) in real life without becoming sexually aggressive. Although there is evidence that negative affective states are associated with deviant sexual fantasies and arousal among sexually aggressive men (McKibben, Proulx, & Lusignan, 1994), deviant sexual arousal is not necessarily equivalent to deviant sexual behavior (Hall, 1989b; Hall et al., 1988; Simon & Schouten, 1991).

Inferring from *post hoc* physiological data that the average sexually aggressive man is more sexually aroused by rape stimuli than the average man who is not sexually aggressive is similar to the observation that the average male professional basketball player is taller than the average man who does not play basketball. Although there are a disproportionately high number of tall persons who play basketball, not all basketball players are tall (e.g., 5′7″ Spud Webb of the Sacramento Kings), and not all tall persons are basketball players (e.g., Abraham Lincoln). Moreover, being tall does not necessarily cause one to play basketball. A tall person must learn to play basketball as a person with sexual arousal in response to deviant stimuli (e.g., rape, child molesting) must learn to be sexually aggressive (Ellis, 1989). Thus, physiological sexual arousal is not sufficient in many instances to produce sexually aggressive behavior nor does it necessarily interact with other variables to produce sexual aggression (Hall & Hirschman, 1991, 1993).

If sexual aggression typically involves sexual arousal during sexually aggressive behavior (Ellis, 1989; Mosher & Anderson, 1986; Quinsey, 1984), why aren't all sexual aggressors sexually aroused by sexually aggressive stimuli? For many men who are sexually aggressive, their motivation appears to be sexual, rather than sexually violent, as a function of distorted cognitions about the meaning and impact of their sexually aggressive behavior. Sexual arousal during sexually aggressive behavior for these men is in response to the sexual, rather than the aggressive, components of the behavior.

Sociobiological Models of Sexual Aggression

The sociobiological approach is somewhat more complex than the physiological sexual arousal model, in that evolutionary variables are posited to contribute to sexually aggressive behavior (Ellis, 1991; Studd & Gattiker, 1991; Thornhill & Thornhill, 1991; Welham, 1990). Sexual behavior, including sexually aggressive behavior, is motivated by biologically based physiological drives (Ellis, 1991). There is also some evidence of a neurological basis of sexual aggression, in that some sexual aggressors exhibit temporal lobe structural deficits (Raine, 1993).

In that copulating with as many females as possible is an optimal reproductive strategy for males in terms of ensuring that they will produce offspring, males tend to be oriented toward short-term sexual relationships that require a minimum of parental investment (Buss & Schmitt, 1993). Females, however, tend to be oriented toward long-term sexual relationships in which their male partners will invest themselves in parenting (Buss & Schmitt, 1993). There exists potential for sexually aggressive behavior when male and female sexual orientations conflict, and natural selection favors men who are able to use force to gain copulatory access to women (Ellis, 1991).

Thornhill and Thornhill (1991) suggested that men use one or more of three types of mating tactics to ensure that they will reproduce progeny: honest advertisement and courtship, deceptive advertisement and courtship, and coercion. Males may feign a long-term commitment to a sexual relationship if they believe that to be the female's objective (Buss & Schmitt, 1993). Sexually coercive behavior is deemed necessary when a man's noncoercive mating tactics are thwarted (Buss & Schmitt, 1993). Evidence of the reproductive motivation in sexually aggressive behavior is that penile-vaginal intercourse is usually involved in rapes of females of reproductive age (12–44), but is uncommon when victims are of pre- or post-reproductive age (Thornhill & Thornhill, 1991).

Although sociobiologists would argue that genetically selected behavior patterns are not rapidly extinguished, the sociobiological model of sexual aggression may be three decades late, in that coercive and noncoercive sexual behavior is currently less dictated by reproductive concerns than it was before the advent of effective contraception (Oliver & Hyde, 1993). Despite the hypothesis that rape is a vestige of a once adaptive behavior, it is unlikely that the motivation for most rapes is impregnating the victim and producing progeny. The observation that rapes typically involve females of reproductive age (Thornhill & Thornhill, 1991) may be more parsimoniously explained as a function of access to victims rather than a function of biological processes. Most rapes are perpetrated by men under 40 years of age (see chapter 4), whose female peers tend to be of reproductive age. Given that the most common type of rape is between acquaintances (Koss, 1993a; Koss et al., 1987), perpetrators typically have social contact with victims before rapes occur. People tend to have contact with their peers in social and work settings, which provide potential perpetrators with access to potential victims. Intercourse also may be less easily accomplished physically with prepubescent victims. Moreover, the mere existence of a behavior is not conclusive evidence that it is an optimal or adaptive solution produced by natural selection (Travis & Yeager, 1991).

Although it has been argued that biological influences over sexual aggression are mediated by an individual's learning experiences (Ellis, 1989; Marshall & Barbaree, 1990a), such experiences may involve learning *not* to be sexually aggressive (Barbaree, 1990). Thus, an implication of the sociobiological model is that sexually aggressive behavior is inevitable (Hall & Hirschman, 1991). Moreover, the model may portray specific racial groups as more likely not to be sexually restrained than others and more likely to engage in short-term mating strategies that are conducive to sexual aggression (Rushton, 1988). Such a portrayal is racist in that there is no consideration of cultural, environmental, and historical events that may make these racial groups disadvantaged (Fairchild, 1991). If sexual aggression is based on evolutionary factors, then intervention implications are not clear, other than removing sexually aggressive genes from the gene pool. Perhaps some of the impetus for the current popularity of the sociobiological model is from those who favor permanent removal of sexually aggressive men from society (see chapter 4).

Summary

Physiological models of sexual aggression posit sexual arousal as the basis of sexually aggressive behavior. Physiological sexual arousal in response to rape stimuli motivates some, but not most, sexual aggressors. However, most sexually aggressive and nonaggressive men exhibit greater sexual arousal in response to consenting than to coercive sexual stimuli. Moreover, many men who exhibit trait sexual arousal to sexually deviant stimuli are not sexually aggressive, nor are many men in whom state sexual arousal to sexually deviant stimuli is induced.

The sociobiological model places physiological sexual arousal in the context of evolutionary factors as a motivation for sexually aggressive behavior. Sexually aggressive behavior is viewed as providing a reproductive advantage. However, the influence of biological factors on sexual behavior is decreasing and much of what is presented as evolution based can be explained with more parsimonious alternative explanations.

Cognitive Models of Sexual Aggression

A male's cognitive distortions about the meaning and impact of sexually aggressive behavior may justify it (Craig, 1990; Hall & Hirschman, 1991). Such cognitive distortions suggest that victims find sexual aggression enjoyable, beneficial, or, at the very least, not harmful. Such cognitive distortions have been referred to as rape myths (Burt, 1980). Rape myths have been defined as generally false, but widely and persistently held, attitudes and beliefs that deny and justify male sexual aggression against women (Lonsway & Fitzgerald, 1994). As with other stereotypes, situations that are consistent with cognitive distortions tend to be recalled, whereas situations that are inconsistent tend to be ignored (Lonsway & Fitzgerald, 1994). For example, a sexually aggressive man may recall an instance of a woman's "token" resistance to sexual activity and inappropriately make the generalization that all women's resistance to sexual activity is token and should be ignored (Ellis, 1989). Cognitive distortions concerning sexual aggression tend to be more accepted by men than by women (Lonsway & Fitzgerald, 1994).

A sexually aggressive man who is angered by a woman may view rape as a justifiable form of retaliation and may not view himself as fully responsible for sexually aggressive behavior because he cannot control his anger (cf. Averill, 1993; DiGiuseppe, Tafrate, & Eckhardt, 1994). A man who perceives provocation may consider himself the victim. Recall O. J. Simpson's describing himself as feeling "like a battered husband or boyfriend" ("Spouse Battering," 1994). A perpetrator also may not perceive himself as responsible for sexually aggressive behavior if he is intoxicated (e.g., "It wasn't me, so I'm not responsible"). Similarly, some sexual aggressors may not believe that sexual aggression can occur between persons involved in a long-term relationship (Johnson & Jackson, 1988). Pornographic depictions may make rape excusable, in that the perpetrator may believe that rape is common and sufficiently nondeviant to be portrayed in the media. Thus, all these disinhibitors serve to make rape less reprehensible and more "normal."

Similar cognitive processes appear to occur among sexual aggressors against children. Society generally does not condone sexual behavior with children, which results in more extreme cognitive distortions to permit sexually aggressive behavior with children vs. adults (Hall & Hirschman, 1992). The cognitive distortion that children enjoy sex with adults may permit child molesters to ignore the inappropriateness of their behavior.

Many sexually aggressive men believe that their behavior is normal and not offensive to women (Koss, Leonard, Beezly, & Oros, 1985). Other men may believe that the expression of sexual lust is sinful and that forced sexual activity is necessary because no one would consent to be overcome by another person's lust (Money, 1988). Some men may believe that sexual aggression is simply an assertion of the masculine gender role (Herman, 1990; Koss et al., 1994). Men who are sexually aggressive against children similarly minimize the impact of their abuse (cf. Lochman & Dodge, 1994).

In sexual situations, many sexually aggressive men may attend to cognitive or situational cues that they believe indicate consent (e.g., she is a friend and not a stranger, she invited me to her apartment, she is intoxicated, "no" may mean "maybe" or "yes") and ignore those cues that indicate nonconsent (Craig, 1990). Some sexually aggressive men have such distorted perceptions of their behavior that sex involving extreme force, such as using a weapon to gain a woman's cooperation to have sex, is not even viewed as rape (Scully & Marolla, 1984). Thus, sexual arousal during many rapes may be in response to the victim's perceived consent rather than to the victim's nonconsent and suffering. Most men's sexual arousal decreases when the victim's suffering is emphasized (Malamuth & Check, 1983; Mosher & Anderson, 1986). Even when a man perceives a situation as rape, he may respond sexually more to the sexual than to the violent aspects of a rape, in that violence combined with sex is typically more sexually arousing than violence alone (Baxter et al., 1986; G. Hall, 1989b).

In that a male forcing a female to engage in sexual behavior is one of the most common forms of sexual aggression (Koss, 1993a), sexual aggression may be rooted in gender differences in sexuality. Children imitate the gender-role behavior modeled by same-gender adults (Bussey & Bandura, 1984; Mischel, 1966) and learn that male behavior is more valued that female behavior (Bem, 1993). A double standard for sexual behavior exists in that women are punished for promiscuous or casual sexual activity, whereas men are not (Oliver & Hyde, 1993; Sprecher, McKinney, & Orbuch, 1987). This double standard is reflected in gender differences in preferences for sexual behavior. The results of a recent meta-analysis of 177 studies suggest that males are more attracted to impersonal sex (i.e., sex that does not involve emotional commitment) than are females, in that large gender differences were found in the incidence of masturbation and in attitudes toward casual premarital sex (Oliver & Hyde, 1993).

Males often utilize short-term mating strategies oriented toward casual sex that may conflict with females' long-term mating strategies oriented toward committed relationships (Buss & Schmitt, 1993). Men fall in love faster than women do (Huston & Ashmore, 1986) and expect sexual activity earlier in developing relationships than women do (Buss & Schmitt, 1993; Clark & Hatfield, 1989; Ellis & Symons, 1990). Indeed, 75% of a sample of college men agreed to have sex when asked by an attractive female confederate, whereas none of a sample of college women agreed to have sex when asked by an attractive male confederate (Clark & Hatfield, 1989). Thus, gender differences in expectations about sexual behavior may result in the potential for sexual aggression.

If many females are unwilling to have casual sexual relationships, then men will force them to do so if they believe they are entitled to have casual sexual relationships (Mosher & Tomkins, 1988). "Macho" men may be the most likely to be sexually aggressive, in that they have adopted a gender-role orientation in which sexuality is associated with dominance over women, which may entail feelings of entitlement to multiple sex partners without emotional investment (Mosher, 1991; Mosher & Sirkin, 1984; Mosher & Tomkins, 1988; Zaitchik & Mosher, 1993). Analogous feelings of entitlement to sex may occur among incestuous fathers who consider their spouse and children property (Herman, 1981). Thus, the goal of sexual aggression for many males is sex, not necessarily forced sex. For example, macho men consider sexually aggressive behavior to be acceptable, but are not sexually aroused and actually express distress, fear, shame, and guilt when imagining themselves committing a rape (Mosher & Anderson, 1986). To the extent that coercive sexual behavior is deemed necessary to get a woman to have sex, it is not considered rape. The following models of sexually aggressive behavior emphasize perpetrators' cognitive distortions that justify sexually aggressive behavior.

A Situational Model of Coercive Sexuality

Craig (1990) has proposed that coercive sexuality in dating relationships is a function of dispositional and situational factors. Dispositional factors that distinguish sexually coercive from noncoercive men include aggressive behavior, cognitive distortions about women and rape, sexual experience, sexual dissatisfaction, family violence, and sexual arousal to the use of force. However, the presence of these dispositional characteristics alone is not sufficient for sexual coercion to occur.

Males having a disposition to sexually coercive behavior may deliberately structure situations to allow them to express their dispositions (Craig, 1990). For example, sexual coercion may be likely to occur in established relationships, when the male pays expenses, and when both persons are intoxicated. In addition, sexually coercive males may selectively attend to cues that they believe to indicate the partner's willingness for sexual activity. These males tend not to view their behavior as sexually coercive or, if they allow that sexually coercive behavior has occurred, to blame the victim (Craig, 1990).

Craig's (1990) identification of cognitive distortions as a causal variable in sexually aggressive behavior appears particularly appropriate in explaining acquaintance rape, which is frequently motivated by such cognitive distortions (Hall & Hirschman, 1991). However, the model does not suggest whether males with certain dispositions are more susceptible to some situational factors than others. For example, would a male who is sexually aroused by force be more disinhibited by apparent sexual cues in a dating situation than a male who had another dispositional factor, such as family violence? Moreover, situational variables may be less influential for a sexual aggressor having a chronic propensity for rule violations than for a sexual aggressor who is motivated more by state variables. The major situational constraint on the former type of sexual aggressor would be the likelihood of getting caught and victim issues, such as perceived consent or blameworthiness, would be secondary (see chapter 3). Although cognitive distortions are a common motivational precursor of sexually aggressive behavior, they may be less central among sexual aggressors whose primary motivation is not cognitive (Hall & Hirschman, 1991, 1992).

Sexual Deviance as an Addictive Behavior

Sexually aggressive behavior has been conceptualized as an addiction to the extent that it is impulsive and causes intense, immediate pleasure at the expense of long-term consequences, and can become compulsive (George & Marlatt, 1989; Herman, 1990). Personal responsibility for addictive behavior is minimized and others are usually blamed (Herman, 1990). Conceptualizing sexual aggression as an addiction underscores that it is not benign or normal behavior and that it is a serious problem that requires extensive time to change (Herman, 1990).

Sexual deviance and other addictions are characterized by similar precursors, including negative emotional states, and by denial that the addictive behavior is problematic (George & Marlatt, 1989). A temporal sequence of affect → sexual fantasy → conscious plan presumably leads to sexually aggressive behavior (Pithers, Marques, Gibat, & Marlatt, 1983). The motivation to engage in sexually deviant behavior is sufficiently compelling that considerations about the legal and social sanctions against such behavior are ignored or minimized (Marlatt, 1989). Although an early discussion of sexual deviance as an addiction conceptualized it as an illness and advocated self-help methods that had been employed in the treatment of other addictions (Carnes, 1983), more recent conceptualizations have emphasized the cognitive aspects of sexual deviance as an addiction, which has resulted in the development of sophisticated cognitive-behavioral treatment interventions (George & Marlatt, 1989; Pithers et al., 1983). The model is cognitive to the extent that cognitive planning, which includes distortions concerning the inappropriateness of sexual aggression, immediately precedes and mediates sexually aggressive behavior (Pithers et al., 1983).

The sequence of affect → sexual fantasy → conscious plan may not be fixed for all sexual aggressors (Hall & Hirschman, 1991). For example, affectively induced physical aggression may occur in the absence of such cognitive planning (Berkowitz, 1990), and impulsive, opportunistic sexual aggression also appears to occur without planning (Prentky & Knight, 1991). Moreover, sexually aggressive behavior has much more serious interpersonal consequences than other addictions, such as smoking, or alcohol or drug abuse (George & Marlatt, 1989). A single relapse with one of the latter addictions is usually not life-threatening. Moreover, relapses with these addictions are not necessarily viewed as failures, but as learning experiences that may assist in preventing future relapses. Conversely, a single relapse episode of sexual aggression is to be avoided at all costs. Relapse prevention with sexual aggressors may be compared to suicide prevention with persons at risk for suicide. Whereas delayed relapse may be beneficial in the treatment of certain addictions (e.g., additional time without being intoxicated), a delayed relapse among sexual aggressors has the same serious consequences as an immediate relapse.

Public sentiments concerning sexual aggressors may reflect a qualitative difference between perceptions of sexual aggression and other addictive behaviors (G. A. Marlatt, personal communication, July 1993). Sympathy is a common response when celebrities or other public figures suffer from nonsexual addictions, such as alcohol or drug abuse. Drug addicts are frequently released from prison without public fanfare after serving their sentences. Although some forms of sexually aggressive behavior may be viewed by society as more "normal" (e.g., acquaintance rape) than others (Herman, 1990; Koss et al., 1994), sexual aggressors who are viewed as deviant (e.g., sexual aggressors who are arrested and convicted, child molesters) are often shunned by society. For example, the neighbors of a sex offender in the Washington state community to which he was released in 1993 burned his house. This man moved to New Mexico to live with his brother, but was subsequently driven out of New Mexico. Entertainer Michael Jackson's payment of a large amount of money to the father of a boy who alleged that Jackson sexually molested the boy attests to the stigma associated with accusations of sexual aggression against children.

Perhaps the contrast in public perceptions of sexual aggression and other addictive behaviors is because the effects of sexual aggression are *interpersonal* whereas many of the effects of other addictions are primarily *intrapersonal* (i.e., they are harmful primarily to the addicted person). Although conceptualizing sexual aggression as an addiction emphasizes the psychological problems of the sexual aggressor, this conceptualization appears not to have changed public perceptions of "deviant" sexual aggressors (e.g., sex offenders, child molesters). The perceived victim in an intrapersonal addiction is the addicted person, who is worthy of sympathy and treatment, whereas the victim of an interpersonal addiction is clearly not the addicted person, who is viewed as worthy of punishment and incarceration (chapter 1, this book; cf. Dent & Arias, 1990). Thus, sexual aggression is similar to other addictions but is also different in important ways.

Attachment Theory and Incest

Alexander (1992) has explained incest in the context of attachment theory. Insecure family attachment is characterized by rejection, role reversal/parentification, and fear/unresolved trauma. Rejecting fathers consider their spouses and children to be their property and minimize the impact of incestuous behavior because they feel entitled to sex. A second common pattern in incestuous families is role reversal, in which daughters engage in parentlike behaviors. The incestuous father again feels entitled to having his sexual needs met by his daughter. The third incestuous family pattern involves a father who may have been abused himself or have experienced the fear of abandonment. His incestuous behavior may represent a maladaptive attempt to resolve his own trauma. These motivational factors for incest appear to be consistent with Hall and Hirschman's (1992) depiction of incestuous behavior as primarily motivated by cognitive distortions.

The family context of incest is recognized in attachment theory. Incest may be more likely in families where mothers and children possess characteristics that make them vulnerable (Alexander, 1992; Trepper & Barrett, 1986). However, the focus on the family context may serve to divert some attention away from the perpetrator's responsibility for sexually aggressive behavior (American Psychological Association Commission on Violence and Youth, 1993; Barrett, Trepper, & Fish, 1990; Browne, 1993; Hall & Hirschman, 1991). Rather than being a symptom of a pathological family system, incest is itself a pathological behavior that is the responsibility of an individual: the perpetrator.

Barrett et al. (1990) have critiqued a family systems approach to incest from a feminist perspective. The systems approach views the whole family system as responsible for incest, not just the perpetrator. Incest is viewed as a symptom of a "sick" family. However, regardless of how "sick" or dysfunctional the family system may be, this is no excuse for perpetrating incest. Family therapy also forces the victim(s) to be in contact with the perpetrator, which may be detrimental to the victim(s). Such a systems approach also may attempt to preserve the family system, rather than remove the perpetrator from the home to reduce the risk of additional sexual abuse. Removal of the incestuous father from the home may be critical to children's safety (Gelles, 1993).

The risk factors reviewed in chapter 4 should be considered in assessing an incestuous father's potential for recidivism. Being in the home is also a particularly high-risk situation for an incest perpetrator. He is faced with the same situational factors in the home that were present when he engaged in incestuous behavior. These situational factors may have led him to exceed the threshold that normally inhibits sexually aggressive behavior and may lead him to recidivate (see chapter 3).

Women and children are often forced from their homes out of fear of the perpetrator. However, the perpetrator is solely responsible for the abuse. Thus, it follows that the perpetrator is responsible for leaving the home to prevent additional abuse. Such a scenario, however, is often unlikely without legal or judicial involvement.

Incest perpetrators' desires to return to reunite with their families whom they have victimized may be at odds with their family's desires. Clinicians working with incest perpetrators should help them consider the possibility of living independently of their families because of the potential for recidivism. A perpetrator's motivation to participate in treatment may be to return to his family, but this goal may not be realistic, even if he successfully completes treatment.

Most families want to remain together after incest has occurred (Barrett et al., 1990). For example, some families may want the perpetrator to return to the family because of economic dependence. Thus, a modified family systems approach might be useful (Barrett et al., 1990). For example, equalizing power in the family may assist in preventing a perpetrator from being overly dominant and perpetrating abuse when the perpetrator is not removed from the home (Barrett et al., 1990). If a perpetrator is to be reunited with his family, *he* should change in treatment rather than expecting the whole family to change, which is the expectation of some systems approaches to the treatment of incest. A gradual reintegration into the family might be better than a sudden reentry.

Summary

The socialization of males and females leads to differing expectations concerning sexual behavior that may result in sexually aggressive behavior when males' expectations are thwarted. "Macho" socialization may be a particular risk factor for sexually aggressive behavior. Yet, most males are not sexually aggressive when their sexual expectations are thwarted and many "macho" men are not sexually aggressive.

Addiction and attachment models of sexual aggression emphasize cognitive distortions that permit sexually aggressive behavior. The addiction model is compelling to the extent that sexual aggression and addictive behaviors are characterized by both impulsivity and compulsivity. However, the cognitive emphasis of the model may limit its applicability to sexual aggression that is not cognitively motivated, and the serious consequences of sexually aggressive behavior may make it different from other addictions. The attachment model of sexual aggression explores the family context of incest, but may unduly deemphasize the perpetrator's responsibility for sexual aggression.

Affective Models of Sexual Aggression

Negative affective states facilitate aggressive acting out. State anger is a common precursor of verbal and physical aggression (Burman, Margolin, & John, 1993; Buss & Perry, 1992; Welsh & Gordon, 1991). Depressive states are also associated with aggressive acting out, and depressive and angry states covary (Berkowitz, 1983; Maiuro, Cahn, Vitaliano, Wagner, & Zegree, 1988). Persons who experience chronically high levels of negative affect may be predisposed to perceive threat in the behavior of others (Krueger et al., 1994). For example, some men may misperceive innocent or trivial acts of a partner as evidence of infidelity, which is a threat to the relationship (Holtzworth-Munroe & Hutchinson, 1993; White & Mullen, 1989). One method of reasserting power in the relationship is to force sexual intercourse, often following physical abuse (White & Mullen, 1989). Negative affect can be provoked by a specific person who is viewed as responsible for the provocation, such as when gender stereotypes are violated by a female leader (Butler & Geis, 1990). However, a range of unpleasant events can provoke the negative affective states that precede aggressive behavior, therefore victims of aggression are not necessarily responsible for provoking it and aggression toward a victim is not necessarily retaliation (Berkowitz, 1990).

Sexual aggression is a maladaptive attempt to cope with negative affective states for persons experiencing affective dyscontrol (Hall & Hirschman, 1991). For males who rape females, the affective motivational precursor tends to be anger, whereas depression tends to be the affective motivational precursor among child molesters. The following models, although they include nonaffective motivational variables, depict the affective dyscontrol that is a motivational precursor for many sexual aggressors.

The MTC Taxonomy of Sexual Aggressors

The Massachusetts Treatment Center (MTC) taxonomy is based on ratings of archival clinical data on institutionalized sexual offenders (Knight & Prentky, 1990; Prentky & Knight, 1991). The MTC taxonomy is reviewed among affective models of sexual aggression because it includes an affectively dyscontrolled subtype. Although the system began as *deductive*, based on extant typologies of sexual aggressors, research on the MTC taxonomy has been primarily *inductive*, insofar as it has been data driven. The dimensions considered in the MTC approach include the amount and meaning of aggression, lifestyle impulsivity, social competence, sexual fantasies, sadism, cognitive distortions, control and dominance, and disinhibitors (e.g., alcoholism, psychosis, senility, mental retardation; Prentky & Knight, 1991). Iterations of this taxonomy began with 4 subtypes and evolved to include as many as 12 subtypes of sexual aggressors. The developers of the taxonomy clearly appear to be complophiles, in that they have described sexually aggressive behavior as having "enigmatic complexity" (Prentky & Knight, 1991).

Hall and Hirschman (1991) have contended that such statistically derived typologies of behavior may yield certain subtypes that are not necessarily clinically meaningful and that descriptive taxonomies do not necessarily correspond with critical motivational factors in sexually aggressive behavior. Offense characteristics may be analogous to a *phenotype*, which does not necessarily reveal information about motivational *genotype*. The complexity of the system also may preclude its use in most research and clinical settings (Hall & Hirschman, 1991).

In one of the only independent attempts to implement the MTC system outside the Massachusetts Treatment Center, Barbaree and his colleagues (Barbaree et al., 1994) simplified the MTC system by categorizing a population of institutionalized sexual offenders into a sexually motivated type and a nonsexual aggressive type, motivated by anger and impulsivity. Relative penile response to rape stimuli was greater for the former type than for the latter type. In addition to these two types, 56% of the population was eliminated from the study because of inaccurate classification using the MTC typology, missing data, or nonresponse to the physiological measures of sexual arousal. Thus, Barbaree et al. (1994) reduced the MTC system to two major subtypes, with the excluded subjects possibly constituting other subtypes. The sexually motivated type corresponds with sexual aggressors who are primarily motivated by physiological sexual arousal, and the nonsexual aggressive type appears to be motivated by affective components. The difficulty in classifying the majority of the subjects (56%) in a sexual-offender population underscores the difficulty in implementing the MTC system.

Theory of the Causes of Courtship Rape

Shotland (1989, 1992) has proposed a typology of rape within the context of dating relationships. Sexual aggression between acquaintances is the most common form of sexual aggression (Koss et al., 1987), and this relational context of sexual aggression has not been well articulated in most other models of sexually aggressive behavior. Anger is a critical component in all forms of sexual aggression in the Shotland (1989, 1992) model, in that anger must be fused with mismatched expectations or sexual arousal or both for sexually aggressive behavior to occur.

In the early stages of a dating relationship before coitus occurs, mismatched expectations about sexual activity between couples provide the initial impetus for sexually aggressive behavior. Mismatched expectations are less likely to cause sexual aggression after couples have been dating for a long time because their partner's sexual expectations are known (Shotland, 1989, 1992). After the couple has been dating but has not had coitus, sexual aggression may represent an effort to assert the man's power in the relationship if he feels that he has been sacrificing his power by exclusive dating, or paying for dates. If a man is sexually aroused at any point in a dating relationship, but frustrated by the woman's refusal of sexual activity, anger and sexual arousal are synergistically enhanced by the excitation-transfer process (Zillmann, 1984). Although rape-supportive attitudes characterize all sexually aggressive men, attitudinal variables (e.g., mismatched expectations, need to assert power, patriarchal beliefs, rape-supportive beliefs) are not sufficient to cause sexual aggression in the absence of sexual arousal fused with anger (Shotland, 1989, 1992).

Rape that occurs among sexually active couples is accounted for by patriarchal attitudes, particularly if the couple is married, which include the man's belief that one of his partner's duties is to sexually satisfy him. Authoritarian conventionalism has been demonstrated to be positively associated with sexually aggressive behavior (Walker et al., 1993). Rape may be particularly likely if the woman has more power (e.g., socially, economically) than the man. Similarly, physical abuse is more likely in relationships in which the husband has less power than the wife in terms of economic status, decision making, and communication skills, than in relationships where there is less power disparity (Babcock, Waltz, Jacobson, & Gottman, 1993). Rape and other aggressive behavior may represent an effort to restore equity in the relationship (Babcock et al., 1993; Hammock, Rosen, Richardson, & Bernstein, 1989).

Some men who are sexually aggressive may not be motivated by anger insofar as they do not view their sexually aggressive behavior as harmful to the victim (Hall & Hirschman, 1991). Moreover, time spent in a relationship does not guarantee that a couple will communicate, understand, or accept each partner's expectations concerning of sexual interaction. Differing expectations, in terms of men's desire for sexual activities that focus on arousal and women's desire for sexual activities that demonstrate love and intimacy, may not necessarily change as a function of time in a relationship (Hatfield, Sprecher, Pillemer, Greenberger, & Wexler, 1988). Thus, the Shotland (1989, 1992) model appears to exclude forms of sexually aggressive behavior that are primarily motivated by cognitive distortions rather than by anger. Such cognitive distortions may be a common motivational factor in sexual aggression between acquaintances (Hall & Hirschman, 1991), including those who are courting.

The Four-Factor Model of Child Sexual Abuse

Finkelhor (1984) proposed that for incestuous or nonincestuous child sexual abuse to occur the perpetrator must: (1) have adequate motivation, (2) overcome internal inhibitions against acting on the motivation, (3) overcome external impediments to committing sexual abuse, and (4) overcome a child's potential resistance to the sexual abuse. All four of these conditions are necessary for child sexual abuse to occur. Motivation for sexual abuse may be sexual or emotional, which is why this theory is reviewed among the affective theories of sexual aggression. Child molesters often have low self-esteem and sex with children may provide feelings of power and dominance. Individual (e.g., impulse control disorder), sociocultural (e.g., child pornography, weak sanctions), and situational (e.g., mother who is not protective of child, emotionally insecure child) factors may cause a perpetrator to overcome internal and external inhibitors and the child's resistance.

The four-factor model does not explain why a child molester's emotional needs could not be as easily met in a nonsexual manner by befriending a child or by physically abusing a child, rather than by sexually abusing a child (Hall & Hirschman, 1991, 1992). The model was also criticized for its emphasis on environmental factors (e.g., mother's or child's resistance) that may be inconsequential to a perpetrator who is intent on being sexually aggressive (Hall & Hirschman, 1992). Although Finkelhor (1984) acknowledged that the primary responsibility for sexually aggressive behavior is with the perpetrator, his emphasis on environmental contingencies may shift some of the focus from perpetrator responsibility for sexually aggressive behavior (American Psychological Association Commission on Violence and Youth, 1993; Browne, 1993; Hall & Hirschman, 1991). Environmental contingencies may affect the likelihood of sexually aggressive behavior, but it is the sexual aggressor's perceptions or misperceptions of these environmental contingencies that may mediate sexually aggressive behavior, rather than the actual contingencies themselves (Hall & Hirschman, 1991).

Summary

Negative affective arousal is often associated with aggression. Data based on the MTC taxonomy suggest that sexual aggressors who are primarily motivated by affective dyscontrol are not characterized by deviant sexual arousal. The theory of courtship rape suggests that anger is fused with sexual arousal or cognitive distortions or both to produce sexually aggressive behavior. Affective motivation, in the form of depression or low self-esteem, may also motivate child molesters, according to the four-factor model. Although the theory of courtship rape implicates anger as present in all forms of courtship sexual aggression, the MTC and four-factor models account for sexual aggression that is not motivated by affective components. However, the MTC model has been overly complex for research and clinical applications, and the four-factor model does not explain why sexual aggression, rather than some form of nonsexual contact, is necessary for a perpetrator to cope with negative emotional states.

Developmental Models of Sexual Aggression

Many sexually aggressive males have experienced negative socialization experiences that facilitate sexually aggressive behavior (Hall & Hirschman, 1991). Parental abuse and neglect, failure to develop adequate social skills, academic problems, and low occupational status are among those negative socialization experiences. These negative experiences create personality problems that increase the likelihood of antisocial behavior, including sexual aggression.

Patterson, Reid, and Dishion (1992) have suggested that the specific progression for physical aggression is: noncompliance with parents → temper tantrums → hitting → assault with an object. An aggressive child's coercive behavior is reinforced insofar as aggressive behavior (e.g., physical punishment) is used to terminate aversive intrusions by other family members (Patterson, DeBaryshe, & Ramsey, 1989). Children displaying temperamental characteristics such as hyperactivity, irritability, and impulsivity may be at particular risk for coercive parenting behavior (McMahon, 1994).

Aggressive children may selectively attend to hostile environmental cues, may tend to interpret others' behavior as having hostile intentions, and may learn to expect that aggressive behavior will be rewarded and will accomplish their goals (Dodge, 1993; Dodge, Bates, & Pettit, 1990; Krueger et al., 1994; Lochman & Dodge, 1994; Lochman & Lenhart, 1993; Slaby & Guerra, 1988). Because of expected rewards for aggressive behavior, young boys are more likely to believe that aggression increases their self-esteem and are less likely than girls to feel guilty about aggression (Perry, Perry, & Weiss, 1989). Such selective information processing among aggressive individuals has been posited to have a biological basis (Moffitt, 1993; Newman & Wallace, 1993). However, the differential reinforcement of boys' and girls' aggressive behavior constitutes a double standard analogous to the double standard for sexual behavior.

Prosocial skills fail to develop in aggressive boys because prosocial behaviors are often ignored or not positively reinforced (Dodge, Pettit, McClaskey, & Brown, 1986; Patterson et al., 1992). This combination of aggressive behavior and poor social skills typically results in rejection by peers (Coie, Belding, & Underwood, 1988; Dodge, Coie, & Brakke, 1982). Such rejection by normal peers often results in forming friendships with deviant peers, who provide support for aggressive behavior in the form of rationalizations and opportunities to be aggressive (Moffitt, 1993; Mosher & Tomkins, 1988; Patterson et al., 1989). Aggressive behavior and poor social skills also result in poor academic performance because the child's noncompliant, undercontrolled behavior interferes with learning (Newcomb, Bukowski, & Pattee, 1993; Patterson et al., 1989). The lack of rewards for conventional behavior in the academic sphere may lead to a dependence on antisocial behavior and on antisocial peers for reinforcement. Alternatively, the relationship between undercontrolled behavior and academic difficulties may not be unidirectional, but may be mediated by underlying factors, including family discord, below-average intellectual functioning, language deficits, and neurodevelopmental delay (Hinshaw, 1993).

Most adolescents who engage in antisocial behavior do not persist in such behavior beyond adolescence (Moffitt, 1993; Rivera & Widom, 1990). However, those that do may either "specialize" in a single type of antisocial behavior, such as sexual aggression, or engage in multiple types of antisocial behaviors (Gillmore et al., 1991; Loeber, 1985). The likelihood of antisocial behavior that persists into adulthood may be a function of the severity of developmental problems.

Although general developmental models explain how aggressive behavior is conditioned, they do not explain why some males become aggressive in a nonsexual manner while other males become sexually aggressive. However, similar to the parental influence postulated in the general developmental models of aggression, parental behavior may also influence the development of sexually aggressive behavior (Marshall, Hudson, & Hodkinson, 1993). Belsky, Steinberg, and Draper (1991) have postulated, from an evolutionary perspective, that children who are insecurely attached to their parents, as a result of coercive family experiences during the first five to seven years of life, may perceive relationships as unpredictable and self-serving.

Although the literature on security of attachment during infancy and subsequent acting-out behavior is inconsistent (McMahon, 1994), failures in parental attachment may contribute to similar failures in peer and romantic attachments (Friedrich, 1990; Hazan & Shaver, 1987, 1990). Insecurely attached children may reach pubertal maturation earlier than children who perceive relationships as enduring and mutually rewarding, and may engage in accelerated sexual activity and temporary relationships (Belsky et al., 1991). For example, boys from divorced families initiate coitus earlier than boys from non-divorced families, independent of parental surveillance (Newcomer & Udry, 1987). Adolescents who do not have adequate adult role models may initiate sex early as an act of independence in an effort to enter the adult world (Elliott & Morse, 1987; Jessor, Costa, Jessor, & Donovan, 1983; Moffitt, 1993; Rodgers & Rowe, 1993). Males having weak confidence in emotional relationships may also seek to coerce females into exclusive sexual relationships (Maccoby, 1991).

Early initiation of sex may result in the oversexualizing of relationships because a person is developmentally unprepared for sex. People who initiate sexual activity after they are developmentally prepared have the capacity to develop the emotional relationships that provide a context for sex. Failure to achieve emotional intimacy in sexual relationships may result in efforts to seek intimacy through sexual behaviors with multiple partners or with weaker, less threatening persons (Marshall, 1989; Marshall & Eccles, 1993). Indeed, early onset of coitus is positively associated with a number of sexual partners (Leitenberg, Greenwald, & Tarran, 1989). However, multiple sexual relationships without emotional intimacy may also cause a young male to view females as objects whose sole purpose is his sexual gratification. A young male may abandon those females who do not cater to his sexual wishes or alternatively may force them to have sex if he perceives his opportunities for sex with other females as limited.

Unlike nonsexually aggressive males, sexually aggressive males, as a result of social skills deficits (Awad & Saunders, 1989; Fagan & Wexler, 1988; Katz, 1990; Shoor, Speed, & Bertelt, 1966), tend not to be bonded to deviant peers (Blaske, Borduin, Henggeler, & Mann, 1989; Prentky & Knight, 1993). Those adolescents who are sexually aggressive and bonded to deviant peers may become generally antisocial via modeling (Ageton, 1983; Moffitt, 1993), whereas those adolescent sexual aggressors who are not bonded to deviant peers may be "specialists" in that their deviance is limited primarily to sexually aggressive behavior. Because adolescents who are sexually aggressive may not be bonded to peers, who influence the sexual behavior of most adolescents (Billy & Udry, 1985a, 1985b; Smith, 1989; Smith, Udry, & Morris, 1985; Udry & Billy, 1987), they may also be particularly susceptible to messages of pornography about sexual relationships (Marshall, 1989; Marshall & Eccles, 1993). Thus, rather than selectively attending to hostile cues from the environment, sexually aggressive males may attend to what they perceive as sexual cues in the environment that may be interpreted as an invitation to engage in sexual or sexually aggressive behavior (Lipton, McDonel, & McFall, 1987). Although sexually aggressive males' social skills may be impaired relative to those of males who are not sexually aggressive (Lipton et al., 1987), males who are sexually coercive with peers may have social skills that are sufficiently intact to form the peer heterosexual relationships that provide the opportunity for sexually aggressive behavior.

Developmental models of consensual heterosexual and coercive sexual behavior are presented in Table 2-1. The starting point for the model is about age 11, when gender segregation ends and boys and girls begin to socially interact (Maccoby, 1988). Intact social skills as a result of supportive, noncoercive parenting allow a young male to develop nonsexual friendships with peer females. Sex is initiated later than in the coercive developmental path, and sexual relationships tend to be lasting and involve emotional investment because of good social skills. Relation-

Table 2-1. Developmental Models of Consensual Heterosexual and
Coercive Sexual Behavior

Consensual Sexual Behavior

Heterosexual friendships because of intact social skills	Later initiation of sex; nonsexual and sexual relationships with females	Lasting sexual relationships because of intact social skills	Nonhostile relations with females because of lasting relationships	Consensual sexual behavior

Coercive Sexual Behavior

Few heterosexual friendships because of poor social skills	Early initiation of sex; heterosexual relationships overly sexualized	Promiscuity because poor social skills prevent lasting relationships	Hostility toward females because of nonlasting relationships	Coercive sexual behavior

ships with females are generally positive and sexual relationships are consensual.

The developmental path to coercive sexual behavior may be a function of inadequate social skills produced by coercive parenting. Sex is initiated early in an effort to attain independent, adult status (Elliott & Morse, 1987; Jessor et al., 1983; Moffitt, 1993; Rodgers & Rowe, 1993), but the failure to find intimacy may result in brief relationships and may motivate the person to seek intimacy in additional sexual contacts (Marshall, 1989). As compared to noncoercive males, sexually coercive males tend to have more sexual partners (Koss et al., 1985; Malamuth, Heavey, & Linz, 1993; Malamuth, Sockloskie, Koss, & Tanaka, 1991). The ability of some sexually aggressive men to engage in consensual sexual relationships suggests that they are sufficiently socially skilled to form such relationships (Muehlenhard & Falcon, 1990). However, the consensual sexual relationships of sexually aggressive men are perceived as short-lived and unsatisfying (Kanin, 1983, 1985), which may suggest that sexually aggressive men's social skills are not adequate. This dissatisfaction may result in generalized hostility toward women and ultimately in coercive sexual behavior.

The developmental models presented in Table 2-1 are applicable to consensual and coercive sexual behavior with peers. However, the developmental path to sexual behavior with significantly younger children may differ from these two models. Child molesters, similar to males who are sexually coercive with peers, may experience an early initiation of sexual activity. Unlike males who are sexually coercive with peers, however, child molesters' sexual initiation tends to be as a victim (Prentky & Knight, 1993). Because child molesters' social skills may be even more impaired than those of males who are sexually coercive with peers (Segal & Marshall, 1985, 1986), many child molesters may not be able to form nonsexual peer relationships. Adolescent child molesters are more easily threatened by peer male-female relationships than nonsexual adolescent offenders (Katz, 1990). However, adolescent males with limited heterosocial interactions usually do not engage in deviant behavior if they have adequate relationships with male peers (Jessor et al., 1983).

What may distinguish child molesters from other adolescents is that their poor social skills do not allow any relationships with female or male peers. Thus, the corrective feedback about inappropriate sexual behavior that is often available from peers is not available to child molesters. Rather than engaging in both consensual and coercive sexual behavior as do males who are sexually coercive with peers, the sexual behavior of adolescent males who molest significantly younger children tends to be exclusively directed toward children. Often, the victims are siblings, who are the most available targets (Johnson, 1988). Although child molesters tend not to engage in other forms of antisocial behavior (Hall & Proctor, 1987), they may be consistent with conceptualizations of delinquents who "specialize" in their delinquent behavior (Loeber, 1985). Insofar as child molesters are most frequently sexually victimized by other males, such modeling results in child molesters being more likely to sexually victimize males than are males who are sexually coercive with peers.

Approximately 50% of adult sexual offenders report that they began sexually offending during adolescence, but this does not necessarily mean that sexually aggressive behavior persists into adulthood for 50% of adolescent sexual offenders (Abel, Mittelman, & Becker, 1985; Davis & Leitenberg, 1987). Most adolescents who engage in antisocial behavior during adolescence do not persist in antisocial behavior beyond adolescence (Moffitt, 1993; Rivera & Widom, 1990), and presumably many, if not most, adolescent sexual aggressors do not persist in their sexually aggressive behavior. Intact premorbid social functioning and opportunities for rewards for nonaggressive behavior in conventional activities (e.g., school, employment, marriage) may deter adolescents who engage in antisocial behavior from continuing a life of acting out (Moffitt, 1993). For sexually aggressive adolescents, opportunities for consenting and satisfying sexual relationships may be a deterrent against persistent sexually aggressive behavior. Thus, adolescent sexual aggressors who have impaired social skills and engage in exclusively coercive sex may be more likely to continue to be sexually aggressive than adolescent sexual aggressors who have the social skills that allow them to engage in consenting sexual relationships. Most adolescent sexual aggressors fit into the latter category, in that 59 to 86% report that they have had consenting sexual experiences in addition to coercive ones (Davis & Leitenberg, 1987). The sexually aggressive behavior of adolescence-limited sexual aggressors may be more influenced by situational factors (e.g., sexual arousal, distorted perceptions of situations, anger) than by a chronic personality-based propensity for acting out across situations (cf. Moffitt, 1993; Rivera & Widom, 1990).

Is coercive sexual behavior simply a normal phase of seeking independent, adult status during adolescence that subsides once young males learn that noncoercive sexual behavior is more rewarding (e.g., Roberts, Abrams, & Finch, 1973)? Adolescent sexually aggressive behavior could be considered normative if normalcy is based on frequency (cf. Moffitt, 1993). In a study of college men, 57.3% admitted to perpetrating unwanted sexual activity (Muehlenhard & Linton, 1987). There is also some evidence that adolescent sexual offenders are less pathological than adolescent nonsexual offenders (Oliver, Hall, & Neuhaus, 1993). Sexually aggressive scripts may be culturally conditioned and sexual aggression may be viewed by some men simply as an assertion of the masculine gender role (Herman, 1990; Koss et al., 1994; Rozee, 1993). Some "mild" forms of sexual aggression that do not involve physical force, such as verbally persuading an unwilling person to have sex or getting a person intoxicated, also may not be viewed as being as serious as other forms of nonsexual physical aggression.

Conceptualizing adolescent sexual aggression as normal may encourage minimization and denial of sexually aggressive behavior (Becker, Harris, & Sales, 1993; National Adolescent Perpetrator Network, 1988). Although sexually aggressive behavior may desist among many adolescent perpetrators, the effects of sexually aggressive behavior may not as easily desist for victims (Briere, 1988; Browne & Finkelhor, 1986; Hanson, 1990; Kendall-Tackett et al., 1993; Koss et al., 1994; Wyatt et al., 1993). If the seriousness of sexually aggressive behavior is defined in terms of impact on victims (Eron, 1987; Hall & Hirschman, 1993, 1994; Hall, Hirschman, & Oliver, 1994), then adolescent sexual aggression must be viewed as pathological behavior, even if it does cease for most adolescent perpetrators. Feminists have argued that the "normal" male socialization toward sexually aggressive behavior does not make sexual aggression acceptable behavior (Herman, 1990; Koss et al., 1994).

✗ Social Learning Models of Sexual Aggression

Social learning models suggest that sexually aggressive behavior is modeled when boys are themselves sexually abused. As parental physical aggression places children at risk for becoming physically aggressive (Dodge et al., 1990), sexual abuse places children at risk for becoming sexually aggressive. Sexually abused children may be rewarded by perpetrators for sexual behavior and learn to use sexual behavior as a strategy for manipulating others (Finkelhor, 1988). Victims of sexual aggression may identify with the aggressor because such identification is more rewarding than a victim identity (Ryan, 1989). More than 25% of a sample of 276 sexually abused children from seven clinical settings touched others' "sex parts," whereas only 6% of a sample of 880 nonabused children at a pediatric clinic did so (Friedrich et al., 1992). Sexual victimization is more characteristic of the developmental histories of adult child molesters than of rapists (Prentky & Knight, 1993; Seghorn, Prentky, & Boucher, 1987).

The social learning model does not explain why most children and adults who are sexually abused do not become sexually aggressive. In a review of recent empirical studies, 21 to 49% of sexually molested children exhibited no symptoms, and symptoms abated within one to one and one half years for 50 to 66% of those who experienced symptoms (Kendall-Tackett et al., 1993). Many men who are sexually aggressive against women also have not experienced childhood sexual abuse (Prentky & Knight, 1993; Seghorn et al., 1987). Moreover, the model does not explain why sexual abuse that is primarily perpetrated by men results in males becoming sexually aggressive with girls (Herman, 1990), which is more common than homosexual sexual aggression (Hall, Maiuro, Vitaliano, & Proctor, 1986). However, proponents of the cycle of abuse have argued that there exist large numbers of undetected female perpetrators of aggression (Herman, 1990).

Feminist Theory

Similar to the social learning model, feminist theory is a developmental model to the extent that attitudes concerning rape are conditioned during a person's development. Thus, male sexually aggressive behavior is not deviant, as in the physiological model of sexual aggression, but a product of normal socialization (Herman, 1990; Koss et al., 1994; Rozee, 1993). Sexual aggression was redefined by feminists from the victim's perspective, rather than from the perpetrator's perspective that has guided many other theories of sexual aggression (Donat & D'Emilio, 1992). Sexual acts that have a negative impact on the victim are sexually aggressive even if the perpetrator did not intend to be sexually aggressive (Hall & Hirschman, 1993, 1994; Hall et al., 1994a). Sexually aggressive behavior is an act of violence that serves to enforce men's societal control over women (Brownmiller, 1975; Clark & Lewis, 1977; Darke, 1990; Donat & D'Emilio, 1992; Herman, 1990; Russell, 1988a), but the impact of sexual aggression is trivialized because of the subordinate status of women in society (Burt, 1980). Feminist theorists have broadened the definition of sexually aggressive behavior to include coercive sexual acts that occur between intimates as well as between strangers (Kanin, 1984; Kanin & Parcell, 1977; Koss et al., 1985).

Given that all men are culturally conditioned, at least to some degree, by sexist influences (Herman, 1990; Koss et al., 1994; Rozee, 1993), feminist theory does not explain why more men are not sexually aggressive. Moreover, the conceptualization of sexual aggression as a violent act does not explain why sexual aggressors are both physically and sexually violent (Ellis, 1989; Hotaling & Sugarman, 1986; Mosher & Anderson, 1986; Quinsey, 1984). However, feminists have recently included sexual motivation as a possible factor in sexually aggressive behavior (Brownmiller, 1975; Donat & D'Emilio, 1992; Estrich, 1987; Koss, 1993b; Koss et al., 1994). The potential for sexual aggression in any form of sexual contact between males and females also may interfere with women's ability to enjoy their sexuality (Donat & D'Emilio, 1992). Similar to the sociological model, another possible limitation of the feminist model is an overemphasis on victim-initiated prevention of sexual aggression, which may divert attention and responsibility from perpetrators (American Psychological Association Commission on Violence and Youth, 1993; Browne, 1993; Hall & Hirschman, 1991).

The Confluence Model of Sexual Aggression

Malamuth, Heavey, and Linz (1993) have proposed that sexual aggression is the result of a convergence of multiple risk variables that interact with environmental factors. Unlike many other approaches to sexual aggression in which there is an almost exclusive focus on clinical research, the Malamuth et al. (1993) model incorporates work from nonclinical areas of psychology, including social, developmental, and evolutionary psychology. Another innovation of this research is that sexual and nonsexual aggression against women is studied within the same framework (Malamuth et al., 1991). The stated goal of Malamuth et al. (1993) was to develop a parsimonious model to predict sexually aggressive behavior. However, the model is complex and Malamuth et al. (1993, p. 90) also contended that "it is necessary to develop more fully 'vertically integrated' multiple-level, complementary explanations of ultimate and proximate causes" of sexual coercion.

Malamuth et al. (1993) suggested that causal factors may not always be exclusively motivational, disinhibitory, or opportunistic, and that some factors may have effects at multiple levels. Such complexity is characteristic of predictive models, which may be less concerned than explanatory models with parsimonious explanations and clinical applicability (see chapter 1). Although the Malamuth et al. (1993) model is complex, it suggests that sexual promiscuity and hostile masculinity are two primary motivational factors that interact to produce sexually aggressive behavior. Given adequate motivation for sexually aggressive behavior, reductions in the inhibition against sexually aggressive behavior and the opportunity for aggressive acts must occur.

Malamuth and his colleagues (1991) appear to posit that physiological sexual arousal and affective components are important predictors of sexually aggressive behavior among the college populations in which the model was developed. However, the sexual promiscuity variable in the Malamuth et al. (1991) study involved age at first intercourse and number of sexual partners, rather than sexual arousal in response to sexually aggressive stimuli, which is the common definition of a sexual preference for rape (Barbaree & Marshall, 1989, 1991; Hall, Shondrick et al., 1993b; Harris et al., 1992). Although it appears that number of sexual partners may include unwilling sexual partners, which would make the sexual promiscuity variable and sexually coercive behavior nonorthogonal, Malamuth (personal communication, November 1993) has stated that subjects were asked to distinguish between coerced and noncoerced sexual experiences. However, sexual promiscuity does allow access to potential victims.

Sexually aggressive men have sexual contact with more persons than nonaggressive men but are less satisfied with their sexual experiences (Kanin, 1983, 1985; Koss & Dinero, 1988). A man who has sex with multiple persons has more opportunities to be sexually coercive than a man who is not having sex or who is having sex in a committed, monogamous relationship in which there is less likelihood of sexual aggression (Buss & Schmitt, 1993). A man who has sex with multiple women has a higher likelihood of meeting women whom he may perceive as vulnerable to sexual coercion than a man who has a limited number of sexual partners. Thus, sexual promiscuity appears to be an opportunity variable rather than a motivational variable.

Sexual promiscuity was not hypothesized to be a singular path to sexual aggression, but was hypothesized to interact with hostile masculinity in facilitating sexual aggression (Malamuth et al., 1993). Men who were hostile toward women and sexually promiscuous were sexually coercive, whereas men who were hostile toward women and not sexually promiscuous were coercive in nonsexual ways (Malamuth et al., 1991). This finding underscores sexual promiscuity as an opportunity variable, insofar as men who are hostile toward women and who also have opportunities to be sexually aggressive (i.e., they are sexually promiscuous) tend to be sexually aggressive, whereas men who are hostile toward women but do not have opportunities to be sexually aggressive tend to be nonsexually aggressive.

The measures used to assess the Malamuth et al. (1991) hostile masculinity construct (hostility toward women, adversarial sexual beliefs, negative masculinity) reflect primarily cognitive components (i.e., beliefs, attitudes) rather than the affective dyscontrol described in other models (e.g., Hall & Hirschman, 1991; Prentky & Knight, 1991). Sexually aggressive men who are impulsive and experience anger dyscontrol problems probably would not be represented in a college population, in that self-control and conformity are prerequisites for entering and remaining in college (cf. Sears, 1986). Thus, to the extent that hostile masculinity is a cognitive variable, the Malamuth et al. (1991) data are consistent with the Hall and Hirschman (1991) model, which suggests that most sexual aggression among college students is motivated by cognitive distortions.

The Malamuth et al. (1993) model has been developed among college students and is not necessarily applicable to other populations in which sexual aggressors may be motivated by other variables. Moreover, the developmental basis of the sexual promiscuity path, which includes parental violence, being physically and sexually abused as a child, and delinquency, may not exist for all types of sexual aggression. The Malamuth et al. (1993) model appears consistent with *early onset* sexual aggressors who initially are sexually aggressive as adolescents or preadolescents (Prentky & Knight, 1993). These early onset sexual aggressors are qualitatively different from *late onset* sexual aggressors, who do not commit offenses as juveniles (Prentky & Knight, 1993). As compared with early onset sexual aggressors, late onset sexual aggressors have better interpersonal, academic, and vocational competence and are less violent. Late onset sexual aggressors also used less pornography than men who began to be sexually aggressive during adolescence.

Summary

Some aggressive behavior has developmental origins. However, sexually aggressive males may have different developmental histories than males who are physically aggressive, in terms of poorer social skills and a tendency to emphasize the sexual aspects of relationships. Sexual abuse and sexist cultural conditioning have been posited as causal variables in sexually aggressive behavior, but many males who are sexually abused or have been exposed to sexist conditioning do not become sexually aggressive. The confluence model of sexual aggression posits a developmental path to the cognitive distortions that lead to sexually aggressive behavior. However, many sexual aggressors have a late onset of sexual aggression that does not include developmental problems.

Conclusion

There are several common elements in the theories reviewed in this chapter. The theoretical models reviewed in this chapter support the four motivational precursors of sexually aggressive behavior proposed by Hall and Hirschman (1991, 1992). However, current theories of sexual aggression tend to be mutually exclusive in their explanations of sexually aggressive behavior (Marshall & Barbaree, 1990a). Proposed causal elements are assumed to be causal for all sexual aggressors (Barbaree & Marshall, 1991), but theories are often population-specific (e.g., college students, incarcerated offenders), are based on data that are difficult to replicate in other settings (e.g., clinical judgments, case history data), or propose a causal sequence of behavior that does not allow for alternative causal sequences (e.g., all sexual aggression begins with early developmental antecedents). Because there is no single theory or set of theories of sexual aggression that is generally accepted, researchers and clinicians lack a common language for communication, which may inhibit theoretical integration and enhance competition between various "camps" of researchers and clinicians. Although various approaches have developed simultaneously, individual approaches typically have not been informed by existing approaches in an integrative sense.

In addition to the mutual exclusivity of theories of sexual aggression, these theories are becoming increasingly complex and less clinically applicable. Although I have eschewed complexity in chapter 1, I advocated multivariate approaches as a reaction to the univariate models that have long dominated the sexual-aggression field (G. Hall, 1990a). However, the Hall (1990a) review was on prediction of sexual aggression, and complexity is useful in predictive models to the extent that it improves prediction. As discussed in chapter 1, the utility of predictive approaches is based on the degree of association between predictor and criterion variables. Conceptual confusion between predictive and explanatory approaches to sexually aggressive behavior may lead to unwarranted comparisons between the two approaches. Although some multivariate models are quite useful for predictive purposes, the clinical implications of these models are unclear (Hall, 1990a). Thus, some complex theoretical models may fail in their intended purpose of being explanatory. At the risk of oversimplifying various theoretical formulations, in this chapter I have attempted to categorize recent theories of sexual aggression based on their major emphases. In response to the need for a comprehensive, yet parsimonious, explanatory model of sexual aggression that is clinically applicable, the quadripartite model (Hall & Hirschman, 1991, 1992) was developed and is reviewed in chapter 3.

3

A Quadripartite Model of Sexual Aggression

Each of the models reviewed in chapter 2 contributes to an understanding of the motivational components of sexually aggressive behavior. I have attempted to integrate the essential components of these theories and have proposed the quadripartite model that is applicable to sexual aggression against women (Hall & Hirschman, 1991) and children (Hall & Hirschman, 1992). This model is explanatory insofar as it is theoretically based and identifies causal variables in sexually aggressive behavior. The model is sufficiently comprehensive to explain different types of sexual aggressors (e.g., incest offenders, extrafamilial child molesters, acquaintance rapists, stranger rapists) but sufficiently parsimonious for clinical applications (Hall, Shondrick, et al., 1993a). The model includes physiological sexual arousal, cognitive distortions, affective dyscontrol, and developmentally related personality problems as motivational precursors of sexually aggressive behavior. Each of these motivational precursors corresponds with a subtype of sexual aggressor that is primarily motivated by one of the four precursors. The major characteristics of each subtype are presented in Table 3-1 from Hall, Shondrick, et al. (1993a).

Support for the physiological, cognitive, and affective components is provided in the theories reviewed in chapter 2 (Hall & Hirschman, 1991,

Table 3-1. Subtypes of Sexual Aggressors

Subtype	Characteristics
Physiological	1. Common among sexual aggressors against children 2. Multiple victims, often male, common 3. Physical violence against victim uncommon 4. Nonsexual aggression uncommon
Cognitive	1. Sexual aggression is planned 2. Less impulsive or violent than other subtypes 3. Lower likelihood of apprehension than other subtypes 4. Acquaintance rape or incest common
Affective	1. Sexual aggression is opportunistic, unplanned, and often violent 2. Sexual and nonsexual aggression common 3. Anger is common among sexual aggressors against adults 4. Depression is common among sexual aggressors against children
Developmentally related personality problems	1. Chronic personality problems 2. Generalized propensity to violate rules 3. Sexual aggression typically violent 4. Poorest treatment prognosis of subtypes

1992). Unlike other models of sexual aggression, our model includes both adjudicated and nonadjudicated men who are sexually aggressive. Although nonadjudicated sexually aggressive men have been described as qualitatively different from adjudicated sexually aggressive men (e.g., Barbaree et al., 1994), there is much overlap between these two groups in their sexually aggressive acts, as well as in the motivation for these acts. The primary difference between an incarcerated rapist and an acquaintance rapist is that the former has been caught whereas the latter usually has not. Moreover, sexual arousal patterns, cognitive distortions, affective dyscontrol, and developmentally related personality problems overlap between adjudicated and nonadjudicated sexual aggressors (Hall, Shondrick, et al., 1993a; Malamuth et al., 1993). Thus, the similarities between adjudicated and nonadjudicated sexually aggressive men warrant their inclusion in a single model of sexual aggression (Hall & Hirschman, 1991).

Although the model has been critiqued as being categorical (Malamuth et al., 1993), Hall and Hirschman (1991) have discussed synergistic interactions that may occur between various motivational precursors. Such synergistic interactions occur most commonly in the developmentally related personality problems subtype. For example, some sexual aggressors with developmentally related personality problems also exhibit deviant sexual arousal (Serin, Malcolm, Khanna, & Barbaree, 1994). Given that some of the more complex models propose developmental paths to sexually aggressive behavior (Malamuth et al., 1991; Prentky & Knight, 1991), the interactions among motivational variables in these models are consistent with the synergistic relations between motivational variables in the developmentally related personality problems motivational precursor in the Hall and Hirschman (1991) model. Although synergistic interactions among motivational precursors are possible for the physiological, cognitive, and affective subtypes, these subtypes tend to be primarily motivated by a single motivational precursor (Hall & Hirschman, 1991, 1992).

Some men who are sexually aroused to sexually aggressive stimuli, or have cognitive distortions about women, or are affectively dyscontrolled, or have developmentally related personality problems, are not sexually aggressive (Hall & Hirschman, 1993). Thus, the presence of one or more of these motivational precursors does not necessarily mean that a person will become sexually aggressive. In an effort to differentiate men who act on these motivational precursors in a sexually aggressive manner from those who do not, we have proposed that sexually aggressive and nonaggressive men have different threshold gradients for sexually aggressive behavior (Hall & Hirschman, 1993).

Inhibitory Thresholds for Sexually Aggressive Behavior

When the appraised benefits of sexually aggressive behavior exceed its appraised threats, then sexually aggressive behavior is more likely to occur than when the converse holds (Bachman, Pasternoster, & Ward, 1992; Berkowitz, 1989; Hall & Hirschman, 1991; Lazarus & Folkman, 1984; Megargee, 1984). Thus, the appraised threats of sexually aggressive behavior serve as a threshold that inhibits sexually aggressive behavior. What are the appraised threats of sexually aggressive behavior? One form of appraised threat is *self threat*. Some men are not sexually aggressive because they may fear legal or societal sanctions against sexual aggression. However, in a study of undergraduate men, 15.7–23.8% reported that they would engage in some form of sexual aggression if they were assured that they would not be caught (Malamuth, 1988a).

The other form of threat that may serve as an inhibitory threshold of sexual aggression is *victim threat*—the threat of harm to the potential victim. Many men who would not be sexually aggressive under any circumstance, even if they would not be detected (Malamuth, 1988a), presumably are not sexually aggressive because of victim empathy or moral considerations (Etzioni, 1988; Megargee, 1984). However, some men may not report that they would engage in sexual aggression because such reporting is socially undesirable (Walker et al., 1993). Nevertheless, sexual aggression is socially undesirable at least partly because of its effects on victims. Thus, a male who is sexually aggressive must believe that the benefits of sexually aggressive behavior (e.g., sexual gratification, sense of power, victim will enjoy rape) are more compelling than either victim threat or self threat.

In a direct test of the self/other threat hypothesis, Bachman et al. (1992) examined the deterrent effects of moral beliefs and formal sanctions (i.e., dismissal from the university and arrest) on college men's self-reported likelihood of engaging in sexual assault. Those men who believed rape to be morally wrong were less likely to engage in sexual assault than men who did not perceive sexual assault as morally wrong, independent of the likelihood of formal sanctions for sexual assault. Conversely, the likelihood of engaging in sexual assault among those men who did not view sexual assault as morally wrong was a function of the likelihood of formal sanctions (Bachman et al., 1992). The men who viewed rape as morally wrong could be conceptualized as not engaging in sexual assault because of the impact of sexual assault on victims (victim threat). Self threat appears to govern the behavior of those men who did not view sexual assault as morally wrong insofar as they would be more likely to engage in sexual assaultive behavior if they were unlikely to be punished.

When a woman refuses to have sex, most men, rather than becoming sexually aggressive, may attempt to persuade her to have sex or may seek another partner (Shotland, 1992). However, a significant minority of males appraise the benefits of sexually aggressive behavior as exceeding its liabilities. Among sexually aggressive males, motivational variables may interact with situational factors that affect the likelihood of sexually aggressive behavior (Malamuth et al., 1993; Marshall & Barbaree, 1990a). Although the need for research on situational factors has been acknowledged, most work has focused on motivational or trait factors (Malamuth et al., 1993; Marshall & Barbaree, 1990a). However, the importance of situational cues is acknowledged even in biologically based models of disinhibition (Newman & Wallace, 1993). The physiological, cognitive, and affective motivational precursors of sexually aggressive behavior are primarily state variables (Hall & Hirschman, 1991) activated by situational determinants. Thus, situational determinants that activate these motivational precursors (e.g., pornographic stimuli, misinterpretation of another person's sexual intentions, anger provocation) may facilitate sexually aggressive behavior in persons who are primarily motivated by one of these three variables.

Neither trait nor state variables are sufficient to produce sexually aggressive behavior (cf. Craig, 1990; Finkelhor, 1984; Shotland, 1989, 1992). For example, state sexual arousal to rape stimuli can be induced in men who are not sexually aggressive (Barbaree & Marshall, 1991), and many men who are not sexually aggressive exhibit trait sexual arousal to pedophilic or rape stimuli (Hall et al., in press; Hall, Shondrick, et al., 1993a). Thus, it is the combination of motivational precursors and situational determinants that facilitates sexually aggressive behavior. However, unlike other theories that do not posit specific person × situation determinants of sexually aggressive behavior (e.g., Craig, 1990), the quadripartite model posits that specific situational variables that are conceptually related to motivational precursors of sexually aggressive behavior evoke sexually aggressive behavior.

Men who are sexually aggressive have lower thresholds for action than do men who are not (Hall & Hirschman, 1993). However, it is obvious that men who are sexually aggressive are not sexually aggressive in every situation in which there are opportunities to be so (Marshall & Barbaree, 1990a). Thus, sexually aggressive men have not "lost control" of their behavior (cf. Marlatt, 1983). Some situations may not be sufficiently sexually arousing, excusable, or provoking for sexually aggressive behavior to occur. Potential sexual aggressors presumably can effectively cope with urges to become sexually aggressive in these low-potency situations (Miner, Day, & Nafpaktitus, 1989).

What situational determinants cause sexual aggressors to exceed the inhibitory threshold for sexually aggressive behavior? For the sexual aggressor who is primarily motivated by physiological sexual arousal, child pornography or violent pornography, in which sexual aggression is portrayed as sexually arousing, as well as sexual fantasies of rape or child molestation, may be stimuli that increase the likelihood of acting out in a sexually aggressive manner (Russell, 1988b). Pornography may be a critical situational determinant of sexually aggressive behavior among child molesters (Carter, Prentky, Knight, Vanderveer, & Boucher, 1987) and the use of violent pornography is also associated with an increase in the self-reported likelihood of sexually aggressive behavior (Demare, Briere, & Lips, 1988). In addition to pornography, more benign stimuli may also be situational determinants of sexually aggressive behavior for a sexual aggressor whose sexual aggression is primarily motivated by physiological sexual arousal. Seeing children in bathing suits at a public swimming pool or nude in a household may be highly arousing to a child molester. For rapists, films that are not necessarily pornographic but that combine sex and violence toward women (e.g., "R"-rated slasher movies) may be highly sexually arousing.

The sexual aggressor who is primarily motivated by cognitive distortions may select situations to be sexually aggressive in which he is unlikely to be blamed or punished. In a large sample of college men, among whom the cognitive subtype of sexual aggressor may be most common (Hall & Hirschman, 1991), 23.8% reported that they would force a woman into sexual acts if they could be assured of not being punished, and 15.7% reported that they would rape if impunity was assured (Malamuth, 1988a). Punishment for rape may be perceived as less likely in the context of a dating relationship or when the victim has engaged in behavior that might make her appear culpable (e.g., the victim initiated the date, wore "provocative" clothing, was drunk, etc.; Allison & Wrightsman, 1993; Muehlenhard, 1988; Shotland, 1992). Such perceptions about perceived culpability for rape may, in part, be factually based in certain jurisdictions. For example, the Broward County, Florida, police stated in May 1994 that a woman who was raped by six men at a nightclub was responsible for the rape because she was engaging in "dirty dancing." This same police department had introduced a rape victim's "provocative" clothing as evidence in a previous case.

Situational factors are particularly influential for the affective dyscontrol subtype (Hall, Shondrick, et al., 1993a). For the sexual aggressor who is primarily motivated by affective dyscontrol, anger provocation may be the situational determinant that causes him to exceed the inhibitory threshold, in that rapists report that generalized anger, as well as anger toward women, was the immediate precursor to their sexually aggressive fantasies and behavior (McKibben et al., 1994; Pithers, Kashima, Cumming, & Beal, 1988). Rapist attack behavior and victim damage also often suggest high levels of anger provocation (Prentky, Burgess, & Carter, 1986). Child molestation may represent an effort to cope with depression-inducing situations (e.g., loneliness) among sexual aggressors against children who have an affective motivation (Finkelhor, 1984; Hall, Shondrick, et al., 1993a; Pithers et al., 1988).

Some sexually aggressive individuals may experience affective overcontrol that is infrequently interrupted by severe episodes of affective dyscontrol (cf. Hershorn & Rosenbaum, 1991; Megargee, 1966). Despite the apparent affective regulation among these persons during periods of affective overcontrol, affective dyscontrol does appear to be a motivational precursor when these persons engage in sexually aggressive behavior. Affective overcontrol may serve as a pressure cooker until affect is released in a dyscontrolled fashion.

Why does affective dyscontrol among some men result in sexual rather than physical aggression? Angry states often involve physiological arousal (Berkowitz, 1990; Welsh & Gordon, 1991) and aggressive acts may reduce such arousal (Koss et al., 1994). There is evidence that anger arousal and sexual arousal to rape stimuli can coexist (McKibben et al., 1994; Yates, Barbaree, & Marshall, 1984), and that anger may enhance sexual arousal among sexually aggressive men (Zillmann, 1984). A similar synergistic process may occur in arousal reduction in that reduction of sexual arousal may also reduce anger arousal (Zillmann, Hoyt, & Day, 1974). Thus, orgasm may dissipate the physiological arousal associated with anger. Similarly, a depressed child molester may choose to interact sexually with the child, rather than to simply befriend or physically abuse the child, because the physiological "high" of sexual arousal may be more powerful in temporarily reducing depressive affect than any positive or powerful feelings gained by simply befriending or by physically abusing the child. Thus, the "advantage" of sexual aggression over physical aggression is a greater reduction in the physiological arousal associated with negative affective states. However, males who are physically aggressive often are also sexually aggressive (Hotaling & Sugarman, 1986), and it is possible that even nonsexual aggression dissipates arousal (Koss et al., 1994). The choice of aggressive outlets for some affectively dyscontrolled sexual aggressors may be circumstantial. In some circumstances (e.g., victim resistance), it may be easier and more convenient to be physically aggressive than to be sexually aggressive.

Situational motivation for sexually aggressive behavior may be less critical for persons primarily motivated by developmentally related personality problems. Antisocial persons tend not to adapt to contingencies because they have experienced noncontingent punishment and reward early in life at home, at school, and with peers (Haapasalo & Tremblay, 1994; Moffitt, 1993; Patterson et al., 1989). Because of a propensity for rule violations in the developmentally related subtype, self threat is the most critical situational determinant of sexually aggressive behavior. Victim threat may not be a deterrent to sexually aggressive behavior because of an egocentric approach to the environment.

Situational determinants of sexual aggression are not exclusively environmentally induced. Situational determinants that cause a person to exceed the inhibitory threshold may be self-induced to the extent that a person may experience physiological, cognitive, or affective states that occur independently of environmental stimulation. For example, a person primarily motivated by physiological sexual arousal may fantasize about molesting a child and be primed to act out this fantasy in the absence of pedophilic input from the environment. Thus, the sexual aggressor is responsible for his response to these situational determinants, and it is not the responsibility of the victim for provoking sexually aggressive behavior (cf. Margolin & Burman, 1993).

I must emphasize that the sexual aggressor's response to the situational determinants is based on his personal interpretation of the situation (Hall & Hirschman, 1991), not necessarily the environmental contingencies themselves (cf. Ellis, 1989; Finkelhor, 1984; Margolin & Burman, 1993). The same situational determinants may not facilitate sexual aggression in other men. For most men, violent pornography, a low likelihood of being prosecuted for rape, and being provoked by a woman do not result in sexually aggressive behavior. Thus, physiological, cognitive, and affective situational determinants alone are *not sufficient* (cf. Craig, 1990; Finkelhor, 1984; Shotland, 1989, 1992) to cause sexually aggressive behavior in the absence of adequate motivation for sexually aggressive behavior (i.e., physiological sexual arousal, cognitive distortions, affective dyscontrol, or developmentally related personality problems).

The gradient of the inhibitory threshold may vary among sexual aggressors (Hall & Hirschman, 1993). The threshold may be relatively high and very potent situational determinants would be necessary to exceed the threshold the first time a person is sexually aggressive, in that the threshold has not previously been exceeded. Sexually aggressive behavior may be reinforced by reward (e.g., sexual arousal) or lack of punishment when the inhibitory threshold is exceeded. In that sexual aggressors are intermittently reinforced insofar as they are not punished each time they offend, such conditioning may be highly resistant to extinction (Ellis, 1989). With repeated offending, the inhibitory threshold may be lowered and less potent situational determinants may be necessary to exceed the threshold. The increased risk of relapse each time a person is sexually aggressive is evidence for threshold lowering (Hall & Proctor, 1987; Hanson, Steffy, & Gauthier, 1993), as is laboratory evidence that suggests that when men are provided multiple opportunities to be aggressive, their aggression increases and their inhibitions about aggressing are reduced (Geen, Stonner, & Shope, 1975). Threshold-lowering as a function of repeated aggression has also been observed for nonsexual aggressive behavior (Holland, Holt, & Beckett, 1982).

Empirical Evidence for the Quadripartite Model

Whereas I have reviewed elsewhere how other theories support each of the four variables as motivational precursors of sexually aggressive behavior (Hall & Hirschman, 1991, 1992), in this chapter I will review some of my recent work with my colleagues that supports the quadripartite model. I have developed two parallel research approaches to support the model. The first approach, *clinical psychopathology*, involves *post hoc* clinical investigations of known sexual offenders, whose behavior has been defined as sexually aggressive by victims and the court system, even if the offender himself may deny the behavior. This approach allows the investigation of presumed motivational precursors of sexually aggressive behavior via between-group comparisons of men who have and have not been sexually aggressive and within-group comparisons of different types of sexual aggressors (e.g., rapists vs. child molesters). However, because these investigations are *post hoc*, hypotheses concerning motivation are inferential in that group differences may be effects (e.g., depression as a reaction to being incarcerated) rather than causes of sexually aggressive behavior. Moreover, the clinical approach does not necessarily allow the direct investigation of situational variables that cause a person with the potential for sexual aggression to act out.

The second approach, *experimental psychopathology*, involves an investigation of basic processes in sexually aggressive behavior via an experimental laboratory paradigm. Parsimonious theories lend themselves to testable hypotheses, and such testing is often conducted in laboratory-based paradigms. The theory of learned helplessness was launched from the laboratory and has helped advance the study of complex human behavior, including depression (Peterson, Maier, & Seligman, 1993). Parsimonious approaches to other complex human behaviors, including psychopathy (Howland, Kosson, Patterson, & Newman, 1993) and addictive disorders (Rohsenow & Marlatt, 1981), have also been developed via laboratory paradigms. If sexually aggressive behavior can be produced in the laboratory, then this approach can allow the direct investigation of situational variables that cause a person to exceed the threshold that normally inhibits sexually aggressive behavior. However, unlike the clinical psychopathology approach, the experimental approach lacks external validity to the extent that certain forms of sexually aggressive behavior (e.g., rape) cannot be simulated in a laboratory setting.

Clinical Psychopathology and Motivational Precursors of Sexually Aggressive Behavior

Unlike other comprehensive theories of sexual aggression, in which separate models for sexual aggression against women and against children have been developed, Hall and Hirschman (1991, 1992) have developed models of sexual aggression against women and against children based on the same four motivational precursors. Although sexual aggressors tend to be "specialized" in their sexually aggressive behavior, insofar as they tend to sexually aggress against either women or children (Hall & Proctor, 1987), similar motivational variables may contribute to sexual aggression against women and against children. Support for a single theory for both types of sexual aggressors is provided in a study of the personality characteristics of inpatient child molesters and rapists (Hall, Graham, & Shepherd, 1991). Child molesters and rapists significantly differed on MMPI Scales 1 and 3, which are measures of physical problems, and Scale 9, which is a measure of physical activity. However, when offender age was controlled (rapists were younger than child molesters), child molester and rapist mean MMPI profiles were not significantly different, which suggests the existence of similar personality characteristics in both groups.

Models in which separate typologies have been developed for child molesters and rapists typically have not considered perpetrator age and physical activity level. Offense characteristics, which are used to differentiate between child molesters and rapists in inductive typologies (e.g., Prentky & Knight, 1991), may mask motivational similarities. For example, the level of physical violence committed in a sexually aggressive act may be a function of the perpetrator's age, with younger perpetrators more capable and likely to be violent than older perpetrators. Yet, both types of perpetrator may be motivated by anger. Thus, offense characteristics may be analogous to a *phenotype* (see chapter 2), whereas personality and motivational variables may be analogous to a *genotype*. Some researchers have suggested that a comprehensive theory of sexual aggression is not possible, and they have advocated the development of specific theories for specific types of sexually aggressive behavior (Marshall & Eccles, 1993). However, such an emphasis on phenotypes may ignore the potential communalities among sexual aggressors (i.e., genotypes) that may simplify the tasks of assessment and treatment (Hall & Hirschman, 1991).

The Hall et al. (1991) study additionally provides support for the existence of two of the four motivational precursors of sexually aggressive behavior proposed by Hall and Hirschman (1991, 1992). A cluster-analytic procedure revealed two subtypes of sexual aggressors, based on their MMPI profiles (Hall et al., 1991). The first subtype, in which MMPI Scale 4 was the most elevated scale in the MMPI profile, corresponds to the developmentally related personality problems motivational precursor of sexually aggressive behavior (Hall & Hirschman, 1991, 1992). MMPI Scale 4 elevations among sexual aggressors suggest a stable, antisocial personality pattern (Hall et al., 1991). This first subtype accounted for approximately 50% of the Hall et al. (1991) sample and is comparable to the 54% of a sample of inpatient sexual offenders who reported that their first sexual offense was before 18 years of age (Prentky & Knight, 1993). The second sexual aggressor subtype in the Hall et al. (1991) data is consistent with the affective dyscontrol motivational precursor of sexually aggressive behavior (Hall & Hirschman, 1991, 1992), in that several MMPI scales were extremely elevated, including Scales 8, 2, and 4. Sexual aggressors against women and against children were both represented in each subtype, which supports the hypothesis that both types of sexual aggression have similar motivational precursors. The clusters in the Hall et al. (1991) study appear to provide relatively unbiased, objective support for two of the four sexual aggressor subtypes proposed by Hall and Hirschman (1991, 1992), in that the clusters were empirically derived rather than predetermined on the basis of a theoretical number of clusters.

Why were only two of the four motivational precursors of sexually aggressive behavior represented in the Hall et al. (1991) data? Perhaps the inpatient sample that was studied did not include all subtypes of sexual aggressors. In an outpatient forensic sample, a cluster-analytic approach revealed three different subtypes in a study of the MMPI profiles of child molesters (Hall, Shepherd, & Mudrak, 1992). The two subtypes in the Hall et al. (1991) study were replicated and a third subtype that corresponds with the cognitive distortions subtype (Hall & Hirschman, 1991, 1992) was additionally revealed (Hall et al., 1992). The MMPI profiles of the subjects in this third subtype were characterized by moderate elevations on Scales 4 and 8, which is consistent with odd, peculiar thinking and behavior, including sexual deviation (Graham, 1987).

Among the subjects in the Hall et al. (1992) study, 44% had MMPI profiles consistent with the developmentally related personality disorders subtype, 17% had MMPI profiles consistent with the affective dyscontrol subtype, and 39% had MMPI profiles consistent with the cognitive subtype. As in the Hall et al. (1991) study, the cluster derivation in the Hall et al. (1992) study was unbiased insofar as the clusters were empirically derived rather than predetermined on the basis of a theoretical number of clusters. The presence of the cognitive subtype in an outpatient sample (Hall et al., 1992) and its absence in an inpatient sample of sexual aggressors may be a function of the types of offenses by the cognitive distortions subtype (e.g., incest offenses, date and acquaintance rape), which may be perceived as less deviant and as not warranting institutionalization. Moreover, although the cognitive subtype of sexual aggressor may be the most common in nonadjudicated populations (Hall & Hirschman, 1991; Koss et al., 1987), the percentage of cognitive subtype subjects in the Hall et al. (1992) forensic sample was a function of arrests. Thus, it is not surprising that the developmentally related personality problem subjects, who have the most chronic problems, constituted the largest percentage of subjects in the Hall et al. (1992) sample. However, persons who engage in antisocial behavior that persists from adolescence into adulthood may be overrepresented in a forensic setting, insofar as they may represent a small percentage of all offenders (Moffitt, 1993; Rivera & Widom, 1990).

A limitation of the Hall et al. (1992) MMPI data in developing an explanatory model of sexual aggression is that personality data do not necessarily imply motivational variables. Moreover, the MMPI profiles of the child molesters in the sample did not significantly differ from those of the nonsexual offenders in the sample who had committed violent (e.g., assault, robbery, kidnapping) and nonviolent (e.g., burglary, forgery, sale of narcotics) offenses. This may be a function of the insensitivity of the MMPI to criminological variables (Hall et al., 1986), given that sexual and nonsexual offenses are qualitatively different. However, sexual aggressors have been found to be similar to nonsexual aggressors on other psychometric measures (Milner & Robertson, 1990). Thus, it appears possible that similar motivational variables characterize sexual and nonsexual aggressors, but that certain situational variables may elicit sexually aggressive behavior.

The Hall et al. (1991, 1992) MMPI studies did not assess physiological sexual arousal, which precluded identification of a physiological sexual arousal/sexual aggressor subtype. However, I have examined the physiological sexual arousal patterns of rapists, child molesters, and community men in response to rape, pedophilic, and consenting-adult sexual stimuli in three other studies (G. Hall, 1989b; Hall et al., 1988; Hall et al., in press). Twenty percent of a sample of inpatient sexual aggressors exhibited sexual arousal in response to verbal depictions of rape that exceeded their sexual arousal in consenting-adult sexual stimuli (G. Hall, 1989b). Forty-five percent of a sample of inpatient sexual aggressors exhibited sexual arousal in response to verbal depictions of sexual intercourse between a man and a female child that exceeded their sexual arousal in response to consenting-adult sexual activity (Hall et al., 1988). Thus, it appears that pedophilic arousal is more prominent among sexual aggressors than is rape arousal. However, the sexual arousal patterns of the rapists of women and child molesters in response to the pedophilic and to the rape stimuli were not significantly different, which suggests that sexual arousal to deviant stimuli does not necessarily correspond to deviant behavior (G. Hall, 1989b; Hall et al., 1988; Simon & Schouten, 1991). In other words, pedophilic arousal was not uniquely characteristic of child molesters nor was rape arousal uniquely characteristic of rapists of women.

Hall et al. (in press) reported that approximately 25% of community men who had not engaged in child molestation exhibited pedophilic arousal analogous to that of the subjects in the Hall et al. (1988) study. Other evidence suggests that sexual arousal to rape stimuli can be induced in men who are not sexually aggressive (Barbaree & Marshall, 1991). Given such overlap in sexual arousal patterns between rapists and child molesters, and between sexual aggressors and men who are not sexually aggressive, it appears that deviant sexual arousal is not sufficient to motivate sexually aggressive behavior. As with the cognitive, affective, and developmentally related personality precursors, situational variables may be required to cause a person who is adequately motivated to be sexually aggressive to exceed the threshold that usually inhibits sexually aggressive behavior (Hall & Hirschman, 1993). Some of these situational variables have been examined in laboratory studies.

Experimental Psychopathology and Disinhibitory Variables

How are situational variables that disinhibit sexually aggressive behavior best examined? In that *in vivo* investigation of rape or child molestation is not possible, some researchers have directly questioned sexually aggressive men about the situational precursors of sexually aggressive behavior (e.g., Pithers et al., 1988). However, such offender descriptions are compromised by memory limitations and distortions that may mitigate the offender's role in the sexually aggressive behavior.

An alternative to retrospective reports is the direct examination of behavior in the laboratory. Physical aggression has been extensively studied in the laboratory by having subjects deliver shocks to another person (Buss, 1961; Geen & Donnerstein, 1983; Taylor, 1986). Much has been learned about the etiology of aggressive acts using this approach. Typically, an hypothesized causal variable (e.g., anger provocation, alcohol) is introduced, and then the subject is allowed to aggress against another person (e.g., shocking another subject).

Laboratory aggression has been criticized as reflective of conformity, rather than deviance, in paradigms in which the aggressor is attempting to teach another person a task and punish deviance by providing feedback via shock (Gottfredson & Hirschi, 1993). For example, administering shock in the typical Buss (1961) laboratory paradigm is inversely associated with delinquent acts as assessed both by self-report and by police records (Gottfredson & Hirschi, 1993). These findings are not surprising, given that the people administering shocks in the Buss paradigm are in a teacher role in which they are instructed to punish deviance. However, laboratory administration of shock is facilitated by theoretically relevant contextual antecedents of aggressive behavior, including negative emotional states (e.g., anger; Carlson, Marcus-Newhall, & Miller, 1990), situational cues (e.g., weapons, opportunity for retaliation, social status of provocateur; Carlson et al., 1990), alcohol (Bushman & Cooper, 1990), and media violence (Donnerstein et al., 1987). In addition, the administration of shock in the laboratory has been demonstrated to have concurrent validity in that it is correlated with written expressions of aggression, and both shock and written expressions of aggression are similarly influenced by theoretically relevant etiological factors, including anger and frustration (Carlson et al., 1989).

Laboratory paradigms of physical aggression have been adapted for the study of sexual aggression by examining men's willingness to aggress against women. Men's aggression in the form of the delivery of a noxious stimulus (e.g., shock, aversive noise) against a female confederate is facilitated when they are angered by the confederate (e.g., Blader & Marshall, 1989; Donnerstein & Hallam, 1978; Malamuth, 1983, 1988b). The delivery of shock to a woman, however, is an analog of physical aggression but may not be analogous to sexual aggression (Hall & Hirschman, 1993, 1994; Hall et al., 1994).

Another criticism of laboratory studies of physical aggression is that subjects in the laboratory may not actually intend to inflict harm (Berkowitz & Donnerstein, 1982; Linz, Donnerstein, & Penrod, 1987). However, recent definitions of aggressive behavior have departed from the traditional emphasis on perpetrator intent (e.g., Baron, 1977) and have focused on the behavior's impact on the victim independent of the perpetrator's intention to be aggressive (Eron, 1987; Hall & Hirschman, 1993, 1994; Hall et al., 1994). Moreover, there may exist some important differences between physical and sexual aggression with respect to intentionality. Discrepancies in perpetrator and victim self-reports of sexual aggression suggest that many men who are sexually aggressive do not consider their behavior to be sexually aggressive (Koss et al., 1987). Fifty-five percent of a large sample of college men indicated ambivalence (20%) or agreement (35%) with the statement "When it comes to sex, females say no but really mean yes" (Dull & Giacopassi, 1987); hence many men may not perceive ignoring a woman's protests as sexual aggression. Because of these perpetrator-victim perceptual discrepancies and disagreement about the victim's nonconsent (Allison & Wrightsman, 1993), intentionality on the part of a perpetrator of sexual aggression may be less critical than it is for a perpetrator of physical aggression, where the harm to the victim is typically less ambiguous. Thus, intentionality may be of more interest in laboratory paradigms of physical aggression (Linz et al., 1987) than in laboratory paradigms of sexual aggression.

Subjects in laboratory studies are typically college students, primarily for reasons of convenience. It has been argued that the behavior of college students is not representative of that of the general population because of the selection for conformity involved in becoming a college student (Gottfredson & Hirschi, 1993; Sears, 1986). However, college students are an appropriate population to study for certain behaviors, such as depression, in that there are high rates of such problems in college populations (Vredenburg, Flett, & Krames, 1993). In that the most common forms of sexually aggressive behaviors may occur in college populations, college samples are an appropriate population to study and are not merely samples of convenience. Thus, studies of sexual aggression among college students are ecologically valid because college-student sexual aggression is the target of interest. The primary purpose of sexual-aggression research with college students is not to generalize to some other noncollege population, as is the case in much social psychological research (Sears, 1986). Moreover, research on sexual aggression in college populations may be less subject to social desirability confounds than research on clinical or forensic samples of sexual aggressors. The anonymity provided in research with college students typically is not possible in research with subjects in clinical or forensic subjects, who have previously been identified as deviant and may perceive situational demands for socially desirable behavior despite assurances of anonymity.

We have defined a subject's actions in the laboratory as sexually aggressive not by a subject's intent but by the potential impact of the actions on the another person (Hall & Hirschman, 1993, 1994; Hall et al., 1994). Laboratory sexual aggression in our paradigm is defined as the presentation of a sexual stimulus to someone who dislikes it, or the presentation of a sexually aggressive stimulus to another person. The inherently reprehensible nature of sexually aggressive stimuli makes the presentation of such stimuli, particularly to a woman, an aggressive act even if it is not explicitly known if the person who is the recipient dislikes such stimuli.

What percentage of men would impose a sexual stimulus on a woman who dislikes such stimuli? In an effort to disinhibit men's presentation of erotic slides to a female, Hall et al. (1994) provided men with a choice of presenting neutral (a clothed man and a clothed woman engaged in a social or sports activity), erotic (a man and a woman nude), explicit erotic (a portrayal of a man and woman engaged in a sexual activity), atypical erotic (explicit portrayals of a man and woman engaged in a sexual activity while wearing costumes and/or utilizing paraphernalia typically associated with atypical sexuality), or autopsy (accident victims) slides under the guise of distracting a female confederate from a visual memory task. About half of the men presented one of the erotic categories of slides under this distraction guise, which appears to have served as justification for presenting erotic slides. Forty-one percent of women showed one of the erotic categories of slides. However, when subjects were told that the female confederate strongly disliked pornography, 72% of the men showed one of the erotic categories of slides, whereas 44% of the women showed one of the erotic slide categories. Thus, the female confederate's dislike of erotic stimuli disinhibited men's showing of such stimuli (Hall et al., 1994).

The subjects could have used the autopsy slides to distract the confederate, in that they were rated by the subjects as equivalent to the erotic slides in distraction value (Hall et al., 1994). However, those subjects who presented erotic slides when the female confederate strongly disliked them were not simply complying with the experimental demand to distract, but were being additionally sexually impositional even if the subjects believed that the most disliked slides would also be the most distracting. Thus, an excuse to be sexually impositional—in this case, the demand to distract—disinhibited sexual imposition. Such an excuse is analogous to other cognitive distortions that serve to justify sexually aggressive behavior (e.g., the woman was drinking or wearing "provocative" clothing, the woman entered the man's apartment; Hall et al., 1994a).

The Hall et al. (1994) laboratory procedure allows the direct investigation of situational variables that cause a subject to exceed the threshold that usually inhibits sexually aggressive behavior (Hall et al., 1994a). The manipulation of a cognitive distortion among college students has been demonstrated to affect slide-showing choice (Shondrick, Hall, & Hirschman, 1992). A common cognitive distortion that is used to justify sexually aggressive behavior is misperceptions about a woman's sexual intent based on her clothing style (Edmonds & Cahoon, 1986). Men and women selected, under the guise of the Hall et al. (1994a) distraction task, neutral, childbirth, autopsy, or erotic slides to show a female confederate (Shondrick et al., 1992). Before selecting the slide category to show, half the subjects were introduced to a female confederate who was "provocatively" dressed (i.e., short skirt, red blouse) and the other half were introduced to the same confederate who was conservatively dressed (i.e., long skirt, white blouse, glasses). Thirty-six percent of the men in the Shondrick et al. (1992) study showed erotic slides to the "provocatively" dressed confederate, whereas only 8% showed erotic slides to the conservatively dressed confederate. Women's showing of the erotic slides was the opposite: Only 4% showed the erotic slides to the "provocatively" dressed confederate, whereas 24% showed the erotic slides to the conservatively dressed confederate. These results suggest the possibility that men may sexually harass women who are perceived as sexually provocative, whereas women may sexually harass women who are perceived as sexually conservative.

The demand to distract the confederates in the Hall et al. (1994) and Shondrick et al. (1992) studies, as well as the fact that the erotic stimuli did not depict sexual aggression, limit the applicability of this methodology to sexually aggressive behavior (Hall & Hirschman, 1994). In an effort to reduce the demand characteristics and to increase the validity of the paradigm, Hall and Hirschman (1994) had subjects select and show either neutral (a neutral conversation between a man and a woman), sexual-violent (a man raping a woman), or violent-sexual (a man physically assaulting a nude woman) vignettes from the film *I Spit on Your Grave* to a female confederate without experimental pretense (e.g., distraction demands).

The reprehensible nature of the sexual-violent and violent-sexual vignettes from the film that have been used in our research (Barongan & Hall, 1995; Hall & Hirschman, 1994) is captured in film critic Roger Ebert's (1988) review.

> "I Spit on Your Grave" is a vile bag of garbage that is so sick, reprehensible, and contemptible that I can hardly believe it played in respectable theaters. But it did. Attending it was one of the most depressing experiences of my life." (Ebert, 1988, p. 310)

It is highly likely that the film would have received two "thumbs down" had it been reviewed on Ebert's television program. Gary Larson's "Amoeba Porn Flicks" cartoon (Figure 3-1) captures the essence of our film-showing procedure.

In a pilot study in which men briefly met the female confederate before selecting and showing the film vignettes, only 1 of 41 men chose one of the sexually violent vignettes. Thus, very few normal men would impose a sexually aggressive stimulus upon a woman. Moreover, it appears that simply viewing the vignettes is not sufficient to facilitate sexually aggressive behavior (cf. Donnerstein, 1980; Donnerstein & Berkowitz, 1981).

THE FAR SIDE   By GARY LARSON

Amoeba porn flicks.

Figure 3-1. Amoeba porn flicks. THE FAR SIDE copyright 1986 FARWORKS, INC./Dist. by UNIVERSAL PRESS SYNDICATE. Reprinted with permission. All rights reserved.

The internal and external validity of the film-showing paradigm is supported by a study by Hall and Hirschman (1994). In a study of the most and least sexually coercive men in a college sample, 52% of the highly coercive men showed one of the sexually violent vignettes, whereas only 8% of the noncoercive men did so. Those subjects who showed the sexually aggressive stimuli reported that the female confederate was more upset and uncomfortable in viewing these stimuli than did subjects who showed the neutral stimulus, despite the confederate's neutral behavior in all film-showing conditions. Of the subjects who showed either the sexual-violent or violent-sexual vignettes, 93% admitted to sexually coercive behavior outside the laboratory setting (i.e., only one of the men who showed these vignettes indicated that he did not engage in sexually aggressive behavior outside the laboratory). However, nearly half of the sexually aggressive men did not show a sexually aggressive film, and it is obvious that the two sexually aggressive films are less socially desirable than the neutral film. Thus, this procedure is probably not suitable for clinical assessment applications (Hall & Hirschman, 1994). Nevertheless, it does not appear that such film showing is particularly susceptible to social desirability influences among college men who are sexually aggressive in real life. Thus, the Hall and Hirschman (1994) laboratory procedure appears to be a viable method of studying the situational variables that may facilitate sexually aggressive behavior.

Barongan and Hall (1995) conducted a study using the Hall and Hirschman (1994) film-showing methodology to investigate the effects of cognitive distortions on the film-showing behavior of an unselected group of 50 college men. As in the Hall and Hirschman (1994) study, those subjects who showed the sexual-violent or violent-sexual vignettes reported that the female confederate was significantly more upset and uncomfortable in viewing these stimuli than did subjects who showed the neutral vignette (Barongan & Hall, 1995). Twenty-eight percent of the men who were exposed to approximately 15 minutes of misogynist rap music showed the sexual-violent vignette, whereas only 4% of men who were exposed to approximately 15 minutes of neutral rap music showed the violent vignette. The misogynist music frequently referred to sex and violence and suggested that women enjoy coercive sex. The neutral music did not refer to sex or violence and was primarily concerned with social-justice issues. These data suggest that cognitive distortions about women may facilitate college men's sexually aggressive behavior against women.

A physiological motivational precursor of sexually aggressive behavior was investigated in a pilot study using the Hall and Hirschman (1994) laboratory paradigm. All subjects had an electrode attached to their wrists and 10 were told that their heart rate increased after viewing the sexual-violent and violent-sexual vignettes, whereas 11 were not given such false feedback. In the false feedback condition, 3 subjects showed the sexual-violent vignette and 3 subjects showed the violent-sexual vignette, whereas only 1 subject showed the sexual-violent vignette and only 1 showed the violent-sexual vignette without the false feedback. In that the heartrate feedback was false, it appears that perceived physiological arousal may serve as an excuse for being sexually aggressive. Extrapolating these findings outside the laboratory context, a man who perceives a sexually aggressive stimulus (e.g., sex and violence combined in media) as highly arousing may believe that he must act on such arousal by being sexually aggressive because this arousal is beyond his control. Perceived arousal may serve as a justification for being sexually aggressive (cf. Averill, 1993; DiGiuseppe et al., 1994; Hanson, Gizzarelli, & Scott, 1994).

The above studies suggest that the laboratory sexually aggressive behavior of men without a predisposition for sexually aggressive behavior is influenced by situational variables. However, the laboratory sexually aggressive behavior of men having a predisposition for sexually aggressive behavior may be less influenced by situational variables. Men who are not selected for sexually aggressive behavior tend not to be sexually aggressive in the laboratory unless there is situational motivation (e.g., "provocative" clothing of female confederate, misogynous music, physiological arousal; Barongan & Hall, 1995; Hall et al., 1994a; Shondrick et al., 1992). However, men with a predisposition for sexually aggressive behavior are sexually aggressive without situational provocation (Hall & Hirschman, 1994). Because the sexually aggressive subjects in the Hall and Hirschman (1994) study constituted an extremely aggressive subsample, they could be conceptualized as analogous to the Hall and Hirschman (1991) developmentally related personality problems subtype. Thus, situational determinants of sexually aggressive behavior may be less important for men having developmentally related personality problems than for men who do not have such developmentally related problems.

Conclusion

Hall and Hirschman (1991, 1992) have proposed a theoretical model of sexually aggressive behavior that is sufficiently comprehensive to incorporate existing theories of sexually aggressive behavior, but sufficiently parsimonious for clinical applications. Physiological sexual arousal, cognitive distortions, affective dyscontrol, and developmentally related personality problems were posited as primary motivational precursors of sexually aggressive behavior. However, because there is a considerable degree of overlap between men who are and who are not sexually aggressive on each of these four precursors, it appears that these variables are not sufficient to cause sexually aggressive behavior. Thus, Hall and Hirschman (1993) have proposed that situational variables may cause men who are adequately motivated by any of these four precursors to exceed the threshold that usually inhibits sexually aggressive behavior. Empirical data from recent clinical psychopathology studies support the existence of the four motivational precursors among both child molester and rapist populations. A new laboratory methodology allows the direct investigation of situational variables that cause men to exceed the inhibitory threshold for sexually aggressive behavior. Evidence among college populations suggests that situational determinants may facilitate sexually aggressive behavior in the laboratory more for males without a predisposition for sexually aggressive behavior than for males with such a predisposition.

II

THEORY-GUIDED ASSESSMENT

4

Predicting Sexually Aggressive Behavior

Unlike the explanatory theoretical models reviewed in part I, predictive models are evaluated solely in terms of their accuracy in predicting behavior. Accurate prediction of sexual behavior is often requested or expected in forensic contexts. Two common questions about alleged sexual aggressors asked by the legal system and by the public are: (1) has the defendant engaged in sexually deviant behavior in the past? and (2) will the defendant engage in sexually deviant behavior in the future? Mental health professionals are often asked by the court system to render expert opinions on these criterion-related questions, often with the intent of having the mental health professional provide definitive answers to these questions (G. Hall, 1990a; Lanyon, 1986). These questions are sometimes asked separately, although they are not mutually exclusive. It is typically assumed that if an alleged sexual offender is sexually deviant, he will sexually reoffend. However, it is also possible that a person could sexually reoffend for other reasons, such as a generalized tendency to violate rules rather than a specific tendency toward sexual aggression. The forensic mental health specialty of sexual-offender assessment has thrived, evidence on the limited accuracy of clinical judgment and psychological testing notwithstanding (G. Hall, 1990a, 1990b; Hall & Crowther, 1991; Murphy & Peters, 1992). Courts have been resistant to suggestions that expert testimony on violent behavior be modified or eliminated (Melton, Petrila, Poythress, & Slobogin, 1987).

Errors in the prediction of sexually aggressive behavior can have severe consequences (G. Hall, 1990a). A dangerous sexual aggressor at liberty places the community at risk. Although clinicians tend to err on the side of predicting sexually aggressive behavior among persons who will not be sexually aggressive and detaining these persons (e.g., G. Hall, 1988), such Type I errors violate individual rights as well as the spirit of the American legal system, which seeks to protect the accused.

The question about whether a person is a sex offender often arises in child custody disputes, in which one parent is accused of sexual abuse (Bresee, Stearns, Bess, & Packer, 1986; Hlady & Gunter, 1990; Jaudes & Morris, 1990; Thoennes & Tjaden, 1990). The accused parent in custody disputes frequently does not have a documented history of being sexually abusive. If the accused parent is determined by the court to be a sexual offender, then custody, and in some cases visitation, is denied.

The second question concerning future behavior often arises in the context of "sexual psychopath" laws, which provide society protection from sexual offenders and provide sexual offenders with rehabilitation (Melton et al., 1987). A decreasing number of states continue to have special laws concerning sexual offenders because of economic constraints, skepticism about treatment efficacy, and generally conservative attitudes (Melton et al., 1987; Small, 1992). Nevertheless, the public remains very concerned about protection from sexual offenders. For example, a law passed in 1990 by the Washington state legislature, which has historically been a leader in sex-offender statutes, requires sexual offenders to be evaluated by clinicians after the offenders have completed their court-mandated sentences to determine if an additional indeterminate sentence is necessary for rehabilitation. Moreover, most states provide some form of sexual-offender treatment through their mental health or corrections departments (Small, 1992).

Personality Profiles of Sexual Aggressors

In diagnosing most psychological problems, clinicians interview clients with the assumption that the client is the best source of information about the problem. Clinicians are trained to establish rapport with the client to gain cooperation, and the client's account of the problem is generally accepted as genuine. Elaborate structured interviews have been developed for diagnostic purposes, with the assumption that self-report is accurate (Endicott & Spitzer, 1978; Robins, Helzer, Croughan, & Ratcliff, 1981).

If traditional diagnostic approaches are utilized with sexual aggressors, it is assumed that they would (1) admit to engaging in sexually aggressive behavior; and (2) admit to some motivation for their sexually aggressive behavior, such as paraphilic urges, that would suggest deviance. Unlike many other psychological disorders, however, the admission of sexually aggressive behavior is extremely socially undesirable (Rogers & Dickey, 1991). Even in prison settings, where inmates have committed a variety of highly socially undesirable acts, sexual offenders dwell at the bottom of the hierarchy, and it is often dangerous for an inmate to be identified as a sexual offender.

The presence of corroborating information, such as victim statements or police investigations, may not deter many sexual aggressors from denying responsibility (G. Hall, 1989a; Lanyon, Dannenbaum, & Brown, 1991; Lanyon & Lutz, 1984; McGovern & Nevid, 1986). In studies in which subjects have openly admitted to sexually aggressive behavior, anonymity was provided and there were no legal or other negative consequences for these admissions (e.g., Abel et al., 1987; Malamuth, 1986; Malamuth et al., 1991). Such conditions of anonymity and impunity are not characteristic of most settings in which sexual aggressors are assessed.

Admission of sexually aggressive behavior typically occurs only under conditions of extreme coercion, such as when a sexual aggressor is threatened with the breakup of his family or when he is facing the prospect of prison if he does not admit engaging in sexually aggressive behavior. Even in such desperate circumstances, however, many sexual aggressors may admit to only the amount of deviant behavior that will gain them credibility (G. Hall, 1989a). Sexual aggressors in clinical or forensic settings are often aware of the "optimal" level of admission for credibility. This typically includes at least partial admission of the offense that brought them to the attention of the evaluator and perhaps admission of other deviant behaviors, depending on the expectations or orientation of the evaluator. For example, some evaluators believe that no sexual aggressors are caught the first time that they offend, or that all sexual aggressors have been sexually abused as children. In these situations, admission of at least some additional sexually aggressive behavior or of being sexually abused would facilitate the sexual aggressor's credibility with the evaluator, whether or not these events had actually occurred. Thus, admissions of behavior that are not documented by corroborating information should be viewed with caution.

Sexual aggressors in forensic settings have also been demonstrated to admit to the "lesser of evils." For example, incarcerated sexual offenders were willing to disclose general psychological problems, but less willing to disclose deviant sexual fantasies (McGovern & Nevid, 1986). In another study of inpatient sexual offenders, self-reported hostility toward women was inversely correlated with a self-report measure of social desirability (i.e., it was socially undesirable), whereas self-reported general hostility was not significantly correlated with social desirability (G. Hall, 1989a). Whereas general hostility may be viewed as a problem that is characteristic of most persons, the admission of hostility toward women by sexual offenders may be socially undesirable because it is characteristic of rapists (G. Hall, 1989a). Even when a sexual aggressor is not being intentionally deceptive, he may engage in unintentional deception as a function of the cognitive distortions about his behavior, as discussed in chapters 2 and 5. Many sexual aggressors may have a poor or distorted awareness of the impact of their sexually aggressive behavior, and this lack of awareness may permit them to engage in sexually aggressive behavior without viewing it as sexually aggressive.

Perhaps more subtle approaches to assessing sexual deviance may be less susceptible to dissimulation than more direct approaches (e.g., "are you sexually attracted to children?"). However, there is much evidence that sexual aggressors who deny sexually aggressive behavior are also generally defensive on self-report measures (Lanyon et al., 1991; Lanyon & Lutz, 1984). Even among sexual aggressors who are relatively nondefensive, self-report measures may not be particularly useful for diagnosis.

When I first began to work with sexual aggressors, I heard talk of a "sex offender profile" based on MMPI data. For example, in case conferences, staff members would examine a patient's MMPI profile, and it would often be claimed that the patient had the "sex offender profile." The 4-8/8-4 MMPI profile allegedly was the child molester profile, and the 4-9/9-4 MMPI profile allegedly was the rapist profile.

My first research project on sexual offenders did suggest that the mean profile for sexual offenders was the 4-8/8-4 MMPI profile (Hall et al., 1986). However, in examining individual sexual offenders' MMPI profiles, the 4-8/8-4 and 4-9/9-4 profiles were no more common than eight other MMPI profiles. The 4-8/8-4 profile accounted for only 7.1% of the profiles in the sample, and the 4-9/9-4 profile accounted for only 5.7%. Thus, the MMPI "sex offender profile" was a myth. The 80% of the sample were no less sexual offenders than the 20% of the sample who had the 4-8/8-4 or 4-9/9-4 "sex offender profiles."

The MMPI may be of some utility in identifying subtypes of sexual aggressors that are associated with theoretically based motivational precursors (Hall et al., 1991, 1992; chapter 3, this book). However, the test is not useful for discriminating between sexual aggressors and "normal" subjects (G. Hall, 1990a; Murphy & Peters, 1992). Moreover, the

MMPI may not be sensitive to personality differences between child molesters and other nonsexual violent and nonsexual nonviolent offenders (Hall et al., 1992). Although the MMPI has been demonstrated to have some utility in predicting sexual aggression in a linear combination of variables, the amount of unique variance in sexual aggression accounted for by MMPI scales is very limited (G. Hall, 1988).

Recent evidence suggests that MMPI subscales specifically designed to assess sexual deviance may have some promise in discriminating sexual offenders, including those who do not admit to sexually offending, from other subjects who did and did not admit to various problems, including subjects undergoing mental health, sanity, child custody, personal injury, and employment evaluations (Lanyon, 1993). However, a potential limitation of the Lanyon (1993) study was that the sexual offenders were evaluated in forensic settings whereas most of the control subjects were not. Thus, the between-group differences could be at least partly a function of greater deviance among forensic vs. nonforensic subjects. Although Lanyon (1993) has suggested that it is premature to apply his findings in clinical settings, these findings are promising in that other available assessment methods are not valid with nonadmitters, who constitute one fifth to two thirds of men evaluated for sexually aggressive behavior in forensic settings (Barbaree, 1991; Lanyon & Lutz, 1984; Marshall, 1994; Pollock & Hashmall, 1991; Scully & Marolla, 1984).

In summary, there exists no unique personality profile of a person who has been or has the potential to be sexually aggressive. However, personality profiles are based on self-report data, which are subject to conscious distortion. An alternative method of assessing sexually aggressors that does not involve self-report is physiological assessment.

Physiological Assessment of Sexual Arousal

The sexual nature of sexually aggressive acts implicates deviant sexual arousal as a cause of sexually aggressive behavior. Physiological sexual arousal has been identified as a motivational factor in various theories of sexual aggression (e.g., Barbaree & Marshall, 1991; Hall & Hirschman, 1991). Although self-report measures of sexual arousal have been advocated by some researchers (Haywood, Grossman, & Cavanaugh, 1990), most researchers and clinicians have used genital measures in the assessment of sexual aggressors.

Several years ago at a small research conference, a distinguished researcher was describing in painstaking detail the procedures of penile assessment of sexual arousal among sexual offenders. The researcher comprehensively covered methods of measurement as well as methods of circumventing faking. I observed another distinguished researcher in the audience who seemed to become increasingly impatient as the presentation approached an hour in length. The second researcher appeared to have a comment to make, but was restraining himself until the end of the presentation. Finally, as the first researcher concluded his presentation, the second researcher exclaimed, "Why don't you just *ask* them" about their sexual arousal instead of going through all the machinations of penile assessment?

Penile measures of sexual arousal have been adopted by researchers and clinicians based on the assumption that self-report of sexual arousal is inaccurate and can be falsely reported. It may be difficult even for perpetrators who admit to engaging in sexually aggressive behavior to admit to deviant sexual arousal (cf. McGovern & Nevid, 1986). Unlike other motivational precursors of sexual aggression, such as affective or developmental problems, which are viewed as common and therefore acceptable, deviant sexual arousal may be viewed as a defining characteristic of sexual deviance by both perpetrators and clinicians (e.g., American Psychiatric Association, 1994; McGovern & Nevid, 1986). Thus, it may be highly socially undesirable to admit to experiencing deviant fantasies or deviant sexual arousal.

Sexual arousal is easily and face-validly measured by penile erection. For some clinicians and researchers, sexual arousal in response to deviant stimuli (e.g., rape, children) has become synonymous with sexually aggressive behavior. Hence, the setting in which sexual arousal is assessed is referred to as the "behavioral laboratory" (Laws & Osborn, 1983). The behavioral-laboratory designation suggests that sexual arousal is the target behavior or at least more important than other behaviors that can be measured. By implication, deviant sexual arousal is indicative of past and potential sexually aggressive behavior. The absence of deviant sexual arousal in an alleged sexually aggressive subject may be taken at face value (i.e., the subject has not been sexually aggressive) or may be viewed as evidence of faking (i.e., the subject is voluntarily inhibiting his deviant sexual arousal).

When a person exhibits sexual arousal in response to deviant or aggressive stimuli, this does not necessarily mean that the person will act on this sexual arousal. Becoming sexually aroused is not a sexually aggressive act. A substantial minority of men who are not sexually aggressive exhibit sexual arousal in response to deviant stimuli, and many sexually aggressive men exhibit "normal" patterns of sexual arousal (Barbaree & Marshall, 1989; G. Hall, 1989b; Hall et al., 1988; Hall et al., in press).

The mean rape index (rape arousal : consenting sexual arousal) for a sample of normal men was .41 and for a sample of rapists was .59 (Baxter et al., 1986). Of the normal men, 17% exhibited a rape index > .8 (Baxter et al., 1986). Although rapists exhibit greater sexual arousal to rape stimuli relative to consenting sexual stimuli than nonrapists do, many rapists exhibit the converse (i.e., greater sexual arousal to consenting stimuli than to rape stimuli), a pattern characteristic of nonrapists (Hall, Shondrick, et al., 1993b). Only 10 to 20% of rapists exhibit rape arousal that exceeds consenting arousal (Baxter et al., 1986; G. Hall, 1989b). Twenty to 30% of normals exhibit sexual arousal in response to pedophilic stimuli that equals or exceeds their arousal to consenting-adult sexual stimuli (Hall et al., in press), whereas 45 to 50% of child molesters exhibit such pedophilic arousal (Barbaree & Marshall, 1989; Hall et al., 1988). In that the range of responses of the deviant population overlaps with the range of responses of the nondeviant population, caution should be exercised in interpreting results of sexual-arousal assessments (cf. Jacobson, Follette, & Revenstorf, 1984).

These findings may be, in part, a result of individual arousability factors (G. Hall, 1989b; Hall et al., in press). Some subjects are more arousable than others to sexual stimuli, independent of sexual or sexually aggressive behavior. Assessing sexual arousal and extrapolating to sexually aggressive behavior is analogous to predicting hypertension from heart rate. Similar to one's heart rate and other autonomic responses, sexual arousal is susceptible to situational influences (e.g., anxiety, arousability).

Another limitation of penile assessments of sexual arousal is faking. Nearly 80% of sexual offenders are capable of inhibiting sexual arousal (G. Hall, 1989b; Hall et al., 1988). If approximately 20% of normals exhibit deviant sexual arousal, as described previously, and approximately 80% of sexual offenders can inhibit sexual arousal, then any given sexual-arousal finding is not necessarily diagnostic. Physiological assessment of sexual arousal may be useful with sexual aggressors who admit engaging in sexually aggressive behavior, but it is not useful with those who deny engaging in sexually aggressive behavior (Freund & Blanchard, 1989). Thus, assessments of sexual arousal may not be useful with the 20 to 66% of alleged sexual aggressors who are evaluated in forensic settings and deny being sexually aggressive (Barbaree, 1991; Lanyon & Lutz, 1984; Marshall, 1994; Pollock & Hashmall, 1991; Scully & Marolla, 1984). Even proponents of physiological assessment of sexual arousal allow that it should *not* be used to determine culpability or potential for sexually aggressive behavior (Harris et al., 1992). Unfortunately, clinicians and legal professionals often ignore such cautionary statements about the limitations of physiological assessment and misuse it.

For some alleged perpetrators, the prospect of undergoing a penile assessment of sexual arousal may cause them to admit that they have engaged in sexually aggressive behavior. However, the threat value of genital assessment or actual results that suggest deviant sexual arousal may also result in false admissions of sexually aggressive behavior during legal proceedings (McConaghy, 1989). Deviance detection via penile assessment is analogous to lie detection via polygraphy (G. Hall, 1990b). The polygraph may also elicit false confessions either because of its threat value or test results. However, the interpretation of autonomic arousal measured by the polygraph is susceptible to some of the same limitations as the interpretation of autonomic arousal measured by genital measures (G. Hall, 1990b).

As may be expected, deviant sexual arousal is also not an adequate predictor of sexually aggressive behavior. In one of the only studies to examine the predictive utility of pedophilic sexual arousal, there was a small but statistically significant *negative* correlation ($-.155$) between a pedophilic sexual-arousal index and subsequent convictions (Rice, Quinsey, & Harris, 1991). Subjects who exhibited greater levels of pedophilic arousal were somewhat *less* likely to be convicted than subjects who exhibited lower levels of pedophilic arousal. Thus, it appears that physiological sexual arousal is more useful as an explanatory construct (e.g., Barbaree & Marshall, 1991; Hall & Hirschman, 1991) than as a predictor variable (see chapter 1).

Abel, Lawry, Karlstrom, Osborn, and Gillespie (1994) have described a new pedophilia screening test that involves ratings of sexual arousal to slides of nude children and adults as well as a "psychophysiological hand monitor that records a noninvasive physiological response to each slide, which is recorded without the patient's awareness." However, more specific information on the latter procedure is not provided. Although the claim is presented that the test can accurately classify pedophiles, data were provided for only 13 "deniers," who presumably were accused of child molestation but denied the accusations. The latter group is of most importance in that it is most similar to perpetrators undergoing evaluations.

To summarize, deviant sexual arousal does not accurately correspond with deviant sexual behavior. Thus, determination of past or potential sexually aggressive behavior is not possible with physiological assessments of sexual arousal. Similar to assessment via self-report, assessment of sexual arousal is subject to deception. There exists no psychological method to definitively determine if a person has been sexually aggressive in the past in the absence of corroborating data. However, when a person has a history of sexually aggressive behavior, it is possible to make clinical predictions concerning future sexual aggression.

Clinical Prediction of Sexually Aggressive Behavior

One of the most widely accepted adages in the study of human behavior is that past behavior is the best predictor of future behavior. This adage forms the basis for accepting students into higher education who have the best grades, for extending credit to persons who have the best histories of paying debts, and for providing automobile insurance to persons having good driving records. There also recently has been public support for using past offenses to determine sentencing of criminals. Washington state allows persons who have committed three felonies to be incarcerated for life (i.e., the baseball analogy, "three strikes, you're out"). A federal "three strikes, you're out" bill has been approved in 1994 for violent felons, and 30 states other than Washington are currently considering such legislation.

The predictive utility of past violent behavior was presented convincingly by John Monahan in his influential 1981 monograph, *Predicting Violent Behavior*. Past sexually aggressive behavior also has been found to be the single best predictor of sexually aggressive behavior (G. Hall, 1990a), apparently because the inhibitory threshold for sexually aggressive behavior may be lowered each time a person is sexually aggressive (see chapter 3). However, the predictive utility of past behavior has been difficult to implement on a practical basis for persons involved in predicting sexually aggressive behavior, who have typically sought and used less accurate methods of prediction, or who have misused past behavior in prediction.

The use of past behavior to predict future behavior is an example of the *actuarial* method of prediction, which involves prediction based on empirically established relations between predictor and predicted variables. *Clinical* prediction involves the individualized study of cases and typically implies the use of human judgment. In a review of 100 comparative studies, the actuarial method has equaled or surpassed the clinical method for predictions concerning neuropsychological diagnosis, medical diagnosis, diagnosis of medical vs. psychiatric disorder, prediction of psychological treatment outcome, length of psychiatric hospitalization, response to electroshock therapy, violent behavior, parole behavior, college grades, and graduate school performance (Dawes, Faust, & Meehl,

1989). Often, the persons making the clinical predictions had access to the same data that were used in the actuarial predictions but were unable to implement the data for accurate prediction.

The actuarial method is also superior to the clinical method in predicting sexually aggressive behavior. G. Hall (1988) reported that a linear combination of offender age, history of arrests for criminal behavior, intellectual functioning, and MMPI scores had an overall accuracy rate of 92% in identifying sexual offenders who were and were not rearrested for sexual offenses against adults over a five-year period following institutional release to the community. The best single predictor—history of arrests for sexual offenses against adults—was correlated .57 with rearrests for sexual offenses against adults, although the correlation between these two variables was .35 in the population from which the subsample for the G. Hall (1988) study was derived (Hall & Proctor, 1987). Moreover, the high accuracy rate of the G. Hall (1988) actuarial formula would probably be reduced with replication.

The accuracy rate for a team of psychiatrists and psychologists, who had access to the same data used in the actuarial formula, was only 53% for predicting rearrests for sexual offenses against adults, which barely exceeds chance (G. Hall, 1988). The team of psychiatrists and psychologists made a decision that sexual offenders were safe (i.e., would not be rearrested) or unsafe (i.e., would be rearrested) based on the offenders' completion or noncompletion of a guided self-help program (MacDonald & DiFuria, 1971). In the prediction of rearrests for sexual offenses against children, neither actuarial nor clinical methods significantly exceeded chance. However, arrests and rearrests for sexual offenses against children were correlated .12, which was statistically significant in the population of sexual offenders (Hall & Proctor, 1987) from which the G. Hall (1988) sample was derived.

It is possible that the relatively poor accuracy in actuarial prediction of sexual offending against children may be a function of victim reporting. Although there is evidence that women are reluctant to report being sexually victimized to authorities (Koss, 1985), adult victims of sexual offenses may be more willing to report their victimization than children because there is less power disparity between men and women than between men and children (G. Hall, 1988). Thus, arrest data may be a somewhat more accurate reflection and a more accurate predictor of the actual behavior of sexual aggressors against women than of sexual aggressors against children.

Why were the clinicians in the G. Hall (1988) study so poor at predicting sexually aggressive behavior? One possibility is the ineffectiveness of the treatment program upon which the dangerousness decisions were based (Furby, Weinrott, & Blackshaw, 1989; G. Hall, 1988). Those sexual offenders who completed the program reoffended at a rate that was not significantly different from those who did not complete the program and were sent to prison to complete their legal sentences (G. Hall, 1988).

Another source of error is revealed in a closer analysis of the clinicians' decisions (G. Hall, 1988). Clinicians were highly accurate at predicting who *would not* reoffend. Clinicians' accuracy rates were 93% for predicting who would not be rearrested for sexual offenses against adults and 86% for predicting who would not be rearrested for sexual offenses against children. This high accuracy is not simply a function of a low base rate of reoffense, in that 26% of the sexual aggressors against adults and 23% of the sexual aggressors against children in the population reoffended. However, clinicians' accuracy rates for predicting who *would* reoffend were only 7% and 17% for rearrests for sexual re-offenses against adults and children, respectively. This overprediction of the potential for aggressive behavior is also common in the prediction of other types of violent behavior (McNeil & Binder, 1991).

It could be argued that the clinicians in the G. Hall (1988) study were doing what was expected of them by protecting the public from potentially dangerous sexual offenders. The clinicians could have improved their accuracy if they had predicted that no sexual reoffenders would reoffend (cf. Faust, 1986), but this would be considered unethical and irresponsible. However, from the civil liberties perspective that has historically guided the American legal and judicial system, this tendency toward false positive, or Type I, errors deprives individual sexual offenders of their rights (G. Hall, 1990a, 1990b). Nevertheless, there is strong public sentiment about keeping "sexually dangerous" persons out of the community, as evidenced by the 1993 Washington state statute to detain sex offenders beyond their legally mandated sentences. Ironically, the G. Hall (1988) study in which clinicians were poor in predicting the dangerousness of sexual offenders took place in Washington state.

Improving Clinical Prediction

What can clinicians do to improve the accuracy of their predictions? Excellent reviews of judgment biases that occur in general clinical decision making appear in Turk and Salovey (1988). Clinicians, like other judges, tend to seek information that confirms their conceptualization of a problem, rather than that which might disconfirm it (Baron, Beattie, & Hershey, 1988; Hogarth, 1987). Moreover, clinical experience may cloud a person's accuracy in prediction insofar as feedback about predictive accuracy is seldom available, and clinicians tend to recall cases that confirm their prediction and to forget or ignore those cases in which their predictions have been incorrect. Such an insular existence may influence clinicians to overgeneralize from clinical experiences, particularly those experiences that are most salient. Thus, a clinician working in a particular setting (e.g., inpatient) may view all sexual aggressors, including those who are not part of the population with whom the clinician is working, as having the same characteristics (e.g., sexual abuse during childhood). Such overgeneralization, however, ignores the heterogeneity of sexual aggressors (see chapter 3).

I have caught myself making such overgeneralizations. For example, when I was working with inpatient sexual offenders, most of whom were child molesters, I found myself being suspicious of men alone with young children in relatively private situations, such as hiking in the woods. Such suspicions are generally irrational, given the low base rate of child molestation. The vast majority of men (over 96%; Hall et al., in press) and women do not molest children.

Clinicians may improve their prediction of sexually aggressive behavior by incorporating valid actuarial predictors into their predictions (G. Hall, 1990a). For example, predictions concerning future violent behavior that are based on past behavior are more accurate than clinical judgment (Mossman, 1994). Hollon and Kriss (1984), however, have contended that clinicians have generally not been influenced by the clinical judgment literature, possibly as a result of hostility toward such research. Such cynicism about research is generally typical of practicing clinicians (Barlow, 1981; Cohen et al., 1986). For example, clinicians may consider discussions with colleagues as more useful than research findings (Cohen et al., 1986). Moreover, research on the limitations of assessment methods that are used with sexual aggressors, such as physiological assessment of sexual arousal, seems to have a limited impact on many practicing clinicians, even when such limitations are offered by proponents of the methods (e.g., Freund & Blanchard, 1989; Harris et al., 1992). Perhaps clinicians believe that their own judgment and methods are no worse than alternative methods. Thus, with respect to the prediction of sexually aggressive behavior, it is useful to examine in an absolute sense how accurate the best predictive methods are.

Actuarial Prediction of Sexually Aggressive Behavior

The finding that past sexual aggression is the best predictor of future sexual aggression is consistent with conceptualizations of recidivists as having antisocial traits (Hall & Proctor, 1987; Knight & Prentky, 1990).

Persons with such antisocial traits tend to have a poor prognosis for changing their behavior. As the number of sexually aggressive acts increases, the threshold inhibiting such acts lowers (see chapter 3). Sexual aggressors who have engaged in a limited amount of sexually aggressive behavior may be more influenced by situational variables, whereas sexual aggressors who engage in multiple sexually aggressive acts may develop a propensity for rule violations that is not primarily mediated by situational influences (Megargee, 1984; Moffitt, 1993).

The Hall and Proctor (1987) data in Figure 4-1 suggest that 25% (18 of 73) of sexual offenders who had one or two previous arrests for rape were arrested for rape after they were released, whereas 50% (3 of 6) of sexual offenders who had three or four previous arrests for rape were arrested for rape after they were released. Thus, it could be argued that these data provide support for the "three strikes, you're out" approach to sentencing. However, if three arrests are used as the criterion for lifetime incarceration, then decisions about dangerousness will be incorrect 50% of the time. Moreover, the Hall and Proctor (1987) findings are based on small numbers, despite the fact that this is one of the larger longitudinal studies of rapist recidivism.

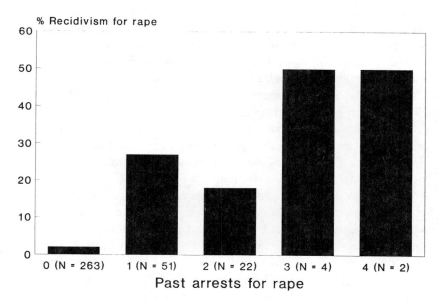

Figure 4-1. Rearrests for rape as a function of past arrests for rape.

Past offenses also appear to have some utility in predicting recidivism among child molesters, although this relationship is somewhat less powerful than it is in predicting rape. In a study in Canada by Hanson et al., (1993) 32% of child molesters with two or more arrests were reconvicted within five years of institutional release, whereas less than 10% of child molesters with one arrest were reconvicted within five years. Approximately 60% of the child molesters having multiple arrests were reconvicted within 20 years postrelease and 30% of the child molesters with one arrest were reconvicted within 20 years. In the Hall and Proctor (1987) study, there was a significant increment for child molesters at four arrests, in that 23% of the subjects having one to three arrests for child molestation was rearrested, whereas 60% of the subjects having four to six arrests was rearrested. However, Hall and Proctor (1987) found a relatively weak association between number of arrests and rearrests for child molestation, primarily because only 1 of the 5 subjects who had five or six arrests was rearrested. These data suggest that incarceration decisions regarding child molesters that are based on past arrests are susceptible to Type I errors. Approximately 40% of child molesters having multiple arrests did not recidivate (G. Hall, 1988; Hanson et al., 1993).

Another reason why it may not be judicious to detain three-time offenders for life is the so-called burnout phenomenon among offenders. G. Hall (1988) reported that younger sexual aggressors against women were at greater risk to reoffend than were older sexual aggressors against women. Figure 4-2 suggests that a burnout in sexual offending against women occurs at 36 years of age. Of the rapists under 36 years of age at the time that they were released from institutions (hospital or prison), 28% sexually reoffended against a woman, whereas only 1 of 8 (12.5%) of the subjects over 35 years of age sexually reoffended against a woman. The one older subject who was 62 years old and sexually reoffended against a woman also had two previous arrests for sexual offending against women, which may have increased his reoffense risk. Incarceration obviously prevents reoffending, but there may be a critical period before the age of 36 during which rapists are at highest risk to reoffend. However, as discussed in conjunction with the data on past offenses, the sample size in the G. Hall (1988) study is probably too small for policy applications.

Subject age was not associated with recidivism for child molesters in either the G. Hall (1988) or Hanson et al. (1993) studies. These data suggest that the burnout phenomenon observed among rapists and other offenders may not occur among child molesters. Perhaps recidivism for child molesters is a function of access to victims. As child molesters age,

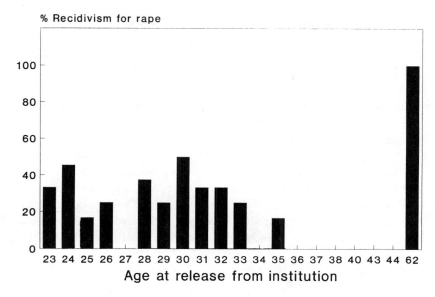

% Recidivism for rape

Age at release from institution

Figure 4-2. Rearrests for rape as a function of age at time of institutional release.

the numbers of their children, nieces, nephews, and grandchildren may increase. These relatives, as well as these relatives' friends, are accessible as potential victims to aging child molesters. Thus, child molesters' recidivism potential as a function of access to victims may not decrease with age.

Thus far I have discussed univariate actuarial approaches. As discussed in chapter 2, complex multivariate approaches have been developed to predict sexually aggressive behavior (e.g., Malamuth et al., 1993). The work of Malamuth and his colleagues has involved anonymously reported sexual aggression in college populations. Prediction among college populations is important because sexual aggression among college students may be one of the most common forms of sexual aggression (Koss, 1993a). Although this work has advanced the conceptual understanding of possible etiological factors in sexually aggressive behavior, the clinical implications of the model are unclear (G. Hall, 1990a). It is unlikely that such complex forms of prediction will be implemented at a practical level with either college student or offender populations. The predictor variables (e.g., multiple measures, historical data) may be difficult and uneconomical to assess on a routine basis. The demand characteristics of the forensic settings in which sexual aggressors are typically seen by clinicians are vastly different from those in the context of Malamuth's research. If clinicians have difficulty implementing single variables, such as past behavior, to improve their prediction, it is highly unlikely that complex, multivariate approaches will be implemented at a practical level. Despite the intention of Malamuth et al. (1993) to develop a predictive model, their model may have more utility as an explanatory than as a predictive approach (see chapter 1).

G. Hall (1988) developed a multivariate actuarial formula for the prediction of sexual aggression in a clinical setting. As discussed earlier, the formula included a linear combination of offender age, history of arrests for criminal behavior, intellectual functioning, and MMPI scores. This formula was highly accurate in predicting sexual aggression against adults: 87% of reoffenders and 93% of nonreoffenders were correctly classified. However, an actuarial formula developed to predict recidivism among child molesters resulted in only 68% accuracy for both reoffenders and nonreoffenders. Clinical and actuarial prediction of child molestation were both inaccurate and not significantly different.

The variables that made unique contributions to explaining the variance in recidivism for sexual aggression against adults were, in descending order of effect size: past sexual offenses against adults, past nonsexual violent offenses, subject age, past sexual offenses against children, and MMPI Scale 5 scores (G. Hall, 1988). Thus, men at risk for committing rape tended to be antisocial persons who had previously committed both sexual and nonsexual violent assaults, and tended to be relatively young. Past sexual offenses against children was a predictor insofar as men who had previously committed sexual offenses against children tended not to be at risk to commit sexual offenses against adults. Finally, MMPI Scale 5 elevations were somewhat associated with risk for sexual aggression against adults. MMPI Scale 5 elevations are suggestive of passivity and self-control (Graham, 1987). However, among persons with antisocial tendencies, such apparent control may mask feelings of anger and resentment (cf. Megargee, 1966). The apparent control may also be brittle, particularly under frustrating circumstances in which aggressive acting out is likely (Graham, 1987). Thus, outward appearance of control or compliance (e.g., with treatment) does not necessarily indicate reduced risk for acting out.

Conclusion

What answers can behavioral science offer to the questions posed at the outset of this chapter? (1) Has the defendant engaged in sexually deviant behavior in the past? (2) Will the defendant engage in sexually deviant behavior in the future? None of the assessment methods reviewed in this chapter can definitively answer the first question. Self-report inventories are compromised by social desirability and defensiveness. Although they possess face validity, physiological measures of sexual arousal are also susceptible to distortion. Moreover, deviant sexual arousal does not correspond very well with deviant sexual behavior. Although some judges and juries would prefer to absolve themselves of the responsibility of answering the "ultimate question" of guilt or innocence, the answer to the ultimate question is a judicial decision, not a clinical one (Blau, 1984). Clinicians do not have the required expertise to render such judicial decisions, particularly when sexually aggressive behavior is involved.

Behavioral science can answer the second question concerning recidivism with some caveats. Probabilistic statements about violence potential are more accurate than absolute statements about whether a person will or will not be violent in the future (Hart, Webster, & Menzies, 1993). Clinicians' predictions about future sexual aggression are less accurate than clinicians' predictions about future safety. Clinicians tend to be more conservative in pronouncing a sexual aggressor to be safe. Considering past sexually aggressive behavior can assist in predicting future sexually aggressive behavior, particularly for rapists, although predictions based solely on multiple arrests for sexually aggressive behavior will be wrong 40 to 50% of the time. However, multivariate combinations of predictors have been relatively accurate in predicting sexual aggression among rapists (G. Hall, 1988; Malamuth et al., 1993).

Is the level of precision that behavioral science can offer in predicting sexually aggressive behavior adequate for social policy purposes? The ratio proposed in the adage of the American legal justice system that it is better for nine guilty persons to go free than for one innocent person to be falsely detained is probably not intended to be prescriptive, particularly with sexual aggressors. However, the accuracy ratio with the "three strikes, you're out" past arrest approach with sexual aggressors would be about 1 : 1 — for every person who is appropriately detained there would be another person who would be falsely detained. Although incarceration is an effective means of protecting the community from sexual aggressors, and there appears to be strong public support for incarcerating violent offenders, it seems unlikely that all potentially violent sexual offenders will ever be locked up with life sentences. Moreover, a 40 to 50% level of imprecision seems unethical and impractical as public policy. A "three strikes" policy would do nothing to protect the community from the two thirds of criminals, many of whom are violent, who are not arrested and convicted (Riveland, 1994).

Perhaps the spirit of the "three strikes, you're out" initiative could be incorporated in a modified manner. Given that many sexual offenders, particularly rapists, tend to "burn out" in their mid-30s, sexual offenders with multiple offenses might be incarcerated until the critical period for recidivism (i.e., 18–35) has passed and then be released into the community under close supervision. Restricting access to potential victims in the community, particularly children, would also be critical.

Being incarcerated with other offenders could be a fertile training ground for future aggression (Moffitt, 1993). However, some level of close monitoring can occur during incarceration, whereas such close monitoring usually cannot occur in the community, where offenders also have access to aggressive peers. Incarceration also may provide the opportunity for treatment interventions. Such interventions should also be followed with treatment after offenders are released into the community. Recent evidence reviewed in chapter 6 suggests the utility of recently developed treatments in reducing sexual offender recidivism.

The actuarial methods reviewed in this chapter are most accurate with sexual aggressors having relatively extensive histories of past sexual aggression. These sexual aggressors are consistent with the developmentally related personality problems subtype in the quadripartite model (Hall & Hirschman, 1991, 1992). However, many sexual aggressors have relatively limited histories of sexual aggression, in terms of behavior for which they are either arrested or not arrested or both. Detection of the potential for sexually aggressive behavior and interventions among these individuals could go a long way toward reducing the most common forms of sexual aggression that occur between acquaintances and are not usually detected by official agencies. The assessment of motivational precursors of sexually aggressive behavior, as well as of situational variables that activate these motivational precursors, may be helpful in identifying risk factors among individual sexual aggressors. Such assessment methods are discussed in chapter 5.

5

Assessment of Motivational Precursors of Sexually Aggressive Behavior

Whereas the task of prediction discussed in chapter 4 is analogous to *psychological testing*, which is oriented toward dichotomous criterion-related questions (e.g., Is the person a sex offender? Will the person reoffend?), the approach presented in this chapter is analogous to *psychological assessment*, which involves the development of a construct or model to explain behavior (Maloney, 1985; Maloney & Ward, 1976; Matarazzo, 1972). Rather than to arrive at a single conclusion about a person, the goal of psychological assessment is to develop a description of a person's psychological characteristics, based on hypothesis testing (Maloney, 1985). Moreover, in the psychological assessment approach, any single test result is interpreted in the context of other clinical data. For example, clinicians using the psychological assessment approach in educational settings may integrate IQ test scores and data on adaptive behavior, rather than using IQ cutting scores alone (e.g., IQ = 70 or 130), in making recommendations for placement in developmentally disabled or gifted programming. Constructs involved in an explanatory model of sexually aggressive behavior (e.g., Hall & Hirschman, 1991; Malamuth et al., 1993; Prentky & Knight, 1991) are important in a psychological assessment context, whereas prediction of sexually aggressive behavior is of secondary importance.

The most basic task in the clinical assessment of sexually aggressive people is to determine the veracity of their self-reports. Dishonesty has been legitimized and elevated to an art form in society. For example, the public has learned *post hoc* that different forms of deception were implemented by some our highest government leaders in the Iran-*contra* scandal. The most blatant form of deception was direct denial. Another form of deception, although perhaps less blatant, was claimed amnesia, which also is a denial of responsibility. Projection was also employed, to the extent that individuals were scapegoated for the scandal. Thus, when our public servants model deception, it is not surprising that deception is viewed as an appropriate defense strategy in society.

The social stigma associated with sexual deviance is probably greater than any other form of deviant behavior (see chapter 4). Sexual offenders are at the bottom of the societal hierarchy, even in prison settings. Whereas the penalty for government fraud may be imprisonment in a "white-collar" institution (e.g., Charles Colson) or no penalty, including the ability to continue to run for public office (e.g., Oliver North), the penalty for sexually deviant behavior typically involves at least a badly tarnished reputation (e.g., president of American University Richard Berendzen; film producer Roman Polanski; although Joey Buttafuoco has been accorded celebrity status by the public following sex with a minor) and often an extended incarceration. Thus, there is extreme pressure not to be honest concerning sexually aggressive behavior.

Given the general social undesirability of admitting sexually deviant behavior and the specific demand to appear nondeviant in the forensic settings in which most sexual aggressors are seen by clinicians, skepticism is warranted. Such skepticism runs contrary to clinicians' training in developing a therapeutic relationship with clients. However, for a clinician to communicate trust in the client's account in a forensic setting is disingenuous because noncompliance with treatment and recidivism typically are nonconfidential information that is reported to legal authorities (Rogers & Dickey, 1991). Moreover, the forensic clinician who communicates trust to the client may be perceived by the client as naive and easily manipulable. Thus, the goal of the initial stages of clinical work with sexual aggressors is empathy and acceptance without collusion (Garland & Dougher, 1991).

Veracity of Perpetrators' Self-Reports

There are several common forms of distortion that are encountered in initial evaluations of men accused of being sexually aggressive. In my research and clinical work with sexual aggressors, I have encountered six common cognitive distortions about sexually aggressive behavior. Each of these distortions serves a defensive purpose. Complete admission of responsibility for sexually aggressive behavior is relatively uncommon. For example, in a prison population, none of the sexual offenders completely admitted responsibility for his sexual aggressive behavior (Barbaree, 1991). Exaggeration of sexually aggressive behavior is also uncommon. Only 1 in over 200 sexual aggressors whom I have assessed in both inpatient and community settings over the past 13 years has overstated the extent of his sexually aggressive behavior. However, fabricated information that minimizes personal responsibility for sexually aggressive behavior is common, which underscores the importance of reviewing corroborating records prior to interviewing persons accused of sexually aggressive behavior. The following distortions are discussed along a continuum of blatancy, beginning with the most blatant form of cognitive distortion, denial.

Denial

This is the Clarence Thomas scenario in which the alleged perpetrator and alleged victim's accounts of events are diametrically opposed. Categorical denial of sexually aggressive behavior is fairly common in forensic evaluation settings. One fifth to two thirds of men evaluated in forensic settings deny engaging in sexually aggressive behavior, despite corroborating evidence to the contrary (Barbaree, 1991; Lanyon & Lutz, 1984; Marshall, 1994; Pollock & Hashmall, 1991; Scully & Marolla, 1984). The veracity of an alleged sexual aggressor's denial should be evaluated by comparing his report of his behavior to victim statements or other corroborating evidence, such as police investigations or presentence evaluations (Rogers & Dickey, 1991). Such corroborating evidence is absolutely necessary to identify cognitive distortions because the sexual aggressor's self-report may be extremely misleading (Herman, 1990). Exclusive reliance on the perpetrator's self-report may lead to the incorrect conclusion that nothing happened or that the offensive behavior was minimal. Even when a sexual aggressor is attempting to be cooperative, his distorted perceptions of his behavior may cause him to deny or minimize acts that are harmful to others (see chapter 2). Perhaps these distortions are a result of recounting a distorted version of sexually aggressive behavior multiple times without being challenged or a result of actually being encouraged by defense attorneys to present such an exculpatory version (Marshall, 1994).

Denial can often be convincing, particularly when a clinician is unprepared for it. During my postdoctoral training, before having any documentation of why he had been referred to the program, I interviewed a man who had been referred to an outpatient anger management program. The man was so convincing in assuring me that he did not have an anger problem that I wrote a note in his chart that this was one of the "rare cases" in which anger management may not be necessary. This note came back to haunt me because the man apparently had been referred for some form of aggressive acting out, which I had been unaware of, and within a few months was referred a second time to the anger management program following additional aggressive behavior. One of my colleagues appropriately chided me for my note about anger management being unnecessary. Since that time, I have refused to see any forensic clients before I have had an opportunity to review corroborating information about them (cf. Marshall, 1994). If clients refuse to have such information released to me, I do not evaluate them.

Cooperation with the assessment process is critical for accuracy. Most assessment methods, such as physiological assessment and self-report, are invalid if the subject is not honest. Thus, denial may preclude accurate assessment of sexually behavior.

Amnesia

Some sexual aggressors claim that they cannot remember being sexually aggressive. Forgetting is qualitatively different from denial. This form of cognitive distortion allows for the possibility that a sexually aggressive act occurred, but the alleged sexual aggressor does not assume responsibility for the act. Reasons offered for amnesia commonly include alcohol or drug intoxication, or elapsed time since the event (e.g., "that was so long ago that I can't remember any details"). Occasionally, the presentation of corroborating data will convince a sexual aggressor to agree that he was sexually aggressive. However, even when agreement on sexually aggressive behavior is reached, the sexual aggressor may maintain amnesia for the events.

Minimization

One fourth to one third of sexual aggressors evaluated in forensic settings admit to engaging in some form of sexual behavior with another person, but minimize its extent or impact or both (Barbaree, 1991; Lanyon & Lutz, 1984; Marshall, 1994; Pollock & Hashmall, 1991). William Kennedy Smith admitted to engaging in sexual behavior with the woman who alleged that he raped her, but he denied that the behavior was rape. A perpetrator's description of the events may be much less extensive than the victim's description in terms of type of activity (e.g., fondling vs. intercourse) and frequency (e.g., "it happened only the one time when I was caught" vs. multiple occasions). Perpetrators may engage in definitional obfuscation. For example, perpetrators may not consider their sexually aggressive behavior to be rape or child molestation, even if the actual sexually aggressive behavior constitutes rape or child molestation.

Unfortunately, plea bargaining in the legal system often serves to reinforce these tendencies to minimize behavior (Marshall, 1994). For example, if a man rapes a woman or child, but is charged with an offense other than rape (e.g., assault, "indecent liberties"), then he may not view his behavior as rape and may see the impact of his behavior as less serious than that which would occur in a rape. During court testimony, I once referred to a man's forced sexual intercourse with a minor female as rape, but the defense attorney objected because the man had not been charged with rape. The judge upheld the objection. One of my favorite legal euphemisms for sexually aggressive behavior is "indecent assault." This term seems to imply that some forms of assault are decent, which is consistent with "macho" notions of the right to be aggressive (see chapter 1).

The cognitive distortions discussed in chapter 3 are often used for minimization. For example, child molesters who do not use physical force to gain their victims' compliance may justify sex as a form of education or an expression of love (Murphy, 1990). Minimization may be perceived as more justifiable in situations in which there are "mitigating" circumstances (e.g., acquaintance rape), but even extreme forms of sexually aggressive behavior can be minimized. For example, rapists have contended that using a weapon to gain a woman's cooperation to have sex is not rape (Scully & Marolla, 1984).

Victim empathy tends to be absent or minimal at best among perpetrators who minimize their sexual aggression (Friedrich, 1990; Hildebran & Pithers, 1989; Murphy, 1990). Dubious assumptions about victims, such as equating a victim's lack of reaction with being unaffected by the sexual behavior, may serve as excuses for sexual aggression (Langevin, Lang, Wright, Handy, & Majpruz, 1989). Moreover, some aggressive males may be insensitive to situations that would create negative emotional reactions for most persons (Lochman & Dodge, 1994) and may not have much empathy because they might not experience extremely negative emotions if they were victimized themselves. Indeed, unwanted sexual contact may be less traumatic for many males than for females (Condy et al., 1987). In other words, even if the perpetrator acknowledges that he is being aggressive, he may take an egocentric perspective of the aggression that does not acknowledge the possibility that others will experience the aggression as more harmful than he does.

Projection

Projection involves admission of sexually aggressive behavior, often even without minimizing its impact, but also displaces responsibility. The basic stance of the sexual aggressor who projects responsibility is that he is the victim. At least 1 in 5 sexual aggressors blames his victim (Pollock & Hashmall, 1991). Victims are often blamed for the perpetrator's sexually aggressive behavior because of the victim's appearance (e.g., "provocative" clothing) or behavior (e.g., "she came on to me," "she was drinking," "she said no but really meant yes"). Victims may also be blamed for provoking anger that makes sexual aggression justifiable. Some sexual aggressors do not necessarily blame the victim, but they may blame the effects of alcohol or drugs (e.g., "I never would have done this if I were sober") or even a "sexual addiction." Another method of portraying the self as victim is to attribute sexually aggressive behavior to being personally sexually abused (Melton, 1992).

There may appear to be an element of legitimacy to such projection of responsibility onto circumstantial factors. Women admit that no sometimes means yes to sex (Muehlenhard & Hollabaugh, 1988), alcohol use is associated with sexual aggression against women (Abbey, 1991; Koss & Gaines, 1993) and children (Pribor & Dinwiddie, 1992), and being sexually abused does place some men at risk for becoming sexually abusive (Friedrich et al., 1992; Rubinstein, Yeager, Goodstein, & Lewis, 1993). However, none of these circumstances absolves a male of responsibility for his sexual behavior. Most persons do not persist with sexual behavior when told no, are not sexually aggressive when intoxicated, and do not become sexually aggressive despite being sexually abused. Thus, the decision to be sexually aggressive is the perpetrator's responsibility (cf. Margolin & Burman, 1993).

Redefinition

Over a third of sexual aggressors admit to assaulting the victim but claim that the assault was nonsexual and that they have some problem that caused them to offend other than a tendency to be sexually aggressive (e.g., anger, alcohol, drugs, stress; Barbaree, 1991; Marshall, 1994; Pollock & Hashmall, 1991). It may be more socially desirable for sexual aggressors to admit to a general problem, such as anger, than to admit to a specific problem that may be perceived as more deviant, such as anger toward women (G. Hall, 1989a; McGovern & Nevid, 1986). Approximately 1 in 4 sexual aggressors also claims that he was sexually aggressive because he was deprived of conventional sexual outlets (Pollock & Hashmall, 1991). Thus, to the extent that the goal of sexually aggressive behavior is sex, it is not viewed by perpetrators as deviant.

Redefinition is similar to projection, except that the perpetrator assumes responsibility for being sexually aggressive. However, perpetrators who use redefinition are unwilling to view themselves as sexually deviant or to be viewed as sexually deviant by others. Thus, specialized treatment for sexually aggressive behavior is viewed as unnecessary, and more general treatment for problems that anyone could experience—such as anger, substance abuse, or stress—is preferred by such perpetrators. The perpetrator's contention is that if he is cured of his general problem, then he will no longer be sexually aggressive.

General problems certainly may exacerbate a person's tendencies to be sexually aggressive. However, general treatment is not an adequate substitute for specialized treatment for sexually aggressive behavior. Nevertheless, a clinician who can offer a comprehensive treatment program, such as those described in chapters 6 and 7, can accommodate a perpetrator's desire for general treatment in the context of a more specialized treatment approach.

Conversion

Stopping sexually aggressive behavior has been compared to religious conversion (Herman, 1990). Some perpetrators will admit that they have been sexually aggressive, but they contend that they will never relapse. Such admission is similar to a confession of sin and conversion in religious contexts. Confession, in and of itself, is viewed as having absolving properties. However, confession and conversion in a religious or nonreligious context that is not followed by behavioral change may serve as a justification of additional transgressions (e.g., "I can do whatever I want to do as long I confess afterward").

Perpetrators who believe that they have reformed may view their problem as having passed and thus not assume responsibility for relapse prevention. However, many reformations by sexual aggressors are temporary. Because most sexual aggressors are not caught the first time they are sexually aggressive, they often have undergone a sequence of sexual aggression followed by guilt and resolve not to relapse, followed by further sexual aggression. Resolve not to relapse is not sufficient to prevent relapse in the absence of specific relapse prevention skills (Marlatt & Gordon, 1985; Marques & Nelson, 1992; Marques, Nelson, West, & Day, 1994). Moreover, even when a sexual aggressor has learned to stop being sexually aggressive, this does not necessarily imply that he has acquired other life skills that are required by society (see chapter 6).

Thus, although the perpetrator admits to engaging in sexually aggressive behavior during treatment, claims of reformation may be as problematic during treatment as some of the other distortions discussed previously because of the perpetrator's belief that no changes are necessary following confession of his "sin."

The first sexual aggressor who I worked with in a clinical setting admitted that he had engaged in child molestation. However, he did not want to discuss child molestation and instead wanted me to help him reduce his feelings of guilt and depression, which were aftereffects of his molesting children. He apparently believed that his admission of molesting a child and his resolve not to reoffend were sufficient to prevent relapse.

Other perpetrators may argue that being arrested or incarcerated has been sufficiently onerous to prevent them from relapsing. However, the fear of punishment tends to wear off. In other words, the fear of punishment may create an initially high threshold for sexual aggression that decreases as a function of time since punishment. Finding God after offending is another form of conversion, although blaming God may become an excuse for relapse when a perpetrator believes God to be responsible for his behavior.

Consenting to participate in treatment may be viewed as an act of conversion by perpetrators and sometimes by their families and therapists (Barrett et al., 1990). However, consent to participate does not necessarily guarantee active participation. Dropout rates among sexual aggressors who begin psychological therapies are about 33% (Abel, Mittelman, Becker, Rathner, & Rouleau, 1988; Chaffin, 1992; G. Hall, 1995a) and are as high as 50% among those who begin psychohormonal treatment (Langevin et al., 1979). Even completion of treatment may constitute a temporary conversion insofar as the perpetrator believes that treatment is complete and that he is "cured" and no longer needs to assume personal responsibility for relapse prevention (Marlatt & Gordon, 1985).

Veracity of Victims' Self-Reports

Although many mental health professionals who evaluate perpetrators of sexual aggression are typically not involved in the evaluation of victims, the assumption of perpetrators' cognitive distortions is predicated on the veracity of victims' accounts of experiences. As discussed previously, corroborating accounts of sexually aggressive behavior from the victim's perspective are mandatory for adequate assessment of perpetrators. Thus, it is important to determine if child and adult victims' accounts of sexual abuse are generally accurate.

Unlike other forms of abuse, in which there often is physical evidence, such as bruises, cuts, or scars, physical evidence is often absent when a person is sexually abused. Although DNA samples from semen have been used to identify perpetrators, semen is not always available, and there is a recent trend for rapists to wear condoms to avoid detection via semen (Wolff, 1994). Moreover, even when semen is available, semen alone does not prove that sexual contact was forced in the absence of other physical evidence of assault. Thus, identification of sexually aggressive behavior is predicated on circumstantial evidence from victims' reports more so than for other forms of abuse (Daro, 1988).

Medical evidence of child sexual abuse is usually inconclusive (Haugaard & Reppucci, 1988). Thus, evaluations of child victims rely heavily on self-report. In laboratory settings, children can accurately report events (Goodman & Helgeson, 1988). However, children's "real life" self-reports outside the laboratory in legal or family (e.g., incest, child custody disputes) settings are potentially compromised by stressors (Faller, 1991; Mikkelsen, Gutheil, & Emens, 1992). Nevertheless, only 4.7 to 7.6% of sexual abuse allegations are estimated by child protection service workers to be false (Everson & Boat, 1989), and there is no evidence that a child can be coached to fabricate a whole event (Levine & Battistoni, 1991). Thus, young children who do not have a working knowledge of sexuality would have difficulty describing sexual contact (e.g., attempted penile-vaginal penetration) in detail without direct experience at the hands of a perpetrator.

An innovative laboratory analog approach that is of particular relevance to the assessment of child sexual abuse has been developed by Saywitz, Goodman, Nicholas, and Moan (1993). In this approach, girls underwent a standardized medical examination with or without a genital examination. Among the girls in the genital examination condition, 86% reported vaginal touch and 69% reported anal touch during direct questioning with anatomically detailed dolls available. *None* of the girls in the nongenital examination condition falsely reported genital touch during free recall or anatomical doll demonstrations.

Clinical methods of evaluation that are less direct than self-report are used with victims who are unable or unwilling to provide details of their victimization. Play with anatomically correct dolls is a popular method assumed to reflect a child's actual experiences of sexual abuse (Boat & Everson, 1988). However, the validity of the use of anatomically correct dolls for assessing sexual abuse with victims may be questionable (Elliott, O'Donohue, & Nickerson, 1993). Nevertheless, anatomical dolls elicit very low rates of false reports of sexual contact among nonclinical samples (Everson & Boat, 1990; Saywitz et al., 1993).

Adults are capable of accurate reports of sexual abuse, as are children. However, how frequent are false accusations of rape among women? About 8% of the reports of rape are considered false, which is higher than the false report rate for other crimes (FBI Uniform Crime Reports, 1991). Nevertheless, FBI data may reveal more about police attitudes than reports of rape that are actually false (Lonsway & Fitzgerald, 1994). Moreover, public perceptions, particularly those of aggressive men who need to justify their aggression toward women, of the frequency of false reports of rape may be inflated by media coverage (Allison & Wrightsman, 1993). The humiliation involved with admission of being a rape victim, including being blamed for the victimization and detailed inquiries into one's sexual history in court proceedings, combined with the low likelihood of rapists being prosecuted, may deter many victims from reporting rape to authorities (Allison & Wrightsman, 1993; Donat & D'Emilio, 1992; Goldberg-Ambrose, 1992). Actual rape incidence has been estimated to be 2 to 15 times *higher* than the number of rapes reported to criminal justice authorities (Koss, 1993a). Thus, false reporting of sexual abuse may be uncommon.

The elicitation by therapists of repressed memories of past sexual abuse have recently been the focus of media attention. In therapy, some adults apparently recall sexual abuse that occurred decades in the past. A sexual abuse suit against Cardinal Joseph Bernardin was dropped in 1994 because the accuser admitted that unreliable memories of abuse in the distant past were elicited during hypnosis. Between 18 and 59% of persons who were abused in childhood report that they forgot being abused (Loftus, 1993). However, analogous to other constructs that are not directly observable, such as "latent" schizophrenia, research on repressed memories is difficult to conduct because most research is based on retrospective reports, which are hard to corroborate. Moreover, it is also difficult to distinguish repression, which involves the unconscious banishment of unacceptable memories that are not subject to voluntary recall (American Psychiatric Association, 1980), from ordinary forgetting, which does not involve repression (Loftus, 1993). In one of the only longitudinal studies on repressed memories, 38% of women known to have been abused 17 years earlier failed to report the abuse (Williams, 1992, cited in Loftus, 1993).

The expectations or suggestions of clinicians, who believe that memories of sexual abuse need to be freed from repression for a client to be psychologically healthy, may influence clients to remember being sexually abused (Loftus, 1993). These clinicians are similar to clinicians who believe that certain factors characterize all sexual aggressors (e.g., all sexual aggressors have committed multiple offenses) and interrogate their clients until the client occasionally admits to the presence of such factors in an effort to placate the therapist. Although some memories of sexual abuse may be confabulated or distorted, the recent popularity of psychological trauma theory has caused many clinicians to believe any client accounts of past abuse (Herman, 1992). Media and popular press presentations of the frequency of sexual abuse may also make persons consider the possibility that they, too, have been sexually victimized (Loftus, 1993). Because clinicians cannot distinguish between genuine and confabulated memories (Loftus, 1993), it appears that accounts of sexual abuse should be regarded with more credibility as a function of the recency of the abuse.

How, then, should victim reports be utilized in the assessment of perpetrators of sexual aggression? It is socially undesirable to admit involvement in sexual aggression, either as a perpetrator or as a victim. Perpetrators are derogated in society, and even in prison are at the bottom of the social hierarchy. Victims also are subject to derogation. Admission to being a victim of sexual aggression often results in the victim's being viewed as responsible for provoking the sexual aggression (Allison & Wrightsman, 1993; Donat & D'Emilio, 1992; Goldberg-Ambrose, 1992). Thus, reports of being sexually victimized or, much more rarely, reports of being sexually aggressive, should be taken seriously. Although false accusations of sexual abuse are possible, they are infrequent and alleged victims' claims of being sexually abused should generally be viewed as more credible than alleged perpetrators' claims of innocence. However, both perpetrators' and victims' memories of events are subject to distortion (Loftus, 1993). Thus, rather than accusing alleged perpetrators of the acts that the victims have claimed, which may be counterproductive clinically (see chapter 6), simply asking perpetrators to account for why the alleged victims have accused them of particular sexually aggressive acts may be more productive. In doing so, however, clinicians can expect alleged perpetrators to employ the cognitive distortions discussed earlier in this chapter. Nevertheless, nonconfrontational presentation of the discrepancies between the perpetrator's and victim's accounts of the events can be an important first step is establishing a therapeutic milieu (Barbaree, 1991; Marshall, 1994). Moreover, a thorough review of the victim's statement communicates to the perpetrator that the clinician is astute and will not be easily manipulable.

Assessment of Situational Disinhibitors of Sexual Aggression

Comprehensive assessment of sexual aggressors involves a consideration of each of the physiological, cognitive, affective, and developmental motivational precursors of sexually aggressive behavior (Hall, Shondrick, et al., 1993a). However, assessment of these motivational precursors alone is not sufficient because many males who exhibit evidence of the motivational precursors may not be sexually aggressive (see chapter 3). In that sexually aggressive behavior appears to be mediated by situational determinants, physiological, cognitive, and affective situational variables that may disinhibit sexually aggressive behavior also should be assessed. In the context of adequate motivation for sexually aggressive behavior, response to situational variables may disinhibit sexually aggressive behavior. Thus, the assessment of the four motivational precursors of sexually aggressive behavior is not adequate without concurrent assessment of situational variables that may cause a person to exceed the inhibitory threshold for sexually aggressive behavior.

A variety of psychological tests traditionally have been used to assess the four motivational precursors (Hall & Hirschman, 1991; Lanyon, 1986). For example, the physiological, cognitive, affective, and developmental motivational precursors have been assessed with domain-specific self-report instruments (Hanson, Cox, & Woszczyna, 1991). The multi-faceted nature of the developmentally related personality problems motivational precursor may make self-report inventories, such as the MMPI-2, more economical than an extended interview that would cover all the areas assessed in such inventories. Knight, Prentky, and Cerce (1994) have recently developed a self-report inventory based on the MTC dimensions that may be useful in assessing the specific developmentally related personality problems of sexual aggressors. However, the transparent nature of self-report test items makes them subject to socially desirable or deceptive responding (see chapter 4). Moreover, support for these traditional measures is based on *post hoc* research with identified sexually aggressive individuals (see chapter 3), and these measures may not adequately assess future risk for sexually aggressive behavior. Self-report inventories often are insensitive to changes in treatment, in that current functioning may not be assessed and historical items are included that cannot change (e.g., past arrests).

Given the susceptibility of psychological testing to dissimulation (see chapter 4), an accurate psychological assessment of a sexual aggressor may not be possible until the defensive distortions discussed earlier in this chapter are modified and there is a modicum of cooperation by the sexual aggressor with the assessment process. Thus, psychological assessments that occur before the sexual aggressor has become cooperative, which is typically when psychological assessments are conducted, may be less useful for clinical purposes than psychological assessments that occur after the sexual aggressor has become cooperative. A defensive sexual aggressor may appear relatively unpathological during an initial assessment but may appear to *increase* in pathology by the end of treatment because he is less defensive and more accurately reports his problems. Because the baseline assessment was not an accurate picture of his pathology, the assessment instruments cannot reveal if the apparent increase in pathology reflects a real increase, no change, or a decrease in pathology.

A sexual aggressor usually becomes cooperative with the assessment process if he believes cooperation is in his best interests. For example, if the admission of problems results in hospitalization or outpatient treatment rather than incarceration, then the sexual aggressor may be less defensive. Another situation in which a sexual aggressor may be cooperative is postsentencing. If a sexual aggressor has nothing to gain by maintaining his innocence, and if his release to the community is contingent upon participation in treatment, then he may view cooperation as advantageous (Marshall, 1994). Clinicians should beware, however, of shrewd sexual aggressors who will exaggerate their problems before a treatment program and minimize them at the end of a treatment program, independent of any treatment effects. Thus, any pre-post treatment changes on psychometric measures must be evaluated in the clinical context. The following discussion of assessment methods is predicated on the assumption that the client is at least minimally cooperative.

Physiological Sexual Arousal

Assessment methods that closely simulate the conditions under which sexually aggressive behavior occurs presumably are more ecologically valid than methods that do not simulate such conditions (e.g., paper-and-pencil tests). Behavioral assessment is a useful method of determining the environmental conditions that elicit behavior (Barrios, 1988). Whereas traditional methods of assessment have been indirect, in that they are removed from the context in which behavior occurs, behavioral assessment strives for direct measurement of behavior that involves *in vivo* observation when possible, and analogue observation when *in vivo* observation is not possible. Obviously, the *in vivo* observation of sexually aggressive acts is not possible or ethical. However, measurement of penile response to deviant sexual stimuli has been widely used as an analog of the conditions under which sexually aggressive behavior actually occurs.

There is more literature on the physiological assessment of sexual arousal than on the other assessment methods discussed in this chapter. Despite the lack of correspondence between physiological sexual arousal and sexually aggressive behavior, physiological assessments may be useful for nondefensive sexual aggressors who have admitted engaging in sexually aggressive behavior (Freund & Blanchard, 1989). However, if a sexual aggressor has admitted to being sexually aggressive and is not defensive, why not just ask him about his sexual arousal instead of conducting a physiological assessment (as the researcher described in chapter 4 proposed)? As discussed in chapter 4, admission of deviant sexual arousal may be highly socially undesirable, even for someone who has admitted to engaging in sexually aggressive behavior, because of the sexual deviance associated with deviant sexual arousal as a cause of sexually aggressive behavior (McGovern & Nevid, 1986). Thus, the physiological assessment of sexual arousal may have a role in the assessment of perpetrators who admit to engaging in sexually aggressive behavior but have not admitted to experiencing deviant sexual arousal.

Sexual arousal in response to deviant stimuli may be more common among sexual aggressors against children than among sexual aggressors against women (Hall, Shondrick, et al., 1993a). Approximately two thirds of sexual aggressors against children exhibit pedophilic patterns of sexual arousal (Hall et al., 1988), whereas only about one third of sexual aggressors against adults exhibit greater or equal arousal to rape stimuli relative to consenting sexual stimuli (G. Hall, 1989b). Insofar as sexual arousal in response to children (Hall et al., in press) or to rape stimuli (Malamuth & Check, 1983) is characteristic of a minority of "normal" men who are not sexually aggressive, the presence of sexual arousal to deviant stimuli in any particular sexual aggressor does not necessarily guarantee that such sexual arousal is the primary motivation for being sexually aggressive. Thus, when sexual arousal to deviant stimuli is detected, a sexual aggressor should be questioned if deviant fantasies or deviant sexual arousal is an immediate precursor to his sexual acting out. In the psychological assessment approach that is advocated in this chapter, any single test result, such as sexual arousal to deviant stimuli, should be verified clinically.

A major problem with most methods to assess physiological sexual arousal is their ecological validity. The sterile, controlled laboratory setting in which these assessments are conducted does not even remotely resemble the situations in which sexually aggressive acts typically take place. After viewing a laboratory in which physiological assessments of sexual arousal were conducted, a former colleague, Greg Gagliardi (personal communication, 1987) described the experience of the subject as "being aroused in unarousing places."

Instructing subjects to allow themselves to become aroused to the stimuli may produce more responses than no instructions concerning sexual arousal (Murphy, Haynes, Coleman, & Flanagan, 1985). Such permission to become sexually aroused to deviant stimuli may approximate conditions under which sexual aggression takes place. However, careful psychological assessment will help determine if sexual arousal under permissive conditions is simply a function of the demand characteristics of the situation.

One innovative suggestion concerning ecological validity is to assess behaviors in the context of situational cues that may mediate them (cf. Marlatt, 1990; Pithers, 1993). Thus, if a person sexually acts out when he is angry, inducing anger would enhance the ecological validity of physiological assessment of sexual arousal. Other situational variables that could be introduced include the presentation of pornography or alcohol consumption (cf. Holtzworth-Munroe, 1992). Caution must be exercised in interpreting sexual arousal that is disinhibited by situational factors, however. Situational variables, such as induced anger, pornography presentation, and alcohol consumption, may disinhibit deviant sexual arousal among men who are not sexually aggressive (Barbaree & Marshall, 1991). Thus, it must be determined whether situationally induced deviant sexual arousal is "normal" or is a motivational precursor to sexually aggressive behavior.

Psychometric Issues. Circumferential measures of penile response have been most commonly used in research on sexual aggressors (Hall, Shondrick, et al., 1993b). Circumferential measures are easier to use than volumetric measures. Most researchers have used maximum amplitude penile responses instead of total response to each stimulus (area under the curve) because of no definite advantage of the total response, greater ease of use, and the greater reliability of the maximum amplitude response (Abel, Blanchard, Murphy, Becker, & Djenderedjian, 1981; Davidson & Malcolm, 1985).

There has been some debate concerning which types of stimuli are appropriate for physiological assessments of sexual arousal. Some researchers and clinicians have used videotapes of sexual acts, but videotaped stimuli tend to create a ceiling effect, such that penile responses to stimuli having different contents (e.g., consenting sex, rape) are all about equal (Abel, Blanchard, & Barlow, 1981). More commonly, audiotaped descriptions of sexual acts have been used to assess rapists and child molesters. In addition, some have used photographs of nude children in assessing child molesters. Although it has been argued that consent cannot be obtained to photograph nude children (W. Murphy, 1993, Association for the Treatment of Sex Abusers meeting, Boston), it also has been argued that in instances in which such photographs are confiscated by authorities (e.g., police), "the damage has been done" and the use of such photographs for clinical purposes may contribute to the prevention of future crimes (H. Barbaree, 1993, Association for the Treatment of Sex Abusers meeting, Boston). In that there is no clear advantage of audiotapes vs. slides in eliciting sexual arousal (Abel, Blanchard, & Barlow, 1981) and because there may exist greater measurement error with slides than with audiotapes (Harris et al., 1992), the use of audiotapes may be preferable.

Another issue related to the type of stimuli used is when such stimuli are presented to adolescent sexual aggressors as part of physiological assessments. There is a very limited literature on the use of physiological assessment of sexual arousal with adolescents (Saunders & Awad, 1988). Exposing adolescents to deviant acts that are novel to them is problematic (Saunders & Awad, 1988). Laboratory studies suggest that exposure to aggressive media can produce aggressive behavior (Donnerstein et al., 1987). Such exposure to aggressive behavior during physiological assessments also is potentially problematic with adult sexual aggressors, as well. However, most clinicians and researchers assume that the acts depicted in assessment stimuli are not novel to adult sexual aggressors, in terms of past fantasies or behavior. Nevertheless, the presentation of such stimuli by clinicians and researchers may also give subjects the impression that these stimuli are condoned to some degree by clinicians and researchers (Freedman, 1988). One method of reducing the negative effects of aggressive media is a debriefing that emphasizes the impact of sexual aggression on victims (Check & Malamuth, 1984; Intons-Peterson, Roskos-Ewoldsen, Thomas, Shirley, & Blut, 1989).

What constitutes a "deviant" level of sexual arousal? Ratios of penile response to deviant stimuli (e.g., descriptions of rape or child molestation, photographs of prepubescent children) vs. nondeviant stimuli (e.g., descriptions of consenting sex between adults, photographs of nude adults) have commonly been used. A variation of the ratio approach is the percentage of full erection, in which penile tumescence in response to a particular stimulus is compared with penile tumescence during a full erection. Cutting scores for deviance have been proposed for these ratio methods (Laws & Osborn, 1983).

Despite their common use in clinical settings, G. Hall (1990c) has demonstrated the lack of clinical utility of ratio scores. A subject exhibiting 1 mm of penile tumescence in response to consenting adult stimuli and 2 mm of tumescence in response to pedophilic stimuli would have the same .50 ratio as subjects exhibiting 5 mm and 10 mm, or 10 mm and 20 mm of tumescence to the respective stimuli. The difference of 1 mm for the first subject could be attributable to measurement error (see chapter 4). However, the third subject, having the same .50 ratio as the other two subjects, would appear to have a clear preference for the pedophilic stimuli (G. Hall, 1990c). A subject exhibiting 10 mm of tumescence to the pedophilic stimuli and 30 mm of tumescence to nondeviant stimuli would have a ratio of only .30, which is not considered deviant by some clinicians (Laws & Osborn, 1983). Yet, in an absolute sense, 10 mm of penile tumescence is a significant response to pedophilic stimuli that may require clinical interventions for the subject with a .50 ratio (10 : 20), as well as for the subject with the .30 ratio (10 : 30). These problems of interpretation also apply to other data transformations, including difference scores (nondeviant score minus deviant score) and standard scores (e.g., z scores). From a psychometric perspective, transformed scores are also less reliable than raw scores (Barbaree, Baxter, & Marshall, 1989; Hall, Shondrick et al., 1993b).

If raw data are more reliable than transformed data, how should they be used in clinical practice? Guidance on this issue can be found in the psychometric concept of the standard error of measurement (SEM), which indicates the margin of error expected in an individual's score as a result of the unreliability of the test (Anastasi, 1988). $SEM = SD_t \sqrt{1 - r_{tt}}$, where SD_t is the standard deviation of the test scores and r_{tt} is the reliability coefficient of the test. Using the Hall et al. (1988) data for penile tumescence in response to audiotapes depicting mutually consenting pedophilic arousal, $SEM = (4.71) \sqrt{1 - .77} = 2.26$. Multiplying the SEM by 2 provides a 95% confidence interval, which is the conventional margin of error ($p < .05$; Anastasi, 1988). Thus the chances are 95 : 5 that an individual's obtained score will fall within 4.52 mm (2 × 2.26) on either side of his *true* score. Given a mean of 4.43 mm penile tumescence in response to the mutually consenting pedophilic stimuli (Hall et al., 1988), there is a 95% chance that during any single plethysmograph assessment that the subject's score will lie between 0 mm (4.43 − 4.52; scores <0 not possible because 0 = no tumescence) and 8.95 mm (4.43 + 4.52). The ±4.52 mm margin of error for the 95% confidence interval suggests that any raw score less than 4.52 mm may not be reliably different from 0. Thus, for clinical purposes, raw scores of about 4.5 mm or greater would be considered interpretable.

Harris et al. (1992) have provided combined SEM data for sexual offenders and nonsexual offenders. The SEMs were 0.43, 0.40, and 1.00 for three different data sets. Using the 95% confidence level, these SEMs suggest a ±.8 mm to ±2 mm margin of error. However, Harris et al. (1992), after using data transformations, interpreted within-group differences among child molesters of less than .6 mm as significant. Such minuscule differences could be a function of measurement error.

Moreover, the *SEM*s for sexual offenders are larger than the combined *SEM* data for sexual offenders and nonsexual offenders that Harris et al. (1992) reported. Using the test reliability coefficients and the standard deviations for sexual offenders' responses to deviant stimuli, the *SEM*s are 1.88, 1.24, and 1.33 for the three data sets. Using the 95% confidence interval, ±3.76 mm, ±2.48 mm, and ±2.66 mm are the margins of error for physiological assessments with sexual offenders. These margins of error underscore the possibility that differences of less than 1 mm are well within the range of measurement error. The clinical significance of such small differences is also questionable (cf. Jacobson & Truax, 1991).

The lower margins of error in the Harris et al. (1992) vs. the Hall et al. (1988) data were a function of the lower *SD* in the Harris et al. data. Lower test reliabilities also increase error. Relatively low test reliabilities are not uncommon with penile measures (Hall, Shondrick, et al., 1993b). Such between-setting differences suggest the importance of examining measurement error in one's particular setting.

Proponents of physiological assessment of sexual arousal have suggested that the only clinical application of such assessment is for treatment and disposition decisions (Harris et al., 1992). If physiological assessment is employed to evaluate the outcome of treatments to reduce sexual arousal to deviant stimuli, then such assessment must be reliable to be useful. If you weigh yourself twice on your bathroom scale and the scale indicates that you have lost weight, is this because of an actual weight loss or the inaccuracy of the scale? Small reductions in penile tumescence following treatment could be a function of phallometric measurement error.

Even if measurement is reliable, the implications of physiological measurement for treatment are unclear. For example, even a reduction in deviant arousal of less than 1 mm or an analogous increase in nondeviant arousal could both result in dramatic evidence of treatment improvement when data transformations are used (e.g., Freund & Blanchard, 1989; Harris et al., 1992). I have advocated the use of raw score data because of the reductions in reliability and interpretive distortions that data transformations cause (Hall et al., 1988). Thus, in keeping with the above discussion of margin of error, a pre- to post-treatment change of 9 mm (2 × 4.5 mm) or greater (e.g., reduction in deviant sexual arousal via aversive conditioning) would be required to ensure no overlap between pre- and post-treatment scores that could be attributable to error, given the *SEM* and *SD* for the Hall et al. (1988) data. To reliably assess change, a pretreatment level of sexual arousal would have to be at least 9 mm of penile circumference, which would have to be reduced to 0 mm for a reliable change. Mean penile circumference scores of 10 mm, 5 mm, and 0 mm are presented. If a subject had a pretreatment penile circumference score of 10 mm, a reduction to 5 mm would be within the margin of measurement error. A 9 mm reduction would be required to exceed the margin of measurement error. Thus, a reduction from 10 mm to 0 mm would constitute a reliable pre-post difference. However, many sexual aggressors are able to voluntarily inhibit their sexual arousal, thus low levels of posttreatment sexual arousal should be regarded cautiously.

From a psychological assessment perspective, the 4.5 mm level or any other cutoff should not be regarded as absolute. If a sexual aggressor complained of a preoccupation with deviant sexual fantasies and arousal, but exhibited penile tumescence of less than 4.5 mm in response to deviant stimuli, such complaints would still constitute evidence of physiological sexual arousal to deviant stimuli that may be associated with sexually aggressive behavior. Such deviant sexual arousal that is imperceptible on physiological measures may be detected with domain-specific self-report measures, such as the Pictorial Sexual Interest Card-Sort (Haywood et al., 1990). Skepticism may be warranted in the converse situation in which a sexual aggressor exhibits high levels of physiological sexual arousal, but denies such arousal. Nevertheless, some men's sexual arousal is a function of arousability factors that may be independent of actual behavior (G. Hall, 1989). Thus, deviant sexual arousal is not necessarily equivalent to deviant sexual behavior (G. Hall, 1989b; Hall et al., 1988; Simon & Schouten, 1991).

The prognosis for change with a sexual aggressor who exhibits physiological sexual arousal to deviant stimuli is a function of the number of times the person has been sexually aggressive. The absolute level of deviant sexual arousal required for a person to act out sexually may decrease as a function of sexually acting out (see chapter 3). In that high levels of deviant sexual arousal can be induced via fantasy, environmental cues (e.g., a woman or child who elicits sexual arousal) are not necessarily critical to mediating sexually aggressive behavior for the sexual aggressor who is motivated by physiological sexual arousal.

Ethical Issues. An ethical issue in the assessment of sexual arousal concerns the qualifications of the clinician conducting such assessments. Similar to the persons who conduct polygraph assessments (Saxe, 1994), many persons who conduct assessments of sexual arousal with alleged perpetrators of sexual aggression are not trained in psychology. The face-validity of physiological measures affords them a guise of objectivity and authority that may easily be misinterpreted. It has been suggested that clinical experience with sexual offenders is one of the most important qualifications of a clinician who works with sexual offenders (O'Connell, Leberg, & Donaldson, 1990). However, as discussed in chapters 1 and 4, clinical experience does not necessarily ensure clinical competence. The clinicians who were unable to accurately predict recidivism in the G. Hall (1988) study all had many years of clinical experience with multiple sexual offenders. Nevertheless, clinicians seeking to gain clinical experience with sexual aggressors will most likely be trained by other clinicians who are already experienced in working with sexual aggressors. Unfortunately, such an apprenticeship system of training may serve to compound clinical inaccuracy.

Perhaps the most important qualification of a person who does clinical work with sexual aggressors is the ability to integrate various sources of data and not interpret any singular test result at face value. Knowledge of the current research literature and the willingness and ability to incorporate research findings into clinical practice is also critical. Such integration is consistent with the psychological assessment approach that is advocated at the beginning of this chapter.

Cognitive Distortions

Many of the common cognitive distortions that sexual aggressors engage in are reviewed at the beginning of this chapter. Any of these cognitive distortions can be employed to justify sexually aggressive behavior. These cognitive distortions may become apparent during an initial interview, in which perpetrator and victim accounts of sexually aggressive acts are compared.

Similar to the assessment of affective dyscontrol, the goal in the assessment of cognitive distortions is to somehow directly observe a person's cognitive distortions. Because cognitive distortions about sexually aggressive behavior are covert and socially undesirable, it may be difficult to observe a person engaging in such cognitive distortions. Scales have been developed that are specifically designed to assess the cognitive distortions of sexual aggressors (Abel, Gore, Holland, Camp, Becker, & Rathner, 1989; Nichols & Molinder, 1984; Stermac & Segal, 1989). However, social desirability is particularly a problem with tests that contain items that deal with obviously deviant behavior (Murphy, 1990; Walker et al., 1993). For example, it is obvious to most adults that sex between adults and children is not an appropriate method of sex education.

An innovative method of assessing the cognitive distortions of sexual aggressors that appears somewhat less transparent than other methods is the Sex Offender Situational Competency Test (Miner, Day, & Nafpaktitus, 1989). In the development of this test, sexual offenders were asked to identify situations that occurred 24 to 48 hours before their sexual offenses that were precursors to their sexual offenses. Subjects taking the test are asked to describe what they would do in these situations. Different sets of situations have been developed for rapists and child molesters. An example of one of the situations for child molesters: You're helping a neighbor who is giving a birthday party for one of her children. She runs out of ice cream and asks you to watch the kids as she runs to the store. What do you do?

Although it may seem obvious that a child molester should not be at a child's birthday party in the first place, or at least avoid being alone with the children and offer to get the ice cream, it is not obvious to many child molesters. Twenty child molesters to whom I administered this test during an initial assessment indicated that they would stay and watch the kids. Although these child molesters may have been indicating what they have actually done in the past, it would be expected that at least some during an initial assessment would recognize the social undesirability of a child molester being alone with children. Or perhaps these child molesters did not view being alone with children as a high-risk situation because they did not consider themselves to be child molesters. Regardless of the reasons for these child molesters' responses to the test, the Sex Offender Situational Competency Test appears to be less transparent than other self-report measures.

One limitation of the Sex Offender Situational Competency Test is its subjective scoring system. Subjects' responses are rated in terms of their coping adequacy. A more objective scoring system, such as that of the Wechsler Adult Intelligence Scale-Revised, in which scoring for common responses is provided, would be desirable. Moreover, some of the situations presented on the test are more transparent than the above example.

The prognosis for change with a sexual aggressor having cognitive distortions is a function of the number of times the person has offended, which may be many because the cognitive subtype may select types of offenses that may not necessarily be perceived as aggressive and may select situations in which he may not be apprehended. Thus, the possibility of multiple offenses for the cognitive subtype is high. Moreover, the likelihood of the cognitive subtype being seen in treatment settings is low in that this subtype of sexual aggressor is not likely to have external pressure to seek treatment (e.g., treatment required by the legal and judicial system) and is unlikely to voluntarily seek treatment because his behavior is not perceived as sexually aggressive or otherwise deviant.

Even when the cognitive subtype of sexual aggressor is treated in clinical settings, treatment outcome may be unknown because he may continue to be sexually aggressive in situations in which he is not detected.

Affective Dyscontrol

Affective dyscontrol may be more readily admitted to as a motivational precursor of sexually aggressive behavior than other motivational precursors because affective problems may be viewed as more common and more acceptable than specific problems of sexual deviance. Many clinicians may be more familiar with affective problems than with other problems that are more unique to sexual aggressors (e.g., deviant sexual arousal, cognitive distortions concerning sexually aggressive behavior). Thus, many clinicians may be more attuned to affective dyscontrol than to other motivational precursors of sexual aggression.

Sexual offenders frequently mention affective problems when asked about immediate precursors to their sexually aggressive acts (Pithers et al., 1988). The admission of common problems, such as anger, may be more socially desirable than the admission of problems more germane to sexual aggression that may suggest personal deviance, such as anger specifically directed toward women or deviant sexual arousal (G. Hall, 1989a; McGovern & Nevid, 1986). Thus, admission of affective problems may constitute a defense against admission of a perpetrator's "real" problems. However, a significant minority of sexual aggressors may actually be motivated by affective dyscontrol (Hall & Hirschman, 1991, 1992; Hall et al., 1993a; Prentky & Knight, 1991). Thus, affective dyscontrol should be assessed in the context of other motivational precursors to determine its relative importance.

The goal of assessments of affective dyscontrol is to accurately assess a person's thoughts and actions in states of affective dyscontrol that lead to sexually aggressive behavior. However, "hot" (i.e., *in vivo*) affective states tend to be minimized under the "cool" cognitive conditions of recalling and describing events (Greenberg, 1991). Thus, recreating situations under which affective dyscontrol occurs and observing a person's behavior under these conditions may be more productive than self-reported recall of affectively laden events.

Affective dyscontrol has commonly been assessed via role playing. Role playing is a form of behavioral assessment that allows a wide variety of stimulus situations to be assessed (Becker & Heimberg, 1988; DiGiuseppe et al., 1994). Role playing involves the replication of contextual conditions and the subject is asked to act as if these contextual conditions are actually occurring. Although role playing is an indirect measure of a subject's behavior in the natural environment (Haynes, 1990), role plays that maximize subject involvement, that use stimulus materials that are relevant to the subject, and that focus on a specific behavioral event are likely to have the most ecological validity (Becker & Heimberg, 1988). Subjects who participate in carefully planned role plays often report how surprised they are at how closely their own reactions mirror the actual events that they are attempting to role-play. Although it may intuitively seem dangerous to provoke anger in aggressive clients, my own clinical experience and that of others (e.g., DiGiuseppe et al., 1994) suggests that aggressive clients do not confuse provocation during role plays with the actual targets of their anger.

As discussed previously in this chapter and in chapter 4, dissimulation may interfere with assessments of sexual aggressors. Role playing may be a particularly effective method of circumventing dissimulation because it is difficult to fake appropriate behavioral responses. Whereas the social desirability of the responses to many self-report measures is transparent, a person who does not have adequate skills usually cannot produce a skilled behavior, such as assertiveness, in a role play. Moreover, even if a person can produce skilled responses (e.g., assertiveness) but does not use these responses in circumstances that might lead to affective dyscontrol (e.g., anger provocation), these circumstances that lead to affective dyscontrol can be replicated in the role play and be paired with the person's skilled responses. Presumably such practice will generalize to real-life settings, although it is the person's prerogative to use his coping skills in provoking situations outside the clinical context.

Rapists are often angry at women (Hall & Hirschman, 1991; Hall, Shondrick, et al., 1993a; Malamuth et al., 1991). Thus, role-playing situations in which a woman is perceived as provoking anger are relevant. Some rapists are not angry with their victim per se, but may be displacing their anger. For example, a rapist may be angry with another woman (e.g., wife, boss) or with another man (e.g., coworker, boss) and choose a less powerful woman to rape. In this instance, the perceived anger provocation by persons other than the victim would be role-played. It is important to emphasize that the provocation in these situations is *perceived* by the sexual aggressor. Aggressive men may perceive provocation from their partners more so than nonaggressive men (Holtzworth-Munroe & Hutchinson, 1993). Even when they perceive provocation, most men do not become sexually aggressive. However, misperceptions result in anger provocation that exceeds the inhibitory threshold in men who are sexually aggressive (see chapter 3).

Depression is more common than anger as an affective motivational precursor of child molestation (Hall & Hirschman, 1992; Hall, Shondrick, et al., 1993a). Because of their poor social skills, potential child molesters may be isolated from adults and this isolation may result in loneliness and depression (Marshall, 1989; Segal & Marshall, 1985). A child molester may believe that he cannot form relationships with peers, so he turns to children for friendship and sexual contact. Analogous to rapists who seek vulnerable victims with whom to be sexually aggressive, child molesters may seek to have sex with children, who may place limited social demands on them relative to peer adults, as a method of coping with their depression. Thus, role playing of depression-inducing events for child molesters typically will involve situations that are not directly induced by children or child victims.

Some sexual aggressors remain passive during role playing. Passivity may represent an effort to inhibit affect or it may reflect the person's actual responses to a provoking situation. Passivity may be particularly characteristic of persons who experience depressive affective dyscontrol, primarily child molesters (Hall & Hirschman, 1992; Hall, Shondrick, et al., 1993a; Pithers et al., 1988). Passive persons may be encouraged to "think aloud" during role playing. The verbal description of thoughts may make these thought processes tangible to a person who may be unaware of them (Beck & Freeman, 1990). In that depressive cognitions are the focus of cognitive therapy, which appears to be effective with depressive disorders (Hollon, Shelton, & Loosen, 1991), identification of such depressive cognitions during role-play situations may be clinically useful.

To the extent that affective provocation that results in sexual aggression is situationally based, the prognosis for change for a sexual aggressor who is motivated by affective dyscontrol is good, relative to the other subtypes. Avoidance of highly provoking situations or learning to adaptively cope with such situations when they occur would presumably be an effective means of relapse prevention. However, as with all sexually aggressive behavior, the prognosis for the affective dyscontrol subtype is a function of the amount of past sexually aggressive behavior.

Assessment of Developmentally Related Personality Problems

As discussed in chapter 3, situational provocation may not be a critical antecedent to sexually aggressive behavior among sexual aggressors having developmentally related personality problems. These sexual aggressors appear to have a propensity for rule violations that is independent of situational influences, other than the likelihood of being punished. Thus, a detailed developmental history may be useful in determining the origin and extent of problems. Although historical data are important in the assessment of all sexual aggressors, such data are of particular importance in the assessment of sexual aggressors who have developmentally related personality problems.

The structured interview that I use in my clinical work with sexual aggressors is in Appendix A. This is a rather lengthy interview, which I abbreviate as the situation warrants. Some redundancy is built into the interview to facilitate a careful, thorough interview. For example, a sexual aggressor may report only the offenses that he was arrested or convicted for, but neglect to discuss other offenses for which he was not caught. Some offenders may be unwilling to spontaneously discuss any offenses for which they were not caught, but many will if they are asked and will not if they are not asked.

As discussed earlier in this chapter, recall of historical data may be distorted because of forgetting, defensiveness, or both. However, careful interviewing across multiple domains (e.g., academic, social, sexual) can yield a sense of the breadth of a person's problems. I typically begin developmental interviews with questions about a person's family life, with particular emphasis on any physical or sexual abuse (cf. Dodge et al., 1990; Friedrich et al., 1992; Haapasalo & Tremblay, 1994; Patterson et al., 1989). Next I determine whether the person had a sense of accomplishment for his academic performance (Ageton, 1983; Patterson et al., 1989). Early peer relationships (i.e., deviant vs. nondeviant) also influence a person's future antisocial behavior (Newcomb et al., 1993; Patterson et al., 1989). Any juvenile legal or psychiatric contact should also be investigated, as should alcohol and other substance abuse.

Sexual development is of particular importance among sexual aggressors. Initiation of sexual relationships at an early age may result in promiscuity as well as the opportunity to become sexually aggressive (see chapter 2). The number and length of sexual relationships and any coercive sexual behavior should be examined. Type and amount of pornography exposure may be associated with juvenile sexual acting out (Marshall, 1989; Prentky & Knight, 1993). Sexual aggressors should also be questioned about early deviant sexual activity, including voyeurism and exhibitionism. Nonsexual aggressive activity also provides data on general impulse dyscontrol (e.g., "What is the most violent thing that you have ever done?"; Monahan, 1981).

Social skills can be assessed with information on the stability of vocational functioning and marital relationships. Difficulties in maintaining employment or relationships may suggest social skills deficits. Aggressive or sexual acting out during adolescence and adulthood are also important in understanding whether such acting out has been chronic or more intermittent. Intermittent acting out followed by periods of self-control may suggest problems that are somewhat more situationally based than chronic acting out. Situationally based problems, to the extent that they can be identified among sexual aggressors having developmentally related personality problems, may have a better prognosis for change than chronic problems, in that problem situations (e.g., provocation) may be altered as well as a person's responses to these problem situations. However, as a result of repetitive sexual acting out that tends to lower the inhibitory threshold against sexual aggression (see chapter 3), sexual aggressors having developmentally related personality problems tend to have a poorer prognosis than sexual aggressors who are motivated by other variables.

Conclusion

A psychological assessment approach is advocated, in which various sources of data are integrated to form an explanatory conceptualization of sexual aggressors. During initial assessments, some sexual aggressors may deny engaging in sexually aggressive behavior and others use several levels of cognitive distortions to justify their sexually aggressive behavior. Victim reports are critical for corroborating sexual aggressors' reports and victim reports tend to be accurate.

There tends to be overlap between sexually aggressive and nonaggressive men on traditional psychometric instruments. However, sexually aggressive men differ from nonaggressive men in their reactions to physiological, cognitive, and affective situational variables. Genital measures are useful in assessing physiological sexual arousal if methodological and clinical caution are exercised. Cognitive distortions may be assessed via interviews and responses to selected high-risk situations. Role playing is appropriate for assessing affective dyscontrol. Sexual aggressors having developmentally related personality problems tend not to be influenced by situational factors. Thus, interviews that emphasize developmental issues may be useful for assessment. Comprehensive assessment that includes attention to physiological, cognitive, affective, and developmental factors will provide a contextual framework for comprehensive treatment interventions.

III

THEORY-GUIDED TREATMENT

6

Is Some Treatment Better than No Treatment for Sexual Aggressors?

Effective treatment for sexual aggressors is essential, in that persons who have engaged in sexually aggressive behavior are at the highest risk to be sexually aggressive in the future (G. Hall, 1990a). However, the conclusion of the comprehensive review of Furby et al. (1989) was that there was no evidence of the effectiveness of treatment for sexual offenders.

The Furby et al. (1989) review sent shock waves though the psychological community, including arguments and counterarguments on the effectiveness of treatment with sexual aggressors. These arguments have corresponded with the setting in which the researchers have conducted their treatment studies. Researchers in institutional settings have been skeptical of the ability of treatment to reduce recidivism (Quinsey, Harris, Rice, & Lalumiere, 1993). Institutionalized samples may include an overrepresentation of sexual aggressors having developmentally related personality problems who have committed multiple acts of sexual aggression and are least amenable to treatment (Hall et al., 1992). Conversely, researchers in outpatient settings, who work with more heterogeneous groups of sexual aggressors who may also be amenable to treatment,

121

have been optimistic about treatment effects (Marshall, 1993; Marshall, Jones, Ward, Johnston, & Barbaree, 1991; Marshall & Pithers, 1994).

Although the Furby et al. (1989) conclusion of no evidence of treatment effects has been quite influential, it may not be an accurate assessment of the treatment models that have been developed since. Furby et al. (1989) allowed that many of the treatment programs they reviewed were obsolete. Moreover, only 7 of the 42 studies in the review directly compared the recidivism rates of treated and nontreated sexual offenders, and these studies were of treatment programs at only three different sites (G. Hall, 1995b). Furby et al. (1989) conducted a qualitative review of the literature because they suggested that methodological problems in most of the studies that they reviewed precluded a quantitative meta-analytic review. State-of-the-art treatment programs have been developed in various settings since the Furby et al. (1989) review, and several treatment studies with adequate methodologies have been conducted.

G. Hall (1995b) identified 12 studies of sexual offender treatment since Furby et al. (1989) reported on the recidivism of treatment and comparison groups that could be included in a meta-analysis. In contrast to Furby et al. (1989), G. Hall (1995b) concluded that treatment was more effective than no treatment or comparison treatments (e.g., interpersonal therapy). Overall, treatment programs yielded a 19% rate of recidivism for sexual offenses, whereas 27% of sexual offenders who were untreated or received comparison treatments sexually reoffended. Thus, it appears that some forms of treatment are superior to other forms of treatment or no treatment. In this chapter, major treatment approaches will be reviewed and critiqued.

Behavioral Treatments

Sexual arousal to deviant stimuli is the primary motivational variable for many sexually aggressive males (Barbaree & Marshall, 1989, 1991; Hall & Hirschman, 1991, 1992; Hall, Shondrick, et al., 1993b; Harris et al., 1992; Lalumiere & Quinsey, 1994; Marshall & Barbaree, 1984, 1990a; Quinsey, 1984; 1986). Thus, it follows that methods to reduce deviant sexual arousal should be effective in reducing sexually aggressive behavior for many sexually aggressive males. Behavioral methods of reducing deviant sexual arousal have been popular among clinicians because they are relatively easy to implement and sexual arousal is also relatively easily assessed as an outcome criterion (see chapter 5). Aversion therapy, which involves classical conditioning of a deviant stimulus (e.g., child) with an aversive stimulus (e.g., aversive fantasy, electrical shock), is the most common behavioral method to reduce deviant sexual arousal (Kelly, 1982).

There are more studies of behavioral methods to reduce deviant sexual arousal than of any other treatment for sexually aggressive males. Most of these behavioral studies report successful cessation of sexually aggressive behavior via behavioral methods, although most of these studies involve single cases or evaluations of treatment with no control or comparison group (e.g., Earls & Castonguay, 1989; Enright, 1989; Hughes, 1977; Hunter & Goodwin, 1992; Johnston, Hudson, & Marshall, 1992; Laws, Meyer, & Holmen, 1978). The longest period without recidivism following behavioral treatment was three years with an exhibitionist (Hughes, 1977). However, follow-up outcome evaluations are more typically one year or less (e.g., Earls & Castonguay, 1989; Hunter & Goodwin, 1992; Laws et al., 1978).

In G. Hall's (1995b) meta-analytic review, three behavioral treatment programs to reduce deviant sexual arousal among sexually aggressive men that included comparison or control groups were evaluated. Follow-up evaluation periods were 1 year (McConaghy, Blaszczynski, & Kidson, 1988), 3.8 years (Rice et al., 1991), and 19 years (Hanson et al., 1993). None of these three programs was significantly more effective in reducing sexually aggressive behavior than no treatment or comparison treatments. In fact, these behavioral programs were slightly *less* effective (i.e., resulted in slightly higher rates of recidivism) than no treatment or comparison treatments (G. Hall, 1995b).

Why are behavioral methods to reduce deviant sexual arousal relatively ineffective in reducing sexually aggressive behavior? One reason may be the heterogeneity of sexual aggressors. Some sexual aggressors are not primarily motivated by deviant sexual arousal (see chapters 2, 3). Thus, a sole treatment focus on deviant sexual arousal may miss other important etiological factors in sexually aggressive behavior. Even some of the early proponents of behavioral methods of reducing deviant sexual arousal in sexually aggressive males contended that the reduction of deviant sexual arousal is but one component of more comprehensive treatment (Marshall & Barbaree, 1978).

Effective reduction of deviant sexual arousal, however, does appear to be effective in reducing sexually aggressive behavior for at least some sexual aggressors. Only 3 of 99 (3%) sexual offenders who volunteered for castration and were castrated in Germany committed additional sexual offenses over an 11-year follow-up period versus 16 of 35 (45%) sexual offenders who volunteered for castration and were not castrated (Wille & Beier, 1989). Most of the castrated subjects did not receive any adjunctive psychotherapy, which is usually a component of antiandrogen drug treatments. Thus, it appears that castration alone was primarily responsible for the differential recidivism rates in the Wille and Beier (1989) study. Although castration of sexual offenders is unlikely to continue in Germany or elsewhere, castration does effectively inhibit testosterone production, which inhibits sexual arousal. Given the apparent effectiveness of castration and the apparent ineffectiveness of behavioral methods in reducing sexually aggressive behavior in controlled studies, it appears possible that behavioral methods are not completely effective in reducing deviant sexual arousal. Perhaps the effects of behavioral methods may wear off over time, as they do in behavioral treatments targeted at other addictive behaviors, such as problem drinking (Marlatt & Gordon, 1985).

Suppression of deviant sexual arousal via behavioral methods may be temporary. Habituation to sexual stimuli may be difficult to accomplish (Julien & Over, 1984) and dishabituation to sexual stimuli may occur following habituation to the same stimuli (Koukounas & Over, 1993). Methods of inducing habituation to deviant stimuli via deliberate exposure to such stimuli (i.e., masturbatory satiation; Marshall, 1979; Marshall & Barbaree, 1978) have been conceptually appealing but have not been supported by empirical evidence (Johnston et al., 1992). This lack of habituation to deviant stimuli suggests that fantasy sexual aggression does not dissipate the motivation to be sexually aggressive. In fact, laboratory evidence suggests that exposure to fantasy aggression via the media actually increases aggressive behavior (Donnerstein et al., 1987).

Reduction of sexual arousal to one deviant stimulus is not necessarily generalizable to other deviant stimuli (Brownell, Hayes, & Barlow, 1977; Hayes, Brownell, & Barlow, 1978), particularly when a subject is motivated not to view stimuli as deviant (e.g., an incest offender undergoing treatment may rationalize that "It's OK to have sex with my daughter's friend because she is not a blood relative"). Reduced sexual arousal in response to one stimulus (e.g., the victim) may not ensure reduced sexual arousal in response to other stimuli (e.g., other children). Behavioral treatment to decrease sexual arousal to each deviant stimulus that potentially could elicit sexual arousal (e.g., all children) is not feasible in many cases. Thus, antiandrogen treatments that have a generalized suppressant effect on sexual arousal may be more appropriate than behavioral methods in reducing deviant sexual arousal.

Hormonal Treatments

Antiandrogen hormonal treatment programs are more effective in reducing sexually aggressive behavior than behavioral treatment programs or no treatment (G. Hall, 1995b). Unlike the effects of behavioral interventions, medroxyprogesterone acetate (MPA), an antiandrogen commonly used in clinical and research settings with sexual aggressors, suppresses all forms of sexual arousal. Such suppression is not limited to particular sexual stimuli. Thus, sexual arousal is suppressed in response to all deviant stimuli. In addition to suppressing sexual arousal, treatments that decrease testosterone may be associated with a general reduction in aggressive behavior (cf. Archer, 1991; Gray, Jackson, & McKinlay, 1991) that cannot be accomplished with behavioral techniques focused on deviant sexual arousal.

Generalized suppression of sexual arousal may also be considered a problem with MPA. A male whose sexual arousal is generally suppressed does not have the opportunity for sexual outlet with consenting partners. Clinical evidence suggests that cyproterone acetate (CPA) suppresses pedophilic arousal, but does not interfere with sexual arousal in response to consenting-adult sexual intercourse and produces fewer side effects than MPA (Bradford, 1990). However, controlled-outcome studies of CPA with sexually aggressive men have yet to be conducted.

Suppression of sexual drive may be accomplished with drugs other than antiandrogens. Some other neuroleptics, such as thioridazine (Mellaril), may produce the same suppression without as many side effects (Bradford, 1993). However, as with CPA, controlled-outcome studies of neuroleptic drugs to reduce sexual aggression have not been conducted.

Sexually aggressive men who participate in hormonal treatment programs are typically self-selected in that these programs tend to be available on a voluntary basis, are invasive (i.e., involve intramuscular injections), and typically require a lengthy time commitment (two to five years; Fedoroff, Wisner-Carlson, Dean, & Berlin, 1992; Meyer, Cole, & Emory, 1992). Thus, it is possible that the most motivated sexual aggressors participate in hormonal treatment programs and that the success of these programs is more attributable to subject motivation for change than to the treatments. However, Fedoroff et al. (1992) found that sexually aggressive men who were sufficiently motivated to participate in five years of psychotherapy recidivated at a significantly higher rate (68%) than sexually aggressive men who participated in five years of psychotherapy combined with hormonal treatment (15%).

It is possible that there may be a disproportionate number of sexual aggressors who participate in hormonal treatments who have hormonal abnormalities and may benefit from such treatments. It is also possible that hormonal treatments may not be effective for all types of sexual aggressors (Marshall & Jones, 1991b) and that those sexual aggressors who have elevated serum testosterone levels constitute a minority of sexually aggressive males (Barbaree, 1990; Lang, Flor-Henry, & Frenzel, 1990). Moreover, it is possible that increased testosterone levels in some sexual aggressors may constitute an *effect* of repeatedly engaging in sexually aggressive behavior rather than a cause of sexual aggression (Raine, 1993). Thus, effective treatments are necessary for males whose sexually aggressive behavior is not primarily motivated by deviant sexual arousal or by hormonal abnormalities.

A major issue with hormonal treatments for sexually aggressive males is compliance with treatment. Antiandrogen drug effects wear off and require regular administration at weekly to monthly intervals (Fedoroff et al., 1992; Meyer et al., 1992). However, such treatments may create the illusion of a cure with no need for continuing compliance with treatment. Two thirds of sexually aggressive men refuse hormonal treatment (Fedoroff et al., 1992; Meyer et al., 1992) and 50% who begin hormonal treatment discontinue it (Langevin et al., 1979). Subjects who want to avoid relapse become drug-dependent. Taking drugs does not help a subject develop problem-solving skills that might result in self-control and independence from drugs. Medical solutions to problems also abdicate an individual's personal responsibility for the problem (Marlatt & Gordon, 1985). However, other available psychological interventions for sexually aggressive males do offer skill acquisition that results in self-control and may be of use in conjunction with hormonal treatments for sexual aggressors having high levels of physiological sexual arousal.

Cognitive-Behavioral Treatments

Cognitive-behavioral treatment programs are more effective in reducing sexually aggressive behavior than behavioral treatment programs or no treatment, but are not significantly more effective than hormonal treatment programs (G. Hall, 1995b). However, cognitive-behavioral programs may be more effective than hormonal treatments for a wider range of sexual aggressors, given the comprehensive nature of cognitive-behavioral programs and the compliance problems with hormonal treatments. Cognitive-behavioral programs are comprehensive in that they typically target deviant sexual arousal, cognitive distortions about sexual aggression, and social skills deficits (Marshall & Barbaree, 1990b). In addition, some cognitive-behavioral programs incorporate relapse-prevention strategies to cope with situational temptations to reoffend. Sexual aggressors' compliance with cognitive-behavioral treatments tends to be greater than compliance rates with hormonal treatments. About one third of sexual aggressors who begin cognitive-behavioral programs drop out (Abel et al., 1988; Chaffin, 1992; G. Hall, 1995a).

Comprehensive Programs

As with theories of sexual aggression (see chapter 1), the most useful treatments for sexually aggressive behavior are sufficiently comprehensive to account for various motivational variables as well as sufficiently parsimonious for applications across clinical settings. Although they have not necessarily been developed within a theory of sexual aggression, comprehensive cognitive-behavioral treatments address most of the primary motivational precursors of sexually aggressive behavior (Hall, Shondrick, et al., 1993a). Moreover, while these cognitive-behavioral programs are comprehensive, they are not overly complex, which allows their application in most clinical settings, although they appear most effective in outpatient settings (G. Hall, 1995b).

A common component of comprehensive cognitive-behavioral programs is the previously reviewed behavioral treatments to reduce deviant sexual arousal. Aversive behavioral treatments to reduce deviant sexual arousal may have cognitive benefits in addition to their classical conditioning properties. Pairing deviant sexual fantasies (e.g., sex with a child) with relevant social consequences (e.g., harm to child, ridicule by others, arrest), instead of the sexual arousal that usually accompanies such deviant sexual fantasies, may assist in changing a sexual aggressor's cognitive distortion that there are no negative consequences of deviant sexual arousal and behavior (Hall, Shondrick, et al., 1993a). Although the long-term effects of behavioral interventions to reduce sexual arousal are limited, they may be a useful starting point in treatment to gain control over sexual preoccupation that could potentially interfere with other aspects of treatment. Moreover, behavioral treatment effects may persist longer if the client is given some responsibility to personally carry out such treatments (e.g., voluntarily pairing deviant sexual fantasies with aversive fantasies or aversive stimuli, such as smelling salts). Some programs also use methods to increase low levels of sexual arousal to adults, which typically involve replacing a deviant sexual fantasy with an appropriate sexual fantasy (e.g., sex with an adult) prior to orgasm (Marshall & Barbaree, 1990b; Quinsey & Earls, 1990). Sex education and treatment of sexual dysfunctions also are offered as needed (Marshall & Barbaree, 1990b).

Treatments to enhance social skills are also common in comprehensive cognitive-behavioral programs for sexual aggressors. Social skills training may be particularly important for sexual aggressors having developmentally related personality problems and for child molesters, who may have poorer social skills than rapists of women (Segal & Marshall, 1985, 1986). The task with persons having extreme social skills deficits is to establish social skills that will assist them in developing peer relationships instead of seeking social support and intimacy with weaker, less threatening, and often significantly younger persons. In addition, social skills training may be effective in modifying cognitive distortions in encoding and decoding social cues, particularly with rapists who may fail to encode women's refusals of sexual overtures (Lipton et al., 1987; McFall, 1990). Social skills training is typically accomplished via role playing, which may also serve the purpose of assessing and treating affective dyscontrol (see chapter 5).

Although social skills training has become a popular component of treatment programs for sexual aggressors, there is no direct empirical evidence that enhanced social skills have a specific effect in reducing sexually aggressive behavior. However, Marshall and Barbaree's (1988) treatment program that primarily consisted of social skills training and behavioral methods to modify deviant sexual arousal was effective in reducing sexual reoffending over two years among child molesters. Insofar as the reduction of sexual arousal was not associated with sexual offending, it appears that the social skills training component in the Marshall and Barbaree (1988) treatment program is the potent element of treatment.

A third common component of treatment programs for sexual aggressors is methods to reduce cognitive distortions. Cognitive distortions about women or children are challenged, the negative consequences of such distorted beliefs are emphasized, and prosocial views are offered as alternatives (Marshall & Barbaree, 1990b). Socratic approaches to cognitive distortions have been advocated as more effective than aggressive, confrontational approaches (Murphy, 1990). Extreme confrontation may have the paradoxical effect of solidifying and even increasing cognitive distortions in some instances (see chapter 7). Therapist confrontation may be reminiscent for sexual aggressors of demeaning parents (Friedrich, 1990).

Methods of increasing empathy for victims of sexual aggression have also been advocated as a method for reducing cognitive distortions (Hildebran & Pithers, 1989; Murphy, 1990; Pithers, 1994). The perception that sexually aggressive behavior creates harm to victims may inhibit sexually aggressive behavior (see chapter 3). The development of such victim empathy is viewed by some clinicians as a prerequisite for other treatment components (Hildebran & Pithers, 1989).

Methods to reduce cognitive distortions are conceptually appealing because many sexual aggressors are motivated by cognitive distortions (see chapters 2 and 3), but these methods have not been evaluated as a specific treatment to reduce sexual aggression. However, in combination with other treatment methods, methods to reduce cognitive distortions have been found to be effective in reducing sexually aggressive behavior among adolescent and adult sexual offenders (Borduin, Henggeler, Blaske, & Stein, 1990; Hildebran & Pithers, 1992; Marshall, Eccles, et al., 1991). Nevertheless, it is unknown whether methods to reduce cognitive distortions are a necessary component of comprehensive treatment programs for sexual aggressors.

Many comprehensive treatment programs for sexual aggressors have a limited focus on aftercare. The implicit assumption is that decreases in deviant sexual arousal and cognitive distortions, and increases in social skills, will persist following treatment and generalize across situations. However, given the difficulty that many sexual aggressors experience in maintaining treatment gains, specific treatment methods have been developed to prevent relapse following a formal course of treatment.

Relapse Prevention

One of the most important innovations in the treatment of sexually aggressive behavior has been the application of the cognitive-behavioral relapse prevention model of addiction (Marlatt & Gordon, 1985) to the treatment of sexual aggression (Laws, 1989; Pithers et al., 1983). Relapse prevention is particularly relevant for treating sexually aggressive behavior because it helps individuals to cope with situational variables that may cause sexual aggressors to exceed the threshold that usually inhibits sexually aggressive behavior (see chapter 3). George and Marlatt (1989) have provided an excellent conceptual rationale for the application of relapse prevention to the treatment of sexual aggressors. I will discuss relapse prevention in detail because I believe that it has much promise as an effective treatment for sexual aggressors and I have used it in my own clinical work (see chapter 7).

The goal of relapse prevention is to maintain a behavioral pattern that is free from sexually aggressive behavior (George & Marlatt, 1989). Punishment, incarceration, and treatment tend to suppress a sexual aggressor's sexually aggressive urges, at least temporarily, but these effects often tend to wear off, presumably because the sexual aggressor does not engage in coping responses in situations in which the risk for relapse is high (e.g., negative emotional states, interpersonal conflict). However, the ability to identify such *high-risk situations* and to engage in a coping response in such high-risk situations increases self-efficacy and decreases the likelihood of a relapse (Marlatt & Gordon, 1985). A coping response for sexual aggressors involves objectively viewing an *urge* to be sexually aggressive as temporary and determinant (George & Marlatt, 1989). When an urge is unrecognized or rationalized, the likelihood of relapse increases (Marlatt, 1985). Another coping response for sexual aggressors is simply avoiding high-risk situations, such as locations frequented by children (George & Marlatt, 1989).

An addicted person may engage in covert actions, known as *apparently irrelevant decisions*, that may facilitate relapse by increasing exposure to high-risk situations (George & Marlatt, 1989; cf. Craig, 1990). For example, a client whom I treated for molesting young boys had purchased a pleasure boat before he entered treatment. The apparent motivation for this purchase was for him to enjoy this boat, and this decision to purchase the boat was apparently irrelevant to his molestation of boys. The boat purchase was an apparently irrelevant decision insofar as this client did not immediately begin attempting to "pick up" young boys in the boat after he had purchased it. However, he later "discovered" that the boat served as a lure for young boys he met, as well as a setting in which to molest them.

For most addictions, a temporary relapse, known as a *lapse*, is not viewed as fatal but is viewed as an expected step in the learning process (Marlatt & Gordon, 1985). Smoking a cigarette or taking a drink for persons in treatment for these addictions is analogous to a person's falling off a bicycle in an effort to learn how to ride the bicycle (Marlatt & Gordon, 1985). However, given the seriousness of even a single relapse episode of sexual aggression (see chapter 2), a reconceptualization of a lapse for sexual aggressors has been advocated (George & Marlatt, 1989). George and Marlatt (1989) have defined a lapse in the context of sexually aggressive behavior as "any occurrence of willful and elaborate fantasizing about sexual offending or any return to sources of stimulation associated with the sexual offense pattern, but short of the offense behavior."

A lapse does not necessarily result in a full relapse if a person can effectively cope with the lapse by interrupting the relapse process. A person's reaction to a lapse may determine whether the lapse will lead to relapse. This reaction has been termed the *abstinence violation effect* (Marlatt, 1985). If a person attributes a lapse to an internal cause that may be perceived as uncontrollable (e.g., "I can't control my sexual urges for children"), then treatment failure may be perceived, a sense of self-efficacy in coping with high-risk situations may be lost, and relapse may result. However, lapses that result from internal causes that are perceived as controllable (e.g., "I have learned how to cope with my sexual urges for children") may prompt future efforts to exert control and thereby prevent relapses (Hudson, Ward, & Marshall, 1992). Alternatively, if a person attributes a lapse to an external cause that may be perceived as controllable (e.g., "I can avoid situations in which there are children"), then a relapse may be less likely because the person is not personally responsible for the lapse (Marlatt, 1985). However, if an external cause is viewed as uncontrollable (e.g., "My daughter keeps coming on to me and I can't avoid her"), this increases the possibility of relapse (Hudson et al., 1992).

A second major component of the abstinence violation effect is affective response to the lapse. A positive affective response (e.g., physiological gratification) increases the likelihood of a lapse leading to a relapse (Marlatt, 1985). Positive affective responses may be common among sexual aggressors who experience lapses. Unlike a "bad trip" with drugs or other negative intoxication experiences, the sexual arousal associated with a sexual aggressor's lapse almost invariably creates a positive affective response, at least temporarily. Treatment interventions emphasize the temporary nature of the positive affect that results from deviant sexual arousal. Negative affect in the form of guilt also often follows a lapse, although such guilt does not invariably follow lapses among sexual aggressors (Pithers, 1993).

Relapse prevention is not intended to be a stand-alone treatment, although relapse prevention principles can be incorporated at any stage of treatment (George & Marlatt, 1989). Relapse prevention is intended to be used in combination with other treatment to prolong positive effects (Laws, 1989). Although relapse prevention has been used with various types of addictions, the conceptualization of sexual aggression as an addiction is not necessary for the application of relapse-prevention concepts to the treatment of sexual aggressors (George & Marlatt, 1989; Marques & Nelson, 1992).

Unlike the previously described hormonal treatments, self-control is the goal of relapse prevention. However, unlike self-help programs for sexual aggressors that have been demonstrated to have limited effectiveness (G. Hall, 1988), relapse prevention is based on psychological concepts and is conducted by professional therapists. In the relapse-prevention approach, recognition of a lapse, which is critical to preventing relapse, is contingent upon self-monitoring. Such self-monitoring makes sense for addictions in which effects are primarily intrapersonal. However, when the effects of a behavior cause harm to others, self-monitoring is more controversial. Thus, relapse-prevention programs for sexual offenders often emphasize control by others (e.g., family members, probation department, employer, etc.; Pithers, 1990). This para-doxical expectation of self-control combined with external monitoring may be perceived by the sexual offender as deceptive and disingenuous (Rogers & Cavanaugh, 1983). Nevertheless, self-control is the ultimate means of relapse prevention, in that omnipresent monitoring is impossi-ble and acts of sexual aggression can take place rather quickly and co-vertly. For example, a child molester can briefly fondle a victim in a public setting where there are crowds, such as a store or park, without detection. External monitoring results in an external motivation that may wear off soon after the external monitoring system subsides (e.g., completion of probation or parole), and excessive reliance on others can externalize responsibility and blame (George & Marlatt, 1989). More-over, the recognition of a lapse, which is critical in preventing relapse, involves a monitoring of a covert event (fantasizing) that is accessible only via self-monitoring. Unless we become a society in which all sexual aggressors are given life sentences in prison, the development of self-control makes sense because most sexual aggressors reach a point during which they are not externally monitored (e.g., postprobation) in which self-monitoring is necessary (George & Marlatt, 1989).

Whereas lapses in other addictions usually involve an external event, such as smoking or drinking, lapses for sexual aggressors involve fan-tasy, which is an intrapersonal event. Thus, sexual aggressors may be particularly susceptible to attributing lapses to internal causes. Urges and lapses usually involve the acknowledgment of deviant sexual arousal, which is considered by many sexual aggressors to be socially undesirable and abnormal (McGovern & Nevid, 1986). Although many sexual ag-gressors experience sexual arousal during coercive situations, they may not label their sexual arousal as deviant and may justify it (e.g., "It wasn't rape—she consented," "She was well developed—she looked older than 14"), which would increase the risk of a lapse or relapse (Marlatt, 1985). However, during treatment sexual aggressors are taught to more accurately perceive coercive sexual activity and learn that their sexual arousal in response to coercive sexual activity is considered deviant.

Whereas in other addictions, urges are commonly experienced by normal persons in response to external cues (e.g., an urge for a drink when passing a bar), the urges of sexual aggressors (e.g., an urge to molest a child when passing a school playground) are not commonly experienced by persons who are not sexual aggressors. There are far more people who smoke, consume alcohol, use drugs, and overeat than there are who are sexually aggressive (particularly against children, in that deviant sexual arousal is more prominent in child molesting than in rape). Thus, it may be difficult for a sexual aggressor to view such an idiosyncratic response (i.e., deviant sexual arousal) as a typical response to an external situation (i.e., "It could happen to anybody in this situation"). Such an external attribution may even be inappropriate to the extent that the potential victim is being blamed for the provocation (e.g., "I wanted to rape her because she was dressed provocatively"). Thus, the key to relapse prevention with sexual aggressors may not necessarily be to attribute urges and lapses to external situations, but to recognize urges and lapses as motivated by internal causes that are *controllable* (George & Marlatt, 1989; Hudson et al., 1992). A sexual aggressor can learn to control deviant sexual arousal, the internal cause of many urges and lapses, via antiandrogen medications or self-administration of behavioral techniques to reduce deviant sexual arousal (e.g., thinking of an aversive consequence of deviant sexual arousal or using a noxious stimulus, such as ammonia, to interrupt deviant sexual arousal).

Current conceptualizations of relapse prevention appear most relevant for sexually aggressive behavior that is motivated by physiological sexual arousal (see chapters 2 and 3). Indeed, it has been suggested that fantasy is a more central component in sexual aggression than in other addictions and that fantasy alone provides more physical gratification for sexual aggressors than for persons having other nonsexual addictions (George & Marlatt, 1989; Laws, 1989). Sexual fantasy is included in the definition of a lapse (George & Marlatt, 1989; Pithers, 1990). Whereas the assessment (e.g., blood alcohol testing) and treatment (e.g., classical conditioning) of internal physiological phenomena have been viewed in the general relapse-prevention model as less critical than the assessment and treatment of situational variables including negative emotional states, interpersonal conflict, or social pressure (Cummings, Gordon, & Marlatt, 1980; Marlatt & Gordon, 1985), both physiological assessment (i.e., penile plethysmography) and classical conditioning (i.e., aversive conditioning) are central components of relapse-prevention applications for sexual aggressors (George & Marlatt, 1989; Laws, 1989). The relapse-prevention approach of acknowledging, accepting, and coping with deviant sexual fantasies seems at odds with the classical conditioning approach of attempting to extinguish these fantasies, which, as discussed previously, appears to be only temporarily effective.

The emphasis on sexual fantasies in the application of the relapse-prevention model to sexual aggressors does not appear relevant for all sexual aggressors. Some sexual aggressors whose primary motivation for sexual aggression is physiological sexual arousal may experience sexual arousal during opportunities for sexual aggression, but may not fantasize about it otherwise (Marshall & Eccles, 1993). Moreover, the general emphasis on physiological sexual arousal in the application of the re-

lapse-prevention model to sexual aggressors does not appear as relevant
for sexual aggressors whose primary motivation for sexual aggression is
cognitive distortions, affective dyscontrol, or developmentally related
personality problems (Hall & Hirschman, 1991, 1992). Although a sexual aggressor who is primarily motivated by cognitive distortions may
justify deviant sexual arousal (e.g., "It isn't really rape if she agreed to go
on a date with me," " . . . if she didn't resist," etc.), justifications themselves play a primary motivational role and may precede sexual fantasy
and arousal in the sequence that leads to sexually aggressive behavior. A
sexual aggressor who is primarily motivated by affective dyscontrol may
be extremely impulsive and opportunistic, and the covert planning (e.g.,
apparently irrelevant decisions) involved in the relapse-prevention model
may be less applicable to this subtype. For example, a sexual aggressor
whom I treated had raped a jogger following an argument with his wife.
He lived in an isolated area in which he had not previously seen joggers,
including this victim, nor had he previously committed any rapes. He
also denied rape fantasies prior to committing the rape; and even if he
did fantasize about rape, his primary motivation for the rape appears to
have been displaced anger rather than sexual arousal. Moreover, any
covert planning that took place had to have been rather instantaneous.
Similarly for a sexual aggressor motivated by developmentally related
personality problems, opportunities for sexual or nonsexual aggression
may be more critical to acting out than covert planning or sexual fantasy.
Although some of these opportunities for aggression may be motivated
by apparently irrelevant decisions or by sexual fantasy, it would be difficult to identify a particular thought pattern or specific fantasy that led to
any particular act of aggression because persons with such developmentally related personality problems tend to have a lifestyle characterized
by impulsivity (Prentky & Knight, 1991). Nevertheless, it appears possible that relapse-prevention conceptualizations could be expanded to accommodate nonsexual motivational variables in sexually aggressive behavior by incorporating paths to sexual aggression in addition to sexual
fantasy and arousal.

Another potential problem with the relapse-prevention approach is
its complexity. Concepts that are useful to clinicians and researchers
(e.g., abstinence violation effect, decision matrix) may be confusing to
clients and may require simplification or at least translation. Complex
treatments make it difficult to comply with treatment requirements (S.
Hall, 1980). Simple, compelling strategies are needed to counteract the
compelling nature of urges to be sexually aggressive. Thus, an emphasis
on a few essential components of relapse prevention may be necessary
for applications with sexual aggressors.

Although the relapse-prevention approach is innovative and holds promise for applications with sexual aggressors, the empirical evidence of its effectiveness is limited. The sexual reoffense rate over an average of seven years for sexual offenders who completed a relapse prevention program was 6%, compared with a sexual reoffense rate of 48% for sexual offenders who did not complete the program (Hildebran & Pithers, 1992). Similar recidivism rates were reported in another program in which relapse prevention methods were incorporated (G. Hall, 1995a). Only 1 of 17 (5.9%) sexual offenders who completed the treatment program committed a probation violation over a 14-month follow-up period, whereas 7 of 13 (53.8%) who were screened from the program for lack of motivation or dropped out of the program committed parole or probation violations or were rearrested, including one subject who was rearrested for sexual assault (G. Hall, 1995a). However, those subjects who were sufficiently motivated to complete the program may have also been more motivated to prevent relapse than those who did not have sufficient motivation to complete the program.

Motivational issues were controlled for in a third study on relapse prevention in which sexual offenders were randomly assigned to treatment or to no-treatment conditions (Marques, Day, Nelson, & West, 1994). However, the sexual reoffense rate over approximately three years for the treatment group (8%) was not significantly different from the sexual reoffense rate of the nontreatment group (13%). The relatively low base rate of recidivism in this study, which precluded a statistically significant treatment effect, apparently is a function of screening the subjects at highest risk for recidivism (i.e., those having three or more previous arrests) from the study.

Future Research

Evidence of the effectiveness of treatments for sexual aggressors is preliminary. Across recent studies and treatment modalities, the reduction in recidivism among sexual aggressors is only 8% (G. Hall, 1995b). Is this an important reduction? It has been argued that *any* reduction in recidivism is important because of reduced harm to victims and lower financial cost to society (Marshall, Jones et al., 1991; Prentky & Burgess, 1990; Quinsey et al., 1993). Marshall et al. (1991) contended that each sexual aggressor who is prevented from relapse saves two or more victims from suffering. However, from a methodological as well as from a social policy perspective, reductions in recidivism should be reliably attributable to treatment (i.e., statistically significant; Quinsey et al., 1993).

G. Hall (1995b) has suggested that statistically significant effects of treatment are nearly impossible to demonstrate, given the relatively low base rates of rearrests for sexual offenses among sexual aggressors. For example, 750 subjects would be required to demonstrate a medium effect of treatment with the recidivism base rate of 27% vs. 19% recidivism following treatment, which G. Hall (1995b) found in his meta-analysis. Moreover, to adequately examine the effects of treatment, which averages about 20 months in recent studies, a follow-up of at least five years would be required (G. Hall, 1995b). Thus, it is incumbent upon clinicians and researchers to conduct outcome research, including aggregating data via cooperative efforts across clinical sites.

An assumption of those who conduct treatment of sexual aggressors without outcome evaluation may be that some treatment, regardless of what type, is better than no treatment. However, participation in some forms of treatment has been positively correlated with recidivism (G. Hall, 1995b), including a behavioral treatment program in which the positive correlation was statistically significant (Rice et al., 1991). In an analogous situation with psychotropic drugs, widespread dissemination and prescription, without outcome evaluation and FDA approval, would be unconscionable. Although I am not advocating federal or state regulation of treatments for sexual aggressors, the drug analogy underscores the potentially harmful effects of treatment and the need for research on treatment effectiveness.

Given the preliminary state of sexual aggressor treatment outcome research, there are multiple issues to be addressed in future research. Rather than simply assuming that a treatment approach is effective because it is conceptually or intuitively compelling, or even because it has been demonstrated to be effective in another setting, the effectiveness of all treatment of sexual aggressors that is conducted should be evaluated. I will discuss several major research issues that may guide future research.

Design Issues

Types of Sexual Aggressors. Most treatments and treatment research on sexual aggression have been conducted with sexual *offenders*, who have been apprehended by the legal system. The treatments reviewed in this chapter are more effective with less pathological sexual offenders, who are typically treated in outpatient settings, than with more pathological sexual offenders, who are typically treated in institutional settings (G.

Hall, 1995b). Thus, it is possible that these treatments may also be effective with sexual aggressors who are not apprehended by the legal system and represent the most common type of sexual aggressor (Koss, 1993a). In that nonapprehended sexual aggressors are unlikely to voluntarily refer themselves to treatment, perhaps the most effective method of reaching them is to implement effective treatment techniques in preventive interventions, as discussed in chapter 9.

Many nonapprehended and first-time sexual offenders are adolescents. There are less treatment outcome data for adolescent sexual aggressors than for adult sexual aggressors. However, cognitive-behavioral methods were effective in reducing sexually aggressive behavior in a small but carefully designed study (Borduin et al., 1990). One important issue in treatment-outcome studies with adolescents is the natural desistence of antisocial behavior (Moffitt, 1993). Possible treatment effects must be disentangled from improvements that would occur even in the absence of treatment.

The most pathological groups of sexual aggressors are another type for which effective treatments are necessary. Treatment interventions are relatively ineffective for sexual aggressors who have extensive offense histories, who are defensive, and who have low motivation for treatment. Sexual aggressors having developmentally related personality problems are overrepresented in the most pathological groups of sexual aggressors. Insofar as their sexually aggressive behavior is relatively independent of situational influences, sexual aggressors having developmentally related personality problems are the most difficult to treat (see chapter 5). Nevertheless, the most pathological sexual aggressors warrant attention from clinicians and researchers because of the large numbers of pathological sexual aggressors in institutions, the extensive number of persons they victimize, and the extensive amount of harm that they cause to victims (Abel et al., 1987; Farrington, Ohlin, & Wilson, 1986; G. Hall, 1990a).

The most pathological sexual aggressors are typically eliminated from samples in treatment-outcome studies because of poor compliance with treatment procedures (G. Hall, 1995b; Marshall, 1994). However, one method of getting the most pathological sexual aggressors to cooperate with treatment interventions is to decrease their denial and minimization of their offenses (Marshall, 1994). Barbaree (1991) and Marshall (1994) have reported that a Socratic method of contrasting incarcerated sexual offenders' accounts of their offenses with their victim's accounts decreased denial and minimization following approximately six hours of treatment.

Types of Treatment. Cognitive-behavioral methods have been demonstrated to have positive effects across settings (Borduin et al., 1990; Hildebran & Pithers, 1992; Marshall & Barbaree, 1988; Marshall, Eccles, et al., 1991). However, these treatment methods were often conducted or supervised by their originators. Bill Marshall, Howard Barbaree, and Bill Pithers all have pioneered the use of cognitive-behavioral methods with sexual aggressors. It is possible that these positive treatment effects were at least partly dependent on the skills of the therapists conducting them, and it remains to be examined whether these positive treatment effects are replicable across settings. G. Hall's (1995a) recent implementation of these cognitive-behavioral methods with rapists and child molesters provides encouraging evidence of the generalizability of these cognitive-behavioral treatments.

Hormonal treatments appear to be effective with some sexual aggressors, but the most commonly used hormonal treatment, MPA, has many negative side effects. CPA may have fewer side effects, but it is yet to be evaluated in a controlled outcome study. Moreover, hormonal treatments have not been examined in combination with cognitive-behavioral treatments. Perhaps hormonal treatments could effectively replace the behavioral component to reduce deviant sexual arousal in comprehensive cognitive-behavioral approaches.

An assumption with comprehensive treatment programs is that all components are necessary for treatment effectiveness. However, this assumption is not necessarily based on empirical evidence. For example, as discussed previously, in the Marshall and Barbaree (1988) treatment program, the behavioral component to reduce deviant sexual arousal was not associated with recidivism. Moreover, some treatment components may be redundant, such as the use of both social skills training and cognitive therapy to reduce cognitive distortions.

In order to determine if particular treatment components are necessary or redundant (or necessarily redundant to the extent that concepts need to be reiterated), the assessment instruments described in chapter 5 could be used pre- and post-treatment to assess improvement. The association between improvement in treatment and recidivism could then be examined. A related research question is whether matching specific treatments (e.g., reduction of cognitive distortions) for specific subtypes of sexual aggressors (e.g., cognitive distortions subtype) is effective.

In order for causal inferences to be made about treatments, comparison or control groups are necessary and random assignment is desirable (Campbell & Stanley, 1963; Kratochwill & Mace, 1983; McConaghy, 1993). Because assignment to a no-treatment control condition may be considered unethical in many settings, alternative treatments are useful as comparison conditions (Marshall, 1993; Marshall, Jones, et al., 1991b; Marshall & Pithers, 1994). Comparison treatments in previous studies have included individual and group therapy (Borduin et al., 1990; Fedoroff et al., 1992; Meyer et al., 1992). In that behavior therapy has been commonly used with sexual aggressors, but appears less effective than other forms of treatment, it could also serve as a comparison treatment, particularly in evaluating hormonal treatments that reduce deviant sexual arousal.

Length of Treatment. In G. Hall's (1995b) recent meta-analysis of treatments for sexual aggressors, the average length of treatment was 20 months. There is no empirical support for an optimal length of treatment. However, lengthy periods of treatment may cause subject motivation to wane. Moreover, long treatment often is complex treatment, which may also contribute to noncompliance (S. Hall, 1980). Practical considerations also dictate abbreviated but efficient treatment. Probation and parole sentences for sexual aggressors in many states are relatively short—often less than two years—and the legal system expects treatment to be completed within the structure of probation or parole.

Definition of Recidivism. The most important outcome criterion for treatment is the prevention of additional sexually aggressive behavior. Official arrest records are typically used as a measure of recidivism. Although such arrest records may underestimate actual behavior, they may be less biased than other methods of assessing sexually aggressive behavior, and any bias presumably would be equally applicable to treatment and comparison groups (Quinsey et al., 1993).

Some studies have examined within-subject changes during treatment, such as reductions in deviant sexual arousal. However, the assessment of within-subject changes may be susceptible to subject defensiveness. Improvement during treatment may paradoxically result in increased recognition and reporting of problems over time. Moreover, recidivism is not necessarily associated with within-subject changes during treatment.

Some researchers have advocated the use of survival analysis methods to analyze length of time until relapse as a measure of recidivism among sexual aggressors (Marques, Day, et al., 1994; Marques, Nelson, 1994). Although delaying relapse among sexual aggressors potentially reduces the absolute number of victims, a delayed relapse has the same serious consequences to victims as an immediate relapse (see chapter 2, this book; G. Hall, 1995b). Thus, delayed relapse is not necessarily an indication of successful treatment. Survival analysis methods may be more useful with other addictions (e.g., smoking, alcohol or drug abuse) in which a single relapse episode is less serious and delayed relapse may be more meaningful as a measure of progress.

Length of Follow-up. In G. Hall's (1995b) meta-analysis, treatment effects were greatest in studies that had follow-up periods following treatment of at least five years. In that most of the comparison and control subjects in the studies that G. Hall (1995b) reviewed had been incarcerated, it is possible that the memory of incarceration deterred recidivism for the initial years following release. Thus, follow-up periods of at least five years may be necessary to demonstrate treatment effectiveness (Tracy, Donnelly, Morgenbesser, & MacDonald, 1983).

Logistical Issues

In a recent survey it was reported that there are more than 1,500 sexual offender treatment programs operating in the United States (Knopp, Freeman-Longo, & Stevenson, 1992). However, only a handful of these programs are generating outcome data. In a review of the sexual-offender recidivism literature, Furby et al. (1989) could identify only 7 studies that directly compared the recidivism of treated and untreated sexual offenders. Since the Furby et al. (1989) review, there have been only 12 studies in which the recidivism of treated sexual offenders has been compared with that of comparison or control groups (G. Hall, 1995b).

Why are there so many treatment programs and so few outcome data? Responsibility for this disparity lies at various levels. Clinicians are often all too eager to apply the most appealing or latest treatment techniques without properly evaluating them. I recently heard of a treatment approach for adolescent sexual offenders that was being used at several agencies, and I inquired at one of the agencies about any published or written materials on the approach. There apparently were no such materials and the various agencies' application of the approach had been based on workshop presentations. No outcome data on the approach were available.

Many clinicians may regard research as an unnecessary intrusion into their work or, at best, a luxury. Such doubts about the value of research decrease the likelihood that clinicians will conduct research or that they will cooperate with researchers who hope to do so. However, such protection of "turf" may obscure the overarching importance of developing demonstrably effective treatments for sexual aggressors.

State legislative agencies also often create impediments to research. Treatment programs created by legislative agencies typically do not include necessary funding for program evaluation. A notable exception is the sexual-offender treatment program supported by the California State

Legislature (Marques, Day, et al., 1994), although elimination of state funding for this program has periodically been threatened (J. Marques, personal communication, April 1992). Rather than being evaluated by scientific methods, state-supported programs are often evaluated by public opinion. Lack of public support, particularly following even a single highly publicized reoffense of a person who has participated in treatment, may outweigh strong evidence of treatment effectiveness. Among sexually aggressive populations having high base rates of recidivism (e.g., 70%), even highly effective treatment programs (e.g., reduction of recidivism to 35%) may be perceived as ineffective in an absolute sense and therefore may be discontinued.

Researchers also bear responsibility for the paucity of treatment outcome data. Complex theories and treatments are difficult to implement in clinical settings. Clinicians and clients may be justifiably suspicious of researchers who develop their ideas in ivory towers for sexual aggressors in the real world. Rivalries among various research camps may also interfere with cooperative efforts that are necessary in adequately replicating treatment effects across settings. Researchers are often slow to modify their pet philosophies to accommodate data that contradict these philosophies (G. Hall, 1980; Kuhn, 1970).

The adequate evaluation of treatments for sexually aggressive behavior is time-intensive and requires relatively long-term periods of funding. However, the development of effective treatments for perpetrators of sexually aggressive behavior apparently is not much of a priority for federal funding agencies. Although national institutes have been established that are exclusively devoted to the treatment and prevention of some addictive behaviors (e.g., alcohol, drug abuse), there is a disproportionately small amount of funding for research on treatment of perpetrators of sexual aggression. Perhaps this federal funding emphasis reflects the perception that persons experiencing some addictions (e.g., alcohol, drug abuse) are victims of their addictions, whereas persons experiencing other addictions (e.g., sexually aggressive behavior) are not (see chapters 1, 2). Unlike persons who are perceived in society as victims, perpetrators of sexual aggression have no lobbyists or others advocating that they receive treatment (Marshall, 1993). Limited research funding may result in methodological limitations that seriously compromise research quality (e.g., nonrandom assignment, no control/comparison groups). Charging clients for services is one approach to addressing funding issues, but this excludes those who cannot pay for services (Marshall & Barbaree, 1990b).

As discussed in chapter 1, sexual aggression may be viewed by many as a women's or children's issue. Hence, interventions to reduce sexual aggression are often targeted at victims. To view sexual aggression as a men's issue involves a radical shift in attitudes and responsibility. Sexual aggression as a men's issue means that all men corporately share at least some level of responsibility for sexually aggressive behavior. Sexual aggression is not an aberration that is the exclusive purview of "nuts" or "perverts," but is the result of a society in which males are dominant and women and children are subordinate. The expression "We have seen the enemy, and the enemy is us," from the "Pogo" comic strip by Walt Kelly, describes the state of affairs. However, such a shift in attitudes and responsibility may be threatening for many men. Unfortunately, there are many proponents of aggression in society (see chapter 1). Until males are recognized at a societal level as responsible for preventing sexual aggression, efforts to conduct research on treatment interventions for perpetrators of sexually aggressive behavior will be severely hampered.

Conclusion

Some forms of treatment are effective in reducing sexually aggressive behavior. Behavioral treatments to reduce deviant sexual arousal appear to have temporary stimulus-specific effects, whereas hormonal treatments to reduce deviant sexual arousal appear to have a more generalized effect of reducing sexually aggressive behavior. Methods to reduce deviant sexual arousal may be most useful with sexual aggressors who are primarily motivated by physiological sexual arousal. Cognitive-behavioral treatments may have broader applications with sexual aggressors, including those motivated by cognitive distortions, affective dyscontrol, and developmentally related personality problems.

Although recent outcome data on treatments for sexual aggressors are encouraging, they are preliminary. Thus, all treatment for sexual aggressors should be considered experimental, which means that it should be systematically evaluated for its effectiveness. The relatively early stage of development of the sexual-aggressor treatment outcome literature does not warrant social policy applications. Yet, there is a proliferation of treatment programs for sexual aggressors, the vast majority of which are not being evaluated for their effectiveness. Given the likelihood that literally hundreds of sexual-aggressor treatment programs will continue to operate without formal evaluation, perhaps suggestions about the necessary effective elements of treatment might be useful. Chapter 7 reviews and critiques treatment methods that are relevant to each of the four primary motivational precursors in the Hall and Hirschman (1991, 1992) model.

7

Theory-Based Treatment of Sexually Aggressive Behavior

Effective treatment can occur by addressing major motivational precursors of sexually aggressive behavior (Hall, Shondrick, et al., 1993a). The most critical areas for treatment intervention should be apparent after a sexual aggressor has been assessed via the methods reviewed in chapter 5. Although there may be more than one variable that motivates sexually aggressive behavior for many sexual aggressors, most sexual aggressors will be primarily motivated by one of the physiological, cognitive, affective, and developmental precursors (Hall, Shondrick, et al., 1993a). Thus, a logical starting point for treatment would be to target a sexual aggressor's primary motivational precursor before addressing other less central issues.

Rather than an assembly-line approach to treatment in which all clients receive the same set of treatment interventions, some tailoring of treatment interventions to individual needs is probably more effective (Marshall & Pithers, 1994). Such a treatment approach is analogous to the psychological assessment approach discussed in chapter 5. It is possible that some treatments are unnecessary for some sexual aggressors. For example, despite the insistence of some clinicians on reducing deviant sexual arousal among sexual aggressors, not all sexual aggressors exhibit deviant sexual arousal (see chapter 2). Such blanket use of a treatment approach is similar to treating all psychiatric patients for schizophrenia. However, comprehensive assessment should prevent the implementation of such a "sheep dip" approach.

The other end of the continuum involves individualized treatments highly dependent on the skills of a particular therapist. Such an approach is not replicable across settings. Most of the treatment methods described in this chapter are sufficiently parsimonious to be replicable, in that they have been successfully implemented by psychologists, graduate students, and other masters-level therapists in two settings with both child molesters and rapists (G. Hall, 1995a). Treatments should be "user-friendly." Users include both therapists and clients. The cognitive-behavioral methods reviewed in chapter 6 are relatively parsimonious, and there is no evidence that more complex treatment methods are more effective than less complex methods.

The critical variables that distinguish many sexual aggressors from other males who are aggressive or nonaggressive are: (1) motivation for sexually aggressive behavior and (2) reactions to situational variables that cause sexual aggressors to exceed the threshold that normally inhibits sexually aggressive behavior (see chapter 3). Table 7-1 from the Hall, Shondrick, et al. (1993a) review summarizes the treatments proposed for the four subtypes of sexual aggressors. The emphasis of Hall, Shondrick, et al. (1993a) was on reducing the motivation for sexually aggressive

Table 7-1. Proposed Treatments for Subtypes of Sexual Aggressors

Subtype	Proposed Treatments
Physiological	Castration
	Psychohormonal treatments
	Aversion therapy
Cognitive	Victim empathy training
	Relapse prevention
Affective	Cognitive therapy of depression
	Pharmacological treatments
	Cognitive-behavioral anger management
Developmentally related Personality Problems	Cognitive therapy
	Social skills training
	Behavior therapy
	Prevention during adolescence

behavior. The treatments described in this chapter address both motivational and situational determinants of sexually aggressive behavior.

Treatment of Cognitive Distortions

Although the sequence of treatment interventions may vary as a function of motivational factors for sexually aggressive behavior, cognitive distortions about sexually aggressive behavior may interfere with a sexual aggressor's initial motivation to participate in treatment. Prochaska and DiClemente (1983) have identified *precontemplation, contemplation, action*, and *maintenance* as stages of change during which treatment interventions may be more or less effective as a function of motivation. Precontemplators tend not to view their addictive behavior as problematic and do not intend to change. Contemplators are open to change and respond to information and feedback about their addictive behavior, although they do not necessarily change it. Persons in the action stage attempt to change their addictive behaviors via active methods such as counterconditioning and stimulus control, which continue during the maintenance stage (Prochaska & DiClemente, 1983). Some of the ineffectiveness of treatment interventions for addictive behaviors may be a function of a lack of attention to these stages of change.

The treatment prognosis is poor for sexual aggressors in the precontemplation (i.e., denial) or contemplation (i.e., admit their behavior, but are not sufficiently motivated to complete a treatment program) stages. Data from my treatment program suggest a 50% recidivism rate among sexual aggressors who either refused or dropped out of treatment (G. Hall, 1995a). Thus, the lack of commitment to complete a treatment program may be associated with risk for recidivism (cf. Daro, 1988). Moreover, interventions to enhance sexual aggressors' motivation may be critical to treatment success. Addressing a sexual aggressor's cognitive distortions about his offenses may expedite the treatment process by moving him into the action stage. Barbaree (1991) and Marshall (1994) have reported success in reducing sexual offenders' denial and minimization and increasing motivation for treatment by systematically comparing and contrasting sexual offenders' accounts of their offending behavior with those of victims. Until a sexual aggressor can recognize that his behavior is problematic, he is unlikely to be motivated to change his behavior.

One initial method of getting a sexual aggressor to consider changing his behavior is to emphasize the self threatening consequences of sexually aggressive behavior (see chapter 3). Potential or actual loss of a marriage, job, or freedom may be sufficiently threatening for some sexual aggressors to contemplate a need for change, even if they do not view their sexually aggressive behavior as wrong. However, self threat is externally motivated and may deter sexual aggression only as long as there is some external pressure for compliance. Following the loss of a marriage or job, a sexual aggressor may not be motivated to prevent relapse. Moreover, after serving a probationary or prison sentence, a sexual aggressor may believe that he has sufficiently paid his debt to society and that he is entitled to reoffend. Behavior change may be limited to selecting situations to be sexually aggressive in which he is less likely to be caught.

Extreme penalties for treatment noncompliance also may elicit temporary compliance until the external demands are lifted. For example, if the penalty for not succeeding in treatment is incarceration, a subject may comply to the extent necessary. However, similar to being involuntarily drafted into the military, the effects of the indoctrination during treatment may not be internalized nor lasting. Thus, self threat may be useful to generate initial motivation but may be insufficient to prevent relapse. Therefore, methods to develop victim empathy are typically introduced after a sexual aggressor exhibits adequate motivation for treatment (Barbaree & Cortoni, 1993; Hildebran & Pithers, 1989; Pithers, 1994).

In the early 1980s, a documentary was televised in which four rape survivors confronted four rapists in an inpatient treatment program. These victims had not been raped by these particular rapists. The confrontation was intensely emotional, with the rape survivors articulately expressing a range of emotions, including anger, fear, and sadness. Some of the survivors were resentful that these men had been given the option of treatment with the possibility of release in the community. These survivors believed that the men should be incarcerated permanently. The treatment program's intended goal of this confrontation was for the rapists to develop empathy for rape victims, based on the assumption that empathy is a deterrent to sexually aggressive behavior (see chapter 3). Each of the four rapists appeared uncomfortable, embarrassed, and genuinely remorseful about committing rape. They pled with the survivors for understanding and forgiveness. The tears that these rapists shed suggested that the treatment program's goal of engendering empathy for the rape victims had been accomplished. Of course, it is quite possible that the social desirability of empathic responding, particularly for the purposes of a televised interview, was salient to these rapists.

What the televised documentary did not cover, however, was what these rapists did after they were released from the inpatient treatment program. I learned that the three men who were eventually released into the community committed additional rapes. The one man who did not reoffend had not been released at the time that I received information on this treatment program.

Why did the rapists' apparently genuine victim empathy have no deterrent effect on their recidivism? These rapists' confrontation with victims appeared to create the emotional involvement that presumably is an effective element of treatment (Greenberg, 1991; Hildebran & Pithers, 1989). However, this confrontation with rape survivors could also have backfired. In a study in which men contemplated exposure to a rape survivor, the men's acceptance of rape myths *increased* (Ellis, O'Sullivan, & Sowards, 1992). Men's exposure to a rape survivor may precipitate an identification with the *perpetrator*, which also occurs among some male victims of sexual abuse (Ryan, 1989). Such identification with the perpetrator may cause men to generate possible excuses for a survivor's rape (e.g., victim responsibility; Ellis et al., 1992). Thus, any victim empathy that was elicited in the rapists during the television documentary may have been eclipsed by justifications for rape, such as those discussed in chapters 2 and 3.

Another potential component of the adverse impact of contact with rape survivors for the rapists was the confrontive nature of the contact. Confrontation may cause therapists to believe that they are influencing clients because they may feel more personally powerful (Garland & Dougher, 1991). However, confrontation may increase resistance and create a defensive posture among clients (Garland & Dougher, 1991; Marlatt, Larimer, Baer, & Quigley, 1993; Murphy, 1990). Confrontation has resulted in paradoxical *increases* in drinking (Miller, Benefield, & Tonigan, 1993) and in rape myth acceptance (Fischer, 1986; Jaffe, Suderman, Reitzel, & Killip, 1992) in programs intended to reduce these behaviors.

When people's sense of freedom is threatened, they may act to restore their freedom. This concept is known in social psychology as *psychological reactance* (Brehm & Brehm, 1981). The confrontation with the rape survivors may have threatened these rapists' sense of freedom. Thus, the rapists' justifications for rape may have represented an effort to restore their sense of freedom.

Direct or vicarious (e.g., filmed) contact with survivors of sexual aggression has been advocated as a method of increasing victim empathy (Hildebran & Pithers, 1989; Pithers, 1994). However, the assumption that contact with survivors of sexual aggression has a universal empathy-eliciting impact appears to be inaccurate. The high frequency of media depictions of violence may desensitize many persons to the effects of violence.

Instead of simply assuming that face-valid methods of increasing empathy for victims are "getting the message across," such methods should be supplemented with an assessment of their impact. For example, after observing a rape survivor's reactions to rape, perpetrators in treatment could be asked to articulate possible justifications for the rape. Processing and having perpetrators challenge such justifications may prevent some of the unintended effects of methods to increase empathy. Personal knowledge of rape victims also appears to engender more empathy than being presented with information about anonymous victims (Barnett et al., 1992). Thus, efforts to personalize victimization, such as having perpetrators imagine that a family member has been victimized, might be productive. Personalizing victimization, however, may not be as effective with perpetrators who have victimized family members. Nevertheless, the goal with incestuous perpetrators is to get them to shift their identification from their own perspective to the victim's suffering.

Presumably, sexual aggressors who are motivated by cognitive distortions select situations to become sexually aggressive in which they are unlikely to be caught or blamed. The goal of empathy training is for sexual aggressors to recognize that sexual aggression is harmful independent of whether they are caught or blamed. However, undetected recidivism is probably more likely with the cognitive subtype than with other subtypes, because sexual aggression is typically committed in situations in which detection is unlikely (e.g., acquaintance rape). Thus, recidivism data may not accurately reflect treatment outcome for many sexual aggressors whose sexual aggression is motivated by cognitive distortions.

One method of attempting to deal with undetected recidivism is to deliberately instruct sexual aggressors to imagine a situation in which a relapse might take place and to also imagine their responses to that situation. This method is known as lapse rehearsal or relapse rehearsal (R. Hall, 1989). Rather than avoiding the possibility of a lapse and inadvertently making a lapse "forbidden fruit," lapse rehearsal allows an analog situation in which a person can rehearse his relapse-prevention skills (George & Marlatt, 1989; R. Hall, 1989). Presumably, such intentional rehearsal will increase the likelihood that a high-risk situation for relapse will not take a person by surprise and that coping responses will be utilized.

Treatment of Deviant Sexual Arousal

Reduction in deviant sexual arousal may assist in the immediate elimination of sexually aggressive behavior for a person who experiences compelling sexual fantasies and arousal. As reviewed in chapter 6, the most effective method of reducing deviant sexual arousal appears to be the pharmacological or surgical reduction of androgens. However, hormonal treatment or castration is not necessarily a panacea for sexually aggressive behavior among persons having deviant sexual arousal. Recidivism rates for sexual aggressors undergoing hormonal treatment range from 3 to 42% (G. Hall, 1995b). Thus, some sexual aggressors are capable of sexual aggression even if their sexual arousal is suppressed. Because hormonal treatments alone are not effective for all sexual aggressors, hormonal treatments are usually not conducted in isolation from other types of psychological treatments. Moreover, approximately 83% of sexual aggressors either refuse hormonal treatment or drop out after they begin treatment (Fedoroff et al., 1992; Langevin et al., 1979; Meyer et al., 1992), possibly because of the need for ongoing invasive drug administration.

Although it is unwise to allow sexual aggressors' preferences to dictate the design of treatment programs, a group of sexual offenders was asked about their preferred forms of treatment (Langevin, Wright, & Handy, 1988). As might be expected, half of the group reported that they preferred to have no treatment. Of the subjects who did want treatment, most preferred individual or group psychotherapy or both. Providing clients with a form of treatment that is consistent with their expectations may facilitate treatment motivation and outcome (Orford & Keddie, 1986). Thus, from a sexual aggressor's perspective, behavioral treatments to reduce deviant sexual arousal may be more desirable than hormonal injections.

Although the effects of aversive behavioral treatments to reduce deviant sexual arousal do not appear to be permanent, these methods may be helpful in the immediate elimination of sexually aggressive fantasies and behavior. The rationale for aversive conditioning of deviant sexual fantasies and arousal that I give clients involves the proverbial cookie jar. Telling a child not to get cookies from the jar is much less effective than having a child eat foul-tasting cookies. Thus, rather than simply telling a sexual aggressor not to engage in deviant sexual fantasies, the goal is to make these fantasies unpalatable.

The relevance of the deviant and aversive stimuli may influence the effectiveness of aversive conditioning (Clarke & Hayes, 1984). Simulating the situational cues that may be associated with sexually aggressive behavior may be desirable to make the conditioning generalizable beyond the clinical setting. For example, the presence of pornography, anger, or alcohol might enhance ecological validity of a deviant fantasy (chapter 5, this book; Pithers, 1993). The premise for introducing such situational stimuli is analogous to that of the stress inoculation model (Meichenbaum, 1985) described below in the section on treating affective dyscontrol. Presumably, a sexual aggressor's suppression of deviant sexual arousal in the presence of disinhibiting stimuli (e.g., pornography, anger, alcohol) in a clinical setting is more generalizable to real-life settings than suppression in a more sterile clinical setting. Given the high percentage of sexual aggressors who may be able to suppress deviant sexual arousal prior to any aversive conditioning (G. Hall, 1989b; Hall et al., 1988), ecological validity may be critical for effective aversive conditioning.

The relevance of aversive stimuli may also affect aversive conditioning. Garcia and Koelling (1966) demonstrated that animals are biologically prepared to associate specific stimuli with particular effects while selectively ignoring other stimuli. Thus, rats learned to avoid sweet-tasting water when nausea was induced but not when they were shocked after drinking sweet-tasting water. In addition, the rats learned to avoid water that was paired with light and noise followed by shock, but did not avoid the "bright, noisy" water when it was followed by nausea induction.

Sexual stimuli often elicit physiological sexual arousal, which suggests that stimuli that elicit physiological responses would be relevant aversive stimuli. Thus, a useful variation on aversive conditioning is "assisted" covert sensitization, in which a noxious physiological stimulus (e.g., ammonia crystals) that elicits a physiological response is used in combination with covert sensitization (Maletzky, 1974). This method can be made "portable" by having clients carry ammonia capsules with them and sniffing the capsules when deviant fantasies occur.

Socially relevant aversive stimuli may also help the effects of aversive conditioning to generalize. For example, pairing fantasies of child molestation with ridicule by others and legal consequences may be more generalizable than pairing these deviant fantasies with some aversive stimulus that is unrelated to child molestation (e.g., pain from a nonspecific source; Hall, Shondrick, et al., 1993a). Such aversive fantasies may need to be tailored to the individual. Some aversive fantasies (e.g., wife leaving, children being derogated because their father is a sexual offender, negative publicity in the media) may be particularly compelling.

With cookies and with deviant sexual arousal, however, classically conditioned aversion may not generalize to all situations (Brownell et al., 1977; Hayes et al., 1978). For example, a classically conditioned aversion to peanut butter cookies may not generalize to cookies that smell and taste differently, such as chocolate chip cookies. Most cookie lovers are able to discriminate between types of cookies that they like or do not like. Similarly, a person may make the attribution that the foul-tasting cookies in his home may be a result of bad cooking, and that cookies baked in other homes may taste better. In an analogous sense, classically conditioned aversion to one child or children is not necessarily effective when a sexual aggressor experiences a new child in a new situation.

It is important to help sexual aggressors develop effective means of coping with situational stimuli that may elicit deviant sexual arousal. Rather than expecting aversive techniques to extinguish sexual fantasies and arousal to all potential deviant stimuli, the relapse-prevention approach suggests that such deviant fantasies are to be expected (George & Marlatt, 1989; Pithers et al., 1983). However, a deviant sexual fantasy does not signify treatment failure, but should be regarded as a temporary lapse. In the relapse-prevention approach, sexual aggressors are taught that lapses can be effectively coped with. One such coping method would be the active implementation of the aversive techniques, such as invoking an aversive fantasy or, as suggested previously, actually sniffing a foul odor as a means of quelling a deviant fantasy. Providing clients an active role in treatment also may help to dispel the notion that the treatment is designed as a cure that requires no follow-up or personal responsibility.

Another method of coping with deviant sexual arousal is to wait until it subsides. The experience of sexual urges has been described as a curvilinear process, including a rise, a crest, and a fall similar to an ocean wave (George & Marlatt, 1989). Hence, George and Marlatt (1989) have described "urge surfing" as a cognitive method of waiting until an urge subsides. A person who experiences an urge to engage in an addictive behavior can imagine himself surfing until he is out of danger of being compelled to act on the urge. Such active methods of coping with deviant sexual arousal may augment the apparently temporary effects of hormonal or behavioral treatments to reduce deviant sexual arousal.

The presence or perception of sexual arousal does not necessitate acting on it. Men may attribute sexual meaning to women's benign behavior, such as friendliness or clothing style (Abbey, 1987; Edmonds & Cahoon, 1986; Shondrick et al., 1992). Such misattributions occasionally result in sexually aggressive behavior. Similar misattributions may occur among men who are sexually attracted to children. Benign behaviors of children, such as a child being nude or a child apparently staring at a man's genitals, may suggest sexual interest to some men. Interventions to correct these distorted perceptions and to help males recognize that their own sexual arousal to such situations is not necessarily shared by the person who is apparently emitting sexual cues may be helpful. For sexual aggressors who believe that "revealing" clothing is an invitation for sex, I suggest that women who frequent nude beaches are not necessarily inviting sex and certainly are not inviting rape.

Many situational stimuli that elicit deviant sexual arousal can simply be avoided (George & Marlatt, 1989). Use of pornography or viewing nonpornographic films that combine sex and violence toward women may be considered high-risk situations for sexual aggressors whose sexual arousal and sexually aggressive behavior is susceptible to these stimuli. Child molesters, who represent the majority of sexual aggressors motivated by physiological sexual arousal, can structure their lives to avoid situations in which children are present (e.g., schools, shopping malls, amusement parks, public swimming pools, beaches, zoos, video game parlors, family reunions). Any employment setting that exposes sexual aggressors to high-risk situations should also be avoided.

Treatment of Affective Dyscontrol

In some instances, affective dyscontrol may serve as a justification for sexually aggressive behavior. If a person believes himself to have acted out during an affective state that was beyond his control, then he cannot be held blameworthy (Averill, 1993; DiGiuseppe et al., 1994). Therefore, a sexual aggressor may be very resistant to learning that he can control his emotions, because he will not have an excuse for his sexually aggressive behavior.

Attribution of sexually aggressive behavior to affective causes may serve a mitigating function. For example, as discussed earlier, as a component of redefining the problem, admitting to a general anger problem may be more palatable to a sexual aggressor than admitting to anger specifically toward women or to deviant sexual arousal (G. Hall, 1989a; McGovern & Nevid, 1986). Thus, some sexual aggressors may be willing to try to control their general anger, but may have a difficult time acknowledging anger specifically toward women.

For both rapists and child molesters, the physiological sexual arousal associated with sexually aggressive behavior may be highly reinforcing because it reduces negative affective states (see chapter 3). However, the physiological "high" from sexual arousal, whether in the context of a consenting or a nonconsenting sexual relationship, is temporary and is often followed by guilt, particularly among affectively dyscontrolled persons (Mosher & Anderson, 1986). Rather than being a deterrent to recidivism, guilt may reduce self-efficacy, which may in turn decrease the likelihood of preventing sexually aggressive behavior (George & Marlatt, 1989).

Rapists and child molesters can be taught that sexually aggressive behavior is not the sole method of coping with negative affective states. The physiological arousal associated with affective dyscontrol can be effectively reduced and controlled via muscle relaxation methods (Deffenbacher, Demm, & Brandon, 1986; Deffenbacher, Story, Stark, Hogg, Brandon, 1987; DiGiuseppe et al., 1994; Novaco, 1976, 1977). Such relaxation can also be accomplished via other methods, such as aerobic exercise. Tricyclic antidepressants also reduce negative affect and may serve as a useful component of a comprehensive treatment approach (Hollon et al., 1991).

Distorted interpretations of environmental cues may lead to provocation in affectively dyscontrolled persons. Analogous to sexual aggressors who attribute sexual meaning to benign cues, persons who experience affective dyscontrol may be predisposed to perceive threat in the behavior of others (Krueger et al., 1994). Cognitive therapy assists persons with affective problems in more accurately processing information (Deffenbacher et al., 1986, 1987; DiGiuseppe et al., 1994; Hollon et al., 1991; Novaco, 1976, 1977). Perceptions of threat often have become reflexive for persons having affective problems. Alternative interpretations and responses to apparently threatening stimuli are encouraged in cognitive therapy. Affective arousal does not necessitate sexually aggressive behavior.

Interventions for affective dyscontrol often include a behavioral component. Many treatment programs for sexual aggressors utilize general social skills training that teaches assertiveness as an alternative to aggressiveness or passivity (Marshall, Jones, et al., 1991). Other programs have a more specific emphasis on anger or depression, which are common affective motivational precursors among sexual aggressors (Hall, Shondrick, et al., 1993a).

Stress inoculation training is particularly useful in modifying maladaptive affective responses to perceived situational provocation (Meichenbaum, 1985). Specific situational cues that provoke negative affect and sexual aggression can be simulated in a role play, as described in chapter 5. One person, usually another client in a group, can be assigned the role of the provocateur and the client can provide detailed input about how the provocateur is to act. Videotaping such role plays can provide useful and powerful feedback to clients. Such videotaped role plays may offer evidence of problems, such as anger toward women, that clients themselves are not aware of. The videotape of the role-play simulation of actual responses to a situation can be carefully reviewed and corrective recommendations can be offered.

Specific behavioral suggestions (e.g., breathe deeply to relax, speak less loudly, sit down rather than stand, give the other person a chance to state his opinion, say what you want rather than what you don't want) are more useful to clients than more general ones (e.g., you should be less angry, you need to change your attitude). The client can then attempt the role play again, this time implementing suggestions for coping.

It is important that the behavior of the person serving as the provocateur is consistent both in the real-life simulation role play and the coping role play. Provocateurs are often tempted to "give in" (i.e., become less provocative) to a person who is demonstrating particularly effective coping responses. However, real-life provocateurs do not always relent in response to effective coping, thus I typically do not have provocateurs "lower the heat" when a client is attempting to implement coping responses.

Treatment of Developmentally Related Personality Problems

Treatment effectiveness varies as a function of psychopathology among sexual aggressors. Treatment is least successful with the most pathological sexual aggressors (G. Hall, 1995b). Sexual aggressors having developmentally related personality problems are among the most pathological sexual aggressors (Hall & Hirschman, 1991, 1992; Hall, Shondrick, et al., 1993a). One of the major problems in attempting to treat sexual aggressors having developmentally related personality problems is that one cannot change a person's history. As discussed in Chapter 4, past sexually aggressive behavior is the best predictor of future sexually aggressive behavior. Thus, a person who has engaged in multiple acts of sexual aggression may remain at high risk for reoffense even if he has completed a treatment program.

Possibly, methods that address primary motivational variables but are not contingent on personal implementation would be useful with the developmental subtype. For example, hormonal treatments do not require any responsibility other than availability for treatment. Nevertheless, the antisocial propensity of many sexual aggressors may be impacted very little by treatments to reduce testosterone. Similarly, antidepressant medication may do little to change ingrained antisocial patterns.

Although the treatment prognosis for sexual aggressors having developmental problems is poor, it may be possible to identify some situational determinants of sexually aggressive behavior. A person's developmental history cannot be changed, but responses to situational provocation may be modified with the treatment methods previously described in this chapter to address physiological, cognitive, and affective motivational precursors. However, situational variables may have limited influence over sexually aggressive behavior that is chronic and cross-situational (see chapter 5).

The burnout phenomenon observed in rapists (see chapter 4) may offer some cause for optimism in treating persons having developmentally related personality problems. Perhaps sexual aggressors having multiple offenses could be incarcerated until their risk for reoffense declines during their mid-30s. Treatment before and following release into the community might further reduce the risk of reoffense. Although the burnout phenomenon occurs with rapists, it typically does not occur with child molesters. In that recidivism among child molesters appears to be associated with access to victims, eliminating access to children may be the best means of preventing recidivism among child molesters in the community (see chapter 4).

Treatment Outcome

It could be argued that a primary treatment focus on physiological, cognitive, and affective motivational variables and reactions to situational variables related to these motivational variables is an overly simplistic approach to the treatment of such a complex and serious problem as sexually aggressive behavior. Isn't simply learning *how* to prevent relapse a superficial approach to symptoms of some larger underlying problem? Shouldn't sexual aggressors learn *why* they are sexually aggressive? Isn't treatment of less than two years too brief to have any lasting effects, given that sexually aggressive behavior is such a serious problem?

The gold standard for any treatment approach for sexual aggressors is its ability to reduce recidivism. G. Hall (1995b) reported in a meta-analysis that hormonal and cognitive-behavioral treatments were effective in reducing sexually aggressive behavior relative to comparison treatments or no treatment. Although these treatments addressed some of the motivational precursors of the quadripartite model (Hall & Hirschman, 1991), none of the treatments was developed in the context of this model.

G. Hall (1995a) implemented the quadripartite model in a treatment study of outpatient child molesters and rapists on probation or parole. Treatments that correspond to the motivational precursors of the quadripartite model suggested by Hall, Shondrick, et al. (1993a) were implemented in the G. Hall (1995a) study. The treatment program in the study involved: (1) 2 months of individual covert sensitization to reduce deviant sexual arousal; (2) 8 months of group therapy focused on cognitive distortions, affective dyscontrol, and relapse prevention; and (3) 2 to 12 months of individual treatment focused on relapse prevention. The treatment manual used in this study is provided in Hall (1995a).

Twenty percent of the subjects referred to the program were screened from treatment because they denied committing a sexual offense or denied a need for treatment (G. Hall, 1995a). Twenty-three percent of the subjects who began treatment dropped out. The subjects who were screened from treatment may be conceptualized as in the precontemplation stage (Prochaska & DiClemente, 1983) because they did not intend to change their behavior. The subjects who dropped out of treatment may be conceptualized as being in the contemplation stage (Prochaska & DiClemente, 1983) because they initially considered change, but did not have the motivation to change their behavior by completing treatment. The subjects who completed treatment (57% of all subjects initially referred to the treatment program) may be considered to be in the action and maintenance stages of change (Prochaska & DiClemente, 1983).

Recidivism was defined by G. Hall (1995a) as any violation of probation or parole conditions. Of the subjects who were screened from the treatment program or dropped out, 53.8% recidivated, whereas only 5.8% ($N = 1$ domestic violence reoffense) of the subjects who completed the treatment program recidivated. Only one subject who was in the group that was screened sexually reoffended. The rest of the reoffenses in the groups that were screened or dropped out of treatment involved domestic violence, theft, public intoxication, and technical violations of probation or parole (i.e., missed meetings with parole or probation officers and failure to get approval for employment).

The subjects in the G. Hall (1995a) study who were sufficiently motivated to complete treatment also were sufficiently motivated to prevent relapse. However, the ability of the subjects who completed treatment to prevent relapse is probably also partly attributable to the effects of the treatment program. The treatment program appears to have been adequately engaging for the 71% of subjects who began and completed treatment. The program also appeared to have general prosocial effects, in that it reduced primarily nonsexual forms of recidivism. The base rate for sexual reoffending in the study was low, thus the impact of the treatment program on sexually aggressive behavior is unclear. Nevertheless, the results of the G. Hall (1995a) study provide preliminary support for a time-limited treatment approach that is based on the quadripartite model. As suggested in chapter 6, future treatment-outcome research is needed in which subjects are randomly assigned to treatments to control for the effects of subject motivation. It also is important to determine the specific effects of treatment components and whether matching of treatments to specific subtypes of sexual aggressors is warranted.

Conclusion

Treatments are available that address the motivation for sexually aggressive behavior and reactions to situational variables that cause the sexual aggressor to exceed the threshold that normally inhibits sexually aggressive behavior. Treatments need not be conducted in a fixed sequence. Interventions that target a sexual aggressor's primary motivational precursor are a logical starting point. A treatment study by G. Hall (1995a) provides preliminary support for the use of a time-limited treatment approach based on the quadripartite model.

What is currently known about treatment pertains almost exclusively to the small percentage of men who have been adjudicated or identified by authorities as being sexually aggressive (G. Hall, 1995b). Most treatment programs for perpetrators target the relatively serious sexual offenders who have been arrested and convicted. Acquaintance and date rapists, who are the most common types of perpetrators, usually do not receive treatment because they are not adjudicated. This situation is analogous to the focus in treatment of alcohol problems. Specialized treatment programs have been designed for persons with the most serious alcohol problems, whereas persons with the most common form of alcohol problems, which are less severe, are the least likely to receive treatment (Kreitman, 1986; Marlatt et al., 1993). It is unknown if treatment is equally effective with nonadjudicated men, although treatment does appear to be more effective with less pathological (i.e., outpatient) than with more pathological (i.e., incarcerated) sexual aggressors (G. Hall, 1995b). However, it is unlikely that sexually aggressive men who are not adjudicated will voluntarily seek treatment for sexually aggressive behavior. Many men who are sexually aggressive do not view their behavior as problematic (see chapter 5), and those who do may avoid treatment out of the fear of being adjudicated. Thus, prevention may be the best method of reducing the amount of sexually aggressive behavior among nonadjudicated men who will not be seen in treatment. Moreover, the poor treatment prognosis for sexual aggressors having developmentally related personality problems also suggests that early preventive interventions are needed (Hall, Shondrick, et al., 1993a). Prevention is addressed in Part IV, with a review of general approaches to preventing aggressive behavior and an application of these approaches to the problem of sexually aggressive behavior.

IV

PREVENTION

8

Protective Factors Against Sexually Aggressive Behavior

Preventive efforts optimally occur before a disorder is fully manifested, thus interventions are targeted toward possible precursors of the disorder, known as *risk factors* (Coie et al., 1993). Such preventive efforts before a disorder occurs have been termed *prelapse* prevention (Hall, Hirschman, 1993). In the case of sexually aggressive behavior, physiological sexual arousal to deviant stimuli, cognitive distortions, affective dyscontrol, and developmentally related personality problems have been identified as motivational precursors to sexually aggressive behavior (Hall & Hirschman, 1991, 1992) that may warrant attention in prevention programs. Table 8-1 presents risk factors for the development of sexually aggressive behavior within the physiological, cognitive, affective, and developmental domains, based on the literature reviews in chapters 2 and 3.

To the extent that similar personality characteristics among sexual and nonsexual offenders suggest similar motivational precursors (Hall et al., 1992), risk factors for sexual aggression may also constitute risk factors for nonsexual forms of aggression. These same risk factors may be associated with other disorders as well, such as sexually transmitted diseases (cf. Coie et al., 1993). Thus, preventive efforts directed at the primary precursors of sexually aggressive behavior may be useful in pre-

Table 8-1. Risk Factors for the Development of Sexually Aggressive Behavior

Physiological
1. Sexual preoccupation
2. Use of pornography, particularly that which involves children or violent images
3. Development of deviant fantasies
4. Masturbation to deviant fantasies
5. Development of sexual arousal patterns to deviant stimuli (e.g., children, rape)

Cognitive
1. Inaccurate perception of social cues (e.g., a person's friendliness = he or she wants sex)
2. Perception of self as victim
3. Blaming others for problems
4. Limited empathy
5. Cognitive distortions about the meaning of sexually aggressive behavior
6. Apparently irrelevant decisions (see chapter 6)
7. Planning of potential sexually aggressive act

Affective
1. Poor awareness of emotional states
2. Emotional constriction
3. Easily provoked
4. Emotional dyscontrol
5. Anger toward women
6. Substance abuse

Developmental
1. Parental divorce
2. Large family of origin
3. Parental neglect
4. Parental physical or sexual abuse
5. Family criminal history
6. Academic difficulties
7. Interpersonal problems
8. Occupational instability
9. Chronic substance abuse

venting multiple disorders. As with effective treatment (see chapter 6), effective prevention of sexually aggressive behavior may focus on reducing the motivation for sexually aggressive behavior and on reducing situational factors that may create risk.

Primary prevention is directed toward the general population to reduce the incidence (i.e., new cases) of a problem (Brantingham & Faust, 1976; Caplan, 1964; Daro, 1988; Levine & Perkins, 1987). *Secondary prevention* is aimed at reducing the prevalence of a problem by targeting high-risk groups (Brantingham & Faust, 1976; Daro, 1988). *Tertiary prevention* involves efforts to ameliorate the long-term symptoms or ramifications of a problem via interventions with victims or perpetrators. Tertiary prevention of sexual aggression has been most common, as reviewed in chapters 6 and 7 with respect to perpetrators. However, the perpetrators who receive treatment usually have been legally convicted and constitute a minority of all perpetrators, in that most perpetrators are not convicted (Koss, 1993a; McCall, 1993).

In addition to interventions to reduce risk factors, a second component of prevention is the development and maintenance of individual and environmental *protective factors* that improve a person's resistance to risk factors and disorder (Coie et al., 1993). In the previous chapters in this book I have examined why men are sexually aggressive. In this chapter, I will review of some protective factors that contribute to men *not* being sexually aggressive.

Protective Factors Against Antisocial Behavior

Many, if not most, adolescent males engage in some form of antisocial behavior (Moffitt, 1993) and many adolescent males also engage in some form of sexually aggressive behavior (Koss et al., 1987; Muehlenhard & Linton, 1987). However, a small minority of adolescents abstains completely from antisocial acts (Moffitt, 1993). Those adolescents who do not engage in deviant behavior constitute such a small, atypical group that some view such nondeviance as deviant (Moffitt, 1993). However, it may be inappropriate to consider some forms of antisocial behavior that have a lasting negative impact on victims, such as sexual aggression, to be "normal" (see chapter 2).

Antisocial behavior for many adolescents is a means of asserting independence from parents and entering the adult world (Moffitt, 1993; Rodgers & Rowe, 1993). However, in circumstances under which adolescents are provided access to adult privileges and responsibilities in a conventional manner, adolescents may be less prone to engage in antisocial behavior. Such access to adult privileges and responsibilities are provided by some cultural or religious groups (Moffitt, 1993). In situations in which adolescents are provided access to adult privileges, they may emulate adults more than peers.

Another factor that may deter adolescents from engaging in antisocial behavior is a lack of contact with antisocial peers (Moffitt, 1993). Structural barriers, such as living in rural areas, may prevent such contact. Moffitt (1993) has also suggested that pathological characteristics may exclude non-antisocial adolescents from peer networks. It is difficult for adolescents to engage in delinquent behavior if they have no friends from whom to learn such behavior (Moffitt, 1994). Thus, an adolescent lacking the requisite social skills to make friends also does not make antisocial friends.

Adult influence and lack of negative peer influence also appear to mediate other adolescent behavior, including substance use and initiation of coitus. A reliance on adults for help and direction and poor social skills characterized abstainers from marijuana use (Shedler & Block, 1990). A self-perception of physical unattractiveness and an inability to enjoy sensuous experiences may have also interfered with marijuana abstainers' interpersonal effectiveness. Similarly, age at first coitus is delayed among adolescents who perceive their parents as more influential than peers (Jessor et al., 1983; Newcomb & Bentler, 1988; Wyatt, 1989). The peer friends of adolescent virgins may share their conservative values (Jessor et al., 1983). Virgins' social relationships with same-gender peers are not impaired, but virgins view themselves as less physically attractive and less competent to establish heterosexual relationships than nonvirgins (Jessor et al., 1983). Virgins tend not to use drugs, are more likely to attend religious activities, and have more years of education than nonvirgins (Jessor et al., 1983; Newcomb & Bentler, 1988; Wyatt, 1989). Unlike Moffitt's (1993, 1994) and Shedler and Block's (1990) conceptualizations of abstainers from antisocial activity and substance use as abnormal, Jessor et al. (1983) stated that virgins were not necessarily psychologically maladjusted relative to nonvirgins, as evidenced by their educational and occupational achievements that exceeded those of nonvirgins. Obviously, those persons who abstain from sexual activity are also not sexually aggressive.

Certain religious and cultural groups may facilitate adult influence relative to peer influence in adolescents' lives (Moffitt, 1993). Such adult influence may be a protective factor against antisocial behavior, including sexual aggression. Moreover, peer influences within these religious and cultural groups may also constitute protective factors. I will discuss religiosity as a potential protective factor against sexually aggressive behavior and also discuss possible reasons for the apparently low prevalence of sexual aggression among some Asian-American groups.

Religious Protective Factors

Society exerts tremendous pressure to engage in sexual relationships, and it is in the context of sexual relationships between acquaintances and intimates that most sexual aggression occurs. Therefore, any influence that restricts relationships, and sexual relationships in particular, is conceivably a deterrent against sexually aggressive behavior. As discussed earlier, religiosity is associated with postponed initiation of coitus among adolescents (Jessor et al., 1983; Newcomb & Bentler, 1988; Sloane & Potvin, 1986; Wyatt, 1989). Religiously oriented women are less likely to be raped than women who are not religiously oriented, probably as a result of limited sexual involvement (Hall & Flannery, 1984). In a recent study, it was found that women raised by conservative Christian parents who integrated their religious values into their family life were the least likely to be sexually abused (Elliott, 1994). Unlike some approaches in which adolescents are instructed to "just say no" without much of a rationale, religiously oriented adolescents may maintain premarital sexual abstinence for moral or spiritual reasons and may also have religiously oriented peers who are supportive of their abstinence. For example, Roman Catholicism may serve as a protective factor against sexual assault in Latino communities (Sorenson & Siegel, 1992).

The perceived self threat (see chapter 3) associated with pre- or extramarital sexual behavior, including sexually aggressive behavior, may be that of violating one's internal moral or spiritual code of ethics more so than external sanctions against sexual aggression, such as arrest and incarceration. Moreover, for religiously oriented persons whose moral code teaches them to respect the rights of others, sexual behavior, including sexual aggression, would be associated with victim threat, in that pre- or extramarital sexual contact may constitute a violation of another person's right not to be sexually active. Such empathy for others could be a deterrent against the cognitive distortions that are motivational precursors to sexually aggressive behavior. Moreover, when sexuality and sexual gratification are not preoccupations in a person's life, it is possible that deviant patterns of physiological sexual arousal are less likely to develop.

Religious institutions may provide adolescents with access to adult privileges, such as leadership, that may deter engaging in antisocial behavior as an attempt to establish independence (Moffitt, 1993). Churches may offer a supportive family environment that is often absent in many families. Many religions value the acceptance of persons who may be rejected in other social or institutional settings. For example, ethnic minority churches are some of the few institutions in which ethnic minority persons have legitimate power in terms of leadership and ownership. These churches offer ethnic minority persons experiences with ethnic minority leaders that are seldom available in other institutional or societal settings.

To the extent that religiosity is a deterrent against premarital sexual contact, it is a deterrent to nonmarital sexual aggression. However, there are also important potentially negative effects of religion on sexually aggressive behavior. Most religions do not prohibit marriage, and much sexual aggression may occur in the context of marriage. The incidence of rape perpetrated by husbands or ex-husbands may be as high as twice that of rapes by acquaintances or strangers (Finkelhor & Yllo, 1985; Russell, 1982). Judeo-Christian and other religions tend to be patriarchal and women are often expected to be subservient to men in marriage.

Religiosity is typically not significantly associated with general attitudes toward rape (Dull & Giacopassi, 1987; Fischer, 1986) or sexually aggressive behavior (Walker et al., 1993), but there is evidence that perceptions of the severity of *marital* rape are *negatively* correlated with Judeo-Christian religiosity (Jeffords, 1984). If men believe that it is their prerogative to be dominant within their marriage and family context, then sexually aggressive behavior could be construed as simply a normal aspect of this dominance. Moreover, religious women may be willing to endure sexual abuse in an effort to honor their commitment to their marriage and family unit (Koss et al., 1994; Torres, 1987).

Corporal punishment is often advocated among fundamentalist religious groups (Grasmick, Bursik, & Kimpel, 1991). Such a rejection of a child's right not to be physically abused may also make it easier to reject a child's right not to be sexually abused. Also, the acceptance and forgiveness advocated by many religious groups may make these groups vulnerable to potential perpetrators, particularly when such acceptance and forgiveness is not accompanied by the expectation of personal responsibility for changing antisocial behavior (see chapter 5).

Religiosity is not a unitary construct, and all forms of religion do not necessarily inculcate sexism. However, most research on sexual behavior that examines religiosity does not consider this heterogeneity of religiosity (Wyatt et al., 1993). Fundamentalist religious beliefs are quite different from nonpatriarchal religiosity that creates respect for human life, particularly women and children, and abhors violence. However, conventional religious beliefs often contain elements of hypocrisy, such as a view of the sanctity of human life that includes opposition to abortion in conjunction with support of capital punishment.

Batson, Schoenrade, and Ventis (1993) have differentiated between religiosity that results in increased compassion toward others versus religiosity that results in the *appearance* of compassion toward others. The latter type of religiosity involves the outward appearance of socially desirable behavior, which may include commitment to traditional religious beliefs and practices such as regular attendance at religious services. However, real-life opportunities to be compassionate tend to be avoided, such as helping a homeless person. Religion is useful to the extent that it provides comfort or social status and becomes dispensable when it no longer serves these purposes or when it inconveniences people by dictating that they act in a manner inconsistent with their personal wishes. Thus, a person who desires to be sexually aggressive might suspend his religiosity if he felt that it would dictate against his desire to be sexually aggressive.

Alternatively, people whose religiosity guides them to be compassionate toward others may be less than conventional in their religious beliefs and practices, but tend to act on their religious convictions in an altruistic manner. Batson et al. (1993) have termed this the *quest* approach to religion. Characteristics of this approach are listed in Table 8-2. The moral principles of a quest orientation would prevent a person from engaging in abusive behavior, including sexual aggression. Men who believe sexual aggression to be morally wrong may be unlikely to engage in sexually aggressive behavior, even when there exist weak sanctions against it (Bachman et al., 1992). Such an orientation could be found in a variety of religions. However, subsuming persons having vastly different religious orientations under a single construct of religiosity probably has contributed to the inconsistent association between religion and behavior (e.g., Wyatt et al., 1993).

In summary, religiosity may serve as a protective factor against sexual aggression to the extent that it limits premarital sexual behavior and provides an alternative to an antisocial lifestyle. Religious beliefs may potentially prevent the development of the cognitive distortions and physiological sexual arousal precursors to sexually aggressive behavior. However, the patriarchal aspects of religion may place some religious persons at risk for engaging in sexually aggressive behavior, particularly in the context of marriage and the family. Thus, the moral and spiritual framework of a nonpatriarchal, nonviolent approach to religion may be a protective factor against sexual aggression, whereas a patriarchal

Table 8-2. Quest Orientation to Religion

1. Approach to religion characterized by complexity, doubt, and tentativeness
2. Life includes a transcendent dimension, not necessarily a clear belief in a transcendent reality
3. Religiosity results in reduced intolerance
4. Religiosity results in increased sensitivity to the needs of others
5. Existential questions posited, clear-cut answers neither obtained nor expected

Source: Adapted from Batson et al. (1993).

approach to religion in which violence against certain groups (e.g., children, women, criminals) is acceptable may constitute a risk factor for sexually aggressive behavior.

Cultural Protective Factors

Mainstream U.S. society is one of the most violent in the world (Fingerhut, Ingram, & Feldman, 1992; Lore & Schultz, 1993; Mercy, Rosenberg, Powell, Broome, & Roper, 1993). Therefore, it may be useful to learn how other cultures prevent violence. Although a recent cross-cultural review of 35 industrialized societies did not support the existence of a rape-free society (Rozee, 1993), the prevalence of sexual aggression may vary across cultural or ethnic groups in the United States (Koss et al., 1987). The deficits of ethnic minority cultures in the United States are typically emphasized in psychological research, but there may be resilient aspects of ethnic minority communities that serve as protective factors against pathology (Hill, Soriano, Chen, & La Fromboise, 1994; Stevenson & Renard, 1993).

Cultures having non-Western origins often emphasize collective values, whereas mainstream U.S. culture stresses individual achievement (American Psychological Association Commission on Violence and Youth, 1993; Hill et al., 1994; Sue & Sue, 1990). Interpersonal conflict and violence tend to be minimal in cultures with collective orientations because individual goals are subordinated to those of the group, social support is high, and competitiveness is low (Triandis, Bontempo, Villareal, Asai, & Lucca, 1988). As discussed in chapter 1, Japan, a collectivist culture, has extremely low rates of violent crime. Similarly, in the United States, arrest rates for violent crimes perpetrated by Asian Americans and Pacific Islanders are about one third the rate of the numbers of Asian Americans and Pacific Islanders in the population (American Psychological Association Commission on Violence and Youth, 1993), which may be a function of a collectivist orientation.

Elsewhere I have discussed protective and risk factors for sexually aggressive behavior associated with several cultures (Hall, 1995, August). For example, social networks in African-American communities may facilitate both competence with peers and in academics (Cauce, Hannan, & Sargeant, 1992). Such academic competence and association with nondeviant peers may serve as protective factors against antisocial behavior (Patterson et al., 1989). Although protective factors against sexually aggressive behavior exist across cultures, I will use Asian-American culture as an example in this chapter because of some of its dissimilarities with mainstream U.S. culture.

The results of a national survey, in which subjects' identities were anonymous, suggest that prevalence rates of sexual victimization are significantly lower for Asian-American women (7%) than for women in other groups (European-American = 16%, African-American = 10%, Latina = 12%; Native American = 40%). Moreover, a low percentage of Asian-American men perpetrate rape (2%) relative to most other groups (European-American = 4%; African-American = 10%, Latino = 7%, Native American = 0%; Koss et al., 1987). Koss et al. (1987) reported that the effect sizes of these statistically significant differences in ethnicity were small. However, to the extent that any reduction in sexually aggressive behavior is important (Marshall, Jones et al., 1991; Prentky & Burgess, 1990; Quinsey et al., 1993), the low percentage of Asian-American women who report being sexually victimized and the low percentage of Asian-American men who report being perpetrators may be potentially important.

Unlike other studies of violence in ethnic minority populations (Lockhart, 1985), Koss et al. (1987) did not use clinical samples or official data, and they controlled for social class to some extent by studying college samples. Although such self-report data may be influenced by social desirability (i.e., Asian Americans find it less socially desirable to report sexual aggression or other forms of violence than other groups; U.S. Commission on Civil Rights, 1992) or the belief of nonanonymity because of the small numbers of Asian Americans in college populations (M. Yoshihama, personal communication, September 1994), the conditions of anonymity may make the data less subject to bias than official reports that require formal contact with the legal system, such as police records. Insofar as most violent crime is intraracial (O'Brien, 1987; Wyatt, 1985) and both Asian American victims' and perpetrators' reports of the prevalence of rape are consistently low (Koss et al., 1987), it appears that sexual aggression is relatively infrequent among Asian Americans.

Relatively low levels of deviance characterize Asian-American communities. Japanese Americans, Chinese Americans, and Asian-Indian Americans have lower rates of child maltreatment, including child sexual abuse, than other groups (Dixon, 1991). Moreover, Asian Americans have lower rates of school problems (Wells et al., 1992), alcohol and drug use (Gillmore et al., 1990; Murray, Perry, O'Connell, & Schmid, 1987; Newcomb, Maddahian, Skager, & Bentler, 1987; Wells et al., 1992) and antisocial behavior than other groups (Maddahian, Newcomb, & Bentler, 1988; Wells et al., 1992) when socioeconomic status is controlled. Preliminary data from the Chinese American Psychiatric Epidemiological Study in Los Angeles suggest that Chinese Americans exhibit rates of mood disorders that are as low as the rates for other groups and rates of anxiety disorders that are lower than those of other groups (S. Sue, personal communication, October 1994). Asian-American academic achievement also exceeds that of other groups (Steinberg, Dornbusch, & Brown, 1992; Sue & Okazaki, 1990). Thus, a male growing up in an Asian-American family may not be exposed to some of the negative experiences that result in developmentally related personality problems associated with sexually aggressive behavior.

Despite the relative absence of antisocial behavior for Asian Americans as a group, problems do exist. Among recent immigrants and groups having lower socioeconomic status, disproportionately high rates of child abuse and neglect, and spousal abuse have been reported (Ima & Hohm, 1991; Uba, 1994). Asian immigrants who have no ethnic community with which to identify may be particularly susceptible to involvement in crime (Uba, 1994). It is possible that high sexual-abuse rates are partly a function of the close monitoring of Asian-American immigrants by social service agencies (Ima & Hohm, 1991). However, the patriarchal aspects of Asian-American families may cause victims of sexual aggression to be more reluctant to report being abused than in other less patriarchal groups (Yoshihama, Parekh, & Boyington, 1991).

Women have a subordinate status and are often oppressed in Asian cultures (Ho, 1990). Thus, some Asian women may believe that they are obligated to comply with a man's sexual advances simply because he is male. Suffering and persevering without complaining and acceptance of fate are Asian women's values that may encourage abuse (Ho, 1990; Yoshihama, 1994; Yoshihama & Sorenson, 1994). Some Asian-American women may not want to report abuse to authorities because they fear that the perpetrator will face discriminatory or even brutal treatment by social service agencies (Hamilton, 1989). Indeed, racial discrimination does exist in the severity of legal charges for sexual assault (Bradmiller & Walters, 1985). Asian-American women are less likely to report dating violence to police than are Latino and African-American women, although Asian-American women are not less likely to report dating violence to police than European-American women (Miller & Simpson, 1991). It is also possible that police may have positive stereotypes of Asian Americans that result in lower arrest rates for various offenses when they are reported, just as negative stereotypes may result in higher arrest rates for other groups (cf. Dembo et al., 1991; Koss et al., 1994). Nevertheless, data consistently suggest that Asian Americans as a group engage in relatively little antisocial behavior.

Perhaps certain aspects of Asian-American culture serve as protective factors against antisocial behavior. Several characteristics valued by traditional Asian culture that promote interpersonal harmony were discussed by Uba (1994) and are listed in Table 8-3. The inhibition of affect and the high value placed on self-control among Asian Americans (Uba, 1994) may serve to prevent the development of the affective dyscontrol associated with sexually aggressive behavior and other nonsexual forms of aggression. Indeed, self-control is the goal of many treatment programs for sexually aggressive behavior (e.g., George & Marlatt, 1989).

In collectivist cultures, the most important relationships are vertical (e.g., parent-child, employer-employee; Triandis, Bontempo, Villareal, Asai, & Lucca, 1988). Social relations tend to be enduring and there is a strong ingroup identity (Triandis et al., 1988). Achievements or failures reflect on one's entire family (Sue & Sue, 1973; Uba, 1994). Social control is accomplished at the family level via guilt and shame (Uba, 1994). To the extent that the Asian-American community is part of one's extended family or ingroup, aggression against others is deterred because violation of other family members is prohibited. In other words, empathy for those perceived as family members prevents aggressive behavior. Thus, sexual aggression against other Asian Americans would be deterred by empathy, or perceived other threat (see chapter 3), and such empathy could reduce the likelihood of the development of cognitive distortions about victims that may constitute a risk factor for sexually aggressive behavior.

Cultural differences also seem to influence the sexual behavior of

Table 8-3. Behaviors that Promote Interpersonal Harmony in Asian Cultures

1. Patience
2. Gentleness
3. Being well mannered
4. Cooperation
5. Being accommodating, conciliatory, and cooperative rather than confrontational
6. Blending in with the group rather than distinguishing oneself for either good or bad behavior
7. Humility and modesty
8. Withholding free expression of feelings
9. Suppression of conflict
10. Avoiding potentially divisive arguments and debates
11. Communicating indirectly
12. Refraining from openly challenging others' perspectives
13. Nonverbal communication
14. Conformity to conventional behavior

Source: Adapted from Uba (1994).

Asian-Americans. Whereas only 40% of a 1982 sample of Chinese-American college students had experienced sexual intercourse (Huang & Uba, 1992), nearly three fourths of a sample of primarily European-American college-age students had experienced sexual intercourse (Jessor et al., 1982). For females in some traditional Asian families, dating may be unacceptable until a certain age or until education is completed (Yoshihama et al., 1991).

Patriarchal cultures, including Asian cultures, may include positive aspects, such as the family nurturance and community aspects of *machismo* in Mexican culture (Sorenson & Siegel, 1992). Similar to some Asian Americans, Mexican-American females are often not allowed to date until late adolescence, which may reduce exposure to situations in which sexual aggression could occur (Sorenson & Siegel, 1992). Moreover, a patriarchal culture that eschews violence against community members may have low levels of sexual assault, unlike mainstream U.S. culture, which is patriarchal and relatively accepting of interpersonal violence (Sorenson & Siegel, 1992).

Unlike non-Asian American groups in which males tend to be more sexually experienced than females (Rodgers & Rowe, 1993), Chinese American men had less sexual experience than Chinese-American women in Huang and Uba's (1992) sample. Perhaps this is because American stereotypes of Asian men are generally negative (e.g., "nerdy," socially inept; Huang & Uba, 1992). Indeed, although they are capable of assertive behavior, many Asian Americans may perceive themselves as nonassertive and socially unskilled (Zane, Sue, Hu, & Kwon, 1991). Huang and Uba (1992) speculated that Chinese Americans may delay sexual intercourse because (1) they want to wait until they are certain that there is adequate emotional commitment; and (2) they may have less positive body images than Caucasians do.

The picture of Asian-American males as perceiving themselves as socially unskilled and relatively unattractive physically (Huang & Uba, 1992) is strikingly similar to the perceptions of the virgins in the Jessor et al. (1983) study and the adolescents who did not use marijuana in the Shedler and Block (1990) study. As with virgins in the Jessor et al. (1982) study, Asian-American males who do not engage in sexual activity also do not engage in sexually coercive activity. Moreover, as with religiously oriented persons, when sexuality and sexual gratification are not central emphases in a person's life, it is possible that deviant patterns of physiological sexual arousal are less likely to develop.

There are potentially negative aspects of Asian cultural limitations on dating behavior. Dating may be done secretly to prevent the loss of social status (Yoshihama et al., 1991). Perpetrators may be able to be sexually aggressive with impunity in such secret dating relationships insofar as females are loathe to disclose the sexual abuse, which would reveal both the abuse and the socially unacceptable dating relationship (Yoshihama et al., 1991). The perpetrator may be able to continue the abuse by threatening the female with exposure of the relationship if she revealed the abuse (Yoshihama et al., 1991).

Is the relative absence of Asian-American deviant behavior a function of cultural influences? A collectivist cultural orientation may explain a lack of aggression against ingroup members, but may not explain the lack of aggression by Asian Americans against non-Asian outgroups. Although ingroup aggression is limited in Japan, outgroup aggression has been extensive in Japan's history, particularly during wartime. For example, the Japanese government recently admitted the large scale physical and sexual abuse of Korean women by Japanese soldiers during World War II, which has been well known and previously documented (Lai, 1986).

The lack of Asian-American aggression against outgroups may be at least partly a function of minority status and discrimination. Sue and Okazaki (1990) have argued that cultural influences are less important than ethnic minority status in explaining Asian-American academic achievement. Asian Americans achieve academically because discrimination has precluded Asian Americans from succeeding in other domains (e.g., business, entertainment, sports). Thus, academic achievement may be perceived by Asian Americans as the sole avenue for overcoming discrimination (Sue & Okazaki, 1990).

Significantly more so than other groups, Asian Americans fear that educational failure will have negative life consequences (Steinberg et al., 1992). Similarly, Asian Americans view police intervention, court time, and jail as more likely consequences for dating violence, and they view these consequences as more severe than do Latinos and African Americans (Miller & Simpson, 1991). Moreover, Asian Americans are more likely than Latinos and African Americans to perceive peer disapproval as a result of dating violence. However, Asian-American perceptions of legal interventions and peer disapproval for dating violence were not significantly different from the perceptions of European Americans (Miller & Simpson, 1991).

Although perceptions of peer disapproval of dating violence among Asian Americans were not significantly greater than that of European Americans, peer norms may influence Asian Americans' behavior. Asian Americans' academic performance tends to be more influenced by their Asian-American peers, who encourage and reward academic performance, than by their parents, who expect high performance but are not necessarily responsive to it in terms of reinforcement or supervision (Steinberg et al., 1992). Peer norms also appear to affect sexual behavior among Asian Americans as they do in other groups (Wyatt et al., 1993). Unlike virginity among mainstream American college students, virginity among Asian-American college students appears normative, insofar as 60% of the Huang and Uba (1992) sample were virgins. Presumably, if most of one's Asian peers are not engaging in coitus, there is less peer pressure toward compulsory heterosexual behavior (cf. Reed & Weinberg, 1984; Rodgers & Rowe, 1993; Wyatt et al., 1993). Having non-Asian peers also affects Asian Americans' sexual behavior. Whereas approximately one third of Chinese Americans who dated only Asians and Asian Americans had experienced coitus, 62.5% of those who dated European Americans had done so (Huang & Uba, 1992). Thus, Asian-American peers tend to have a conservative effect on Asian Americans' behavior, and the more limited the amount of sexual behavior, the more limited are the opportunities for aggressive sexual behavior.

Influences that deter antisocial behavior among Asian Americans are not necessarily applicable to other groups (cf. Catalano et al., 1993; Steinberg et al., 1992; Sue & Okazaki, 1990). The amount of sexual contact among non–Asian American college students is unlikely to decrease to the relatively low levels of sexual contact among Asian-American college students. Nevertheless, delaying coitus until a person is developmentally capable of making an emotional commitment may serve as a deterrent to sexually aggressive behavior. Early onset of coitus is positively associated with a number of sexual partners (Leitenberg et al., 1989), and sexually aggressive males are more likely to be sexually promiscuous than nonaggressive males (Malamuth et al., 1991) because promiscuity results in increased opportunities for sexual aggression (see chapter 2).

The low rates of antisocial behavior among Asian Americans may also have implications for prevention in non-Asian groups. Peer support appears to contribute to nondeviance among Asian Americans. Group identification may result in a sense of responsibility to help other group members avoid deviant behavior. Such group identification can be encouraged via cooperative education (Johnson & Johnson, 1989). Cooperation is a cultural value that may facilitate empathy and a lack of aggression among Asian Americans. Conversely, competition is highly valued in American society and is even fostered in the American educational system. However, cooperative learning experiences may actually facilitate achievement rather than hinder it (Johnson & Johnson, 1989).

Thus, aspects of Asian-American culture may serve as deterrents against the developmentally related personality problems, affective dyscontrol, cognitive distortions, and physiological sexual arousal that are motivational precursors to sexually aggressive behavior. Similar to persons having a religious orientation, the relatively limited sexual contact between unmarried Asian Americans may preclude opportunities for sexually aggressive behavior. Another similarity between Asian-American culture and religiosity is a patriarchal orientation, which may be used as an excuse to justify sexually aggressive behavior in a domestic context. However, some aspects of a culturally based patriarchal orientation, such as a sense of community and family nurturance, are not necessarily negative influences.

Conclusion

Mainstream American culture is one of the most violent in the world. However, there are certain religious and cultural communities within American culture whose values appear to deter sexually aggressive behavior. Religious and cultural factors that limit or delay heterosexual contact serve as deterrents against sexually aggressive behavior, insofar as heterosexual contact provides the opportunity for sexually aggressive behavior to occur (Malamuth et al., 1991). Religious and cultural influences may be transmitted by parents and reinforced by peers.

The American Psychological Association Commission on Violence and Youth (1993) recommended that cultural values be incorporated into violence-prevention programs in minority cultures. However, cultural or religious values that deter violent behavior may also be useful in violence-prevention programs for the majority group in the United States. Stevenson and Renard (1993) have suggested that racial socialization can enhance family functioning. Racial socialization includes parental instruction about societal racism, educational struggles, extended family relevance, spiritual or religious awareness, culture and cultural pride, and childrearing values (Stevenson & Renard, 1993). Although preventive interventions may need to be individually tailored for different ethnic groups (Catalano et al., 1993), the general principles of racial socialization appear useful to both ethnic minority and majority groups. Racial issues are not specific to persons of color but are also of relevance to European Americans (Helms, 1990).

Socialization toward non-Western cultural values may be viewed as elitist and racist. However, advocating that the positive aspects of non-Western cultures be adopted is no more racist than advocating feminist socialization is sexist. Perhaps the relatively greater acceptance of feminist values among social and behavioral scientists and in society is associated with the large number of women in society. White males may hold more feminist attitudes because they have more control over other groups and are less threatened by these groups, including White females, who are needed by White men as mothers, sisters, lovers, and wives (Williams, 1985). Conversely, Americans whose ancestors were from non-Western cultures have constituted a minority in terms of actual numbers as well as in societal power. The American majority has a history of controlling the sexual and nonsexual behavior of ethnic minority groups (Wyatt, 1994). Thus, there is less impetus in the majority group to consider non-Western values as an alternative.

Both religion and culture have been criticized as being patriarchal. Certain religious and cultural influences may delay the initiation of sexual relationships. However, patriarchal aspects of religion and culture that excuse sexual aggression in the context of the subordination of women are not preventive factors against sexual aggression once sexual relationships are initiated. Nevertheless, family nurturance and a sense of community may actually be *positive* aspects of patriarchal cultures that may also protect against sexual aggression (Sorenson & Siegel, 1992). Although specific religious and cultural influences may not be applicable across cultures, the current discussion of religion and culture suggests that positive parental and peer influences may serve as protective factors against sexual aggression. Thus, programs intended to reduce the risk of sexual aggression may direct their efforts toward enhancing positive parental and peer influences.

9

Reduction of Risk Factors for Sexually Aggressive Behavior

Is it ever too late to attempt to prevent sexually aggressive behavior? My answer to this question is a qualified no. Even when a person has committed multiple sexual offenses, there is about a 50% chance that he will not reoffend, and this likelihood may be reduced with preventive detention during critical periods of risk, by limiting access to potential victims, and with treatment interventions (see chapters 4, 6). Males in situations in which they are on the verge of sexually aggressive behavior can interrupt the sequence that leads to sexually aggressive behavior by using cognitive-behavioral methods, particularly relapse prevention, described in chapter 7.

Is it ever too *early* to attempt to prevent sexually aggressive behavior? My answer again is no. Once deviant patterns of behavior are established, it may be difficult to undo them, and early onset of deviant behavior is typically associated with severity (Coie et al., 1993; Rivera & Widom, 1990). Among sexual aggressors, those who first experience problems during childhood are at higher risk for recidivism and are more difficult to treat than those whose problems are less chronic (Hall & Hirschman, 1991). Effective preventive efforts with potential perpetrators of sexual aggression benefit not only the perpetrators but also potential victims and all of society in terms of the potential psychological and financial costs of sexual aggression (Daro, 1988; Prentky & Burgess, 1990).

Insofar as antisocial behavior may stabilize as early as age 5 or 6 (Loeber, 1982; Olweus, 1979), early preventive interventions may be imperative. Moffitt (1994) has suggested that primary prevention of violent behavior should occur before age 3. However, children may not be capable of understanding and retaining existing interventions to prevent sexual abuse until they are about school age (Daro, 1988; Haugaard & Reppucci, 1988). Preventive efforts should occur at the latest during late adolescence before 18 years of age (Moffitt, 1993).

The primary focus of the interventions described in Chapters 6 and 7 is the individual perpetrator. Although such *tertiary prevention* efforts with sexual aggressors usually focus on sexual offenders, who constitute a minority of all sexual aggressors (Koss, 1993a; McCall, 1993), this small percentage of sexual aggressors who are adjudicated may commit a disproportionately high percentage of sexually aggressive acts (Abel et al., 1987; Farrington et al., 1986). Thus, the development of effective interventions with this group could dramatically reduce crime (cf. G. Hall, 1990a; Moffitt, 1994). However, repeat sexual offenders, who often have developmentally related personality problems, are among the least amenable to existing treatment interventions (Hall & Hirschman, 1991, 1992; Hall, Shondrick, et al., 1993a). Moreover, sexual aggressors at the greatest risk for recidivism are those having a history of sexually aggressive behavior (see chapter 4), and treatment interventions cannot change a person's history.

One promising area of tertiary intervention is with adolescent sexual aggressors. Adolescent sexual aggressors often do not have the ingrained patterns of sexually aggressive behavior that adult sexual aggressors do, and they may be less pathological than adolescent nonsexual offenders (Oliver et al., 1993). Outcome data reported by Borduin et al. (1990) suggest that cognitive-behavioral multisystemic treatment is effective treatment with adolescent sexual offenders.

It is possible that the motivational precursors of sexually aggressive behavior and sexually aggressive behavior itself are recursive. In other words, repeated acts of sexual aggression may foster the development of deviant sexual arousal, distorted cognitions, and hostility toward women that may place a person at risk for additional sexually aggressive behavior. Thus, stopping sexually aggressive behavior after the first time it occurs may also have a role in preventing the development of motivational precursors of sexually aggressive behavior. Nevertheless, preventive interventions before males become sexually aggressive have the potential to be more effective and to have a broader societal impact than those interventions focused on males who have already begun to sexually act out.

Certain general risk factors for abuse have been identified that may warrant *secondary prevention* efforts. Perhaps the most predictive risk factor for perpetrating aggression is being male. Although many males are not physically or sexually aggressive, many more males than females perpetrate aggression, particularly sexual aggression (see chapter 1). Young males having conduct disorders may be at risk for subsequent antisocial behavior, and there exist many family-based interventions that appear effective in ameliorating the effects of conduct disorders (McMahon, 1994). To the extent that there exists a genetic transmission of general antisocial tendencies, boys of antisocial parents are at risk for perpetrating antisocial behavior (Mednick, Gabrielli, & Hutchings, 1984). Single and teen parents, low socioeconomic status or isolated families, parents of handicapped children, parents undergoing crises, and parents who experience conflict with their children may be at risk to abuse their children (Wolfe, 1987). Lower class parents are more likely to use physical discipline, authoritarian parenting, and less frequent verbal and cognitive stimulation (Patterson et al., 1989). However, unlike child abuse and neglect, which are often associated with poverty, sexual abuse occurs across the socioeconomic spectrum (Daro, 1988; Peters et al., 1986). Poor attachment bonds within families may be more specifically associated with the risk of child sexual abuse (Alexander, 1992).

Although the heterogeneity of high-risk families makes their identification difficult, a profile of a family at high risk for sexual abuse is one where the mother is absent or is unavailable because of disability, where there is mother-daughter or parental conflict, where the mother's educational status is less than father's, or where there is the presence of a stepfather (Melton, 1992). Sexually abused boys are at risk for perpetrating sexually aggressive behavior (Groth, 1979; Friedrich et al., 1992; Swift, 1979). Adult males at risk for violence against women include refugees, rural-urban migrants, unemployed men, alcoholics, and men in the process of separation and divorce (Koss et al., 1994).

Whereas the primary focus of tertiary secondary prevention is on actual or potential perpetrators, *primary prevention* typically focuses on factors in the potential perpetrator's environment. The discussion earlier in this chapter on protective factors suggests that parents and peers are appropriate foci for preventive efforts in the potential perpetrator's environment. A review of preventive interventions that enhance positive parental and peer influences that may deter sexually aggressive behavior follows.

Interventions in the Home

A mother's responsivity to an infant helps develop a secure attachment (Booth, Spieker, Barnard, & Morisset, 1992). Such responsivity includes sensitivity to a child's behavioral cues, responsivity to a child's distress, ability to foster social-emotional growth, and ability to foster cognitive growth. The development of a secure attachment between infant and parent may foster positive peer relationships and prevent later sexual and nonsexual acting out (Alexander, 1992; Belsky et al., 1991; Booth et al., 1992; Friedrich, 1990).

It has been suggested that the caregiving and relational responsibilities that society relegates to women in families make it unlikely for females to perpetrate sexual aggression (Barrett et al., 1990). Moreover, incestuous fathers tend to lack empathy for their child and tend not to be involved in child-care responsibilities (Williams & Finkelhor, 1990). Thus, sexual-abuse prevention programs for fathers may include parenting skill training (Daro, 1991).

As with mother-child attachment, an emphasis on father-child attachment is important in preventing sexual aggression, including the father's equal responsibility for the care and security of the child (Alexander, 1992). However, fathers have traditionally been ignored in the psychological literature on parenting interventions (Forehand, 1993). Moreover, most parenting courses have difficulty attracting fathers because they are more oriented toward mothers and may inadvertently communicate that childrearing is the mother's domain (Daro, 1991).

Daro (1988) suggested that the following interventions are important in preventing the sexual abuse of children:

1. Increasing the parent's knowledge of child development and the demands of parenting
2. Enhancing the parent's skill in coping with the stresses of infant and child care
3. Enhancing parent-child bonding, emotional ties, and communication
4. Increasing the parent's skills in coping with the stress of caring for children with special needs
5. Increasing the parent's knowledge about home and child management
6. Reducing the burden of child care
7. Increasing access to social and health services for all family members

Preschool children who are at risk for conduct disorders engage in a cycle of acting out, punishment, and rejection by parents (Landy & Peters, 1992; Patterson et al., 1989). Children who develop conduct disorders during the preschool and early school-age years may have the poorest long-term prognosis (Kazdin, 1987a; McMahon, 1994; Moffitt, 1993). An aggressive child's coercive behavior is reinforced insofar as parents use aggressive behavior (e.g., physical punishment) to terminate aversive intrusions (Haapasalo & Tremblay, 1994; Patterson et al., 1989). Thus, parents can be trained in stress and anger management so as not to scapegoat the child, as well as in ways of effectively controlling their children's behaviors without using physical punishment (Petersen & Brown, 1994). Parent interventions focused on monitoring children, prosocial fostering, discipline, and problem solving were associated with a reduction in teacher ratings of child antisocial behavior at school (Dishion, Patterson, & Kavanagh, 1992). Such parent interventions may be successfully implemented during home visits by nurses or paraprofessionals (Petersen & Brown, 1994).

Education and communication between parents and children about sex is also important in preventing sexual abuse (Parrot, 1991b). However, overly liberal or repressive attitudes about sex may both pose problems. Parents who communicate liberal attitudes about sexuality but who do not also respect sexual boundaries may put their children at risk for incest (Friedrich, 1990; Wyatt et al., 1993). Parents having liberal attitudes about sex should be explicit about when and with whom nudity and masturbation should occur (Wyatt et al., 1993). Children in such families also need to be aware that everyone does not share their liberal values (Wyatt et al., 1993).

Parents with repressive attitudes concerning sexuality may also put their children at risk for incest (Wyatt et al., 1993). It may be particularly difficult for a child who lacks sexual information to effectively withstand sexual advances, and the secrecy about sexual behavior may allow sexual abuse to occur without detection (Wyatt et al., 1993). Most adolescents look more to their peers than to their parents for information about sex, but peer influence about sexuality tends to be even greater among women who receive limited information from their parents about sexuality (Wyatt et al., 1993).

Parents may deny that their child is a perpetrator of sexual abuse or may blame the victim. Victims of sexual abuse are often punished by their parents for engaging in sexual behavior (Parrot, 1991b). However, parents need to teach boys to respect a "no" from a female (Parrot, 1991b). Moreover, parents need to develop empathy for victims and recognize that the perpetrator, not the victim, is responsible for deciding to become sexually aggressive (see chapter 1).

Early interventions serve as deterrents against some of the developmentally related personality problems that lead to sexually aggressive behavior. Parent-child attachment may assist a child in the development of empathy that may prevent the development of cognitive distortions about sexual aggression. Parental openness concerning sex education may prevent the development of sexual preoccupation and deviant sexual arousal that may motivate sexually aggressive behavior.

Prevention of antisocial behavior via parent training may be more effective with preadolescents (Kazdin, 1987b) than with adolescents (Patterson et al., 1989). Parenting patterns and antisocial behavior may be better established by adolescence. Moreover, influence over children's behavior shifts from their parents to their peers as they enter school. Thus, school-based interventions with a focus on a child's peers are needed to supplement interventions in the home.

Interventions in Schools

It is difficult for me to convincingly communicate to my two-year-old daughter the value of sharing toys and taking turns when other older children on the playground are grabbing toys away from her and not taking turns. Similarly, it is difficult to teach children to appreciate racial and cultural differences in a racist society. Thus, the effects of positive parenting may be enhanced or negated by children's peer involvement, which becomes increasingly influential at school.

Those children who gravitate toward antisocial peers tend to be those who fail academically (Patterson et al., 1989). Thus, efforts to increase rewards in academic settings may discourage children from seeking rewards from delinquent peers (Patterson et al., 1989). Patterson et al. (1989) suggest that prevention programs should include parent training, social skills training for the child, and academic remediation. Early intervention before the child experiences academic failure may be effective. Preschool intervention programs have been designed to help parents enhance their children's academic achievement (Levenstein, 1992; Weikart & Schweinhart, 1992).

Bonding

Hawkins et al. (1992) have designed a model program involving interventions during the first through fourth grades to bond children to their families and schools as prevention against drug use and antisocial behavior (Hawkins et al., 1992). The program is based on a social development model, which posits the importance of secure attachments via bonding with others. Bonding in the program is defined as: (1) attachment, a positive emotional or affective feeling toward others; (2) commitment, a sense of investment in a social unit; and (3) belief in the general morals or values held by a social unit. The three major components of the program are: (1) parent training, (2) child skills training, and (3) proactive classroom management. Such multilevel intervention appears necessary for effective prevention, insofar as competence in one domain (e.g., academic) is not necessarily associated with competence in others (e.g., family, peers; Cauce et al., 1992).

Parents are trained to identify desirable and undesirable behaviors in their children, to teach expectations for behavior, and to provide positive consequences for desired behaviors and moderate negative consequences for undesired behaviors in a consistent and contingent fashion (Hawkins et al., 1992). Parents are also trained to support their children's academic achievement via providing a positive learning environment at home, helping their children to develop reading and math skills, learning to communicate effectively with teachers, and supporting their children's progress. Children are trained in communication, decision making, negotiation, and conflict-resolution skills. High-risk children are targeted who exhibit early conduct disorders, peer rejections, and involvement with antisocial peers.

The proactive classroom management component trains teachers to provide clear expectations about behavior, and contingent encouragement and praise for student effort and progress (Hawkins et al., 1992). Teaching methods include interactive teaching, in which teaching objectives are modeled and mastery is expected of students before proceeding to more advanced work, and cooperative learning, which involves the use of small interdependent groups of students as learning partners in which success is contingent on the whole group's performance.

The Hawkins et al. (1992) prevention program appears effective. At the beginning of the fifth grade, children in the intervention group engaged in significantly less alcohol initiation and less delinquent behavior than children in a control condition. Although this program was not specifically designed to prevent sexually aggressive behavior, there is evidence that many of the positive effects of the Hawkins et al. (1992) program are the same factors that may delay the age of first coitus. Wyatt et al. (1993) reported the following factors that delayed age of first coitus among a community sample of adolescent females:

1. Family harmony
2. Parents' provision of education about sexuality and sexual boundaries
3. Absence of school problems
4. Absence of peer problems
5. Absence of violence
6. Absence of substance abuse
7. Absence of criminal activity
8. Emphasis on academic achievement

To the extent that delayed initiation of coitus decreases the opportunities for sexual aggression, it is probable that the bonding facilitated by the Hawkins et al. (1992) prevention program indirectly reduces sexually aggressive behavior. Delayed initiation of coitus may serve to reduce the development of deviant sexual arousal that may be associated with sexual preoccupation for some males. Moreover, the development of positive affect toward others may prevent affective dyscontrol. A sense of commitment to a social unit may be analogous to the sense of community in cultural groups that may serve as a source of empathy and a deterrent against cognitive distortions about sexually aggressive behavior. A general effect of the Hawkins et al. (1992) program also appears to be a reduction in the likelihood of negative childhood experiences that result in developmentally related personality problems.

Sexual Abuse Education

Perhaps the most popular school-based approach to sexual abuse prevention has been via sex education. In that 90% of children are in public schools (Coie et al., 1993), school-based programs are economical and avoid the stigma of identifying individual children or families at risk for sexual abuse (Daro, 1991). A combination of a few "universal" prevention programs, as well as programs targeted at high-risk individuals, for entire schools may could go a long way toward preventing various disorders (Coie et al., 1993).

Sexual abuse prevention education appears successful in transmitting facts about what sexual abuse is, in improving children's ability to identify body parts and what constitutes good and bad touching, in facilitating communication between children and parents about the problem of sexual abuse, and in increasing children's disclosure of sexual victimization (Finkelhor & Strapko, 1992). Programs that include active involvement (e.g., role plays) tend to be more effective than programs primarily consisting of passive exposure (e.g., film, discussion) or individual study

(Finkelhor & Strapko, 1992). Usually the training and use of teachers is less obtrusive than an outside person as the educator (Haugaard & Reppucci, 1988).

Older children are better able to benefit from sexual abuse prevention education than younger children (e.g., preschool, primary grades; Finkelhor & Strapko, 1992; Melton, 1992). Poor retention of information on sexual abuse in young children (e.g., preschool age) suggests that repetition of sexual abuse information is required (Haugaard & Reppucci, 1988). Moreover, "booster" sexual abuse prevention sessions are needed for children of all ages, insofar as prevention information can be forgotten in as little as one or two months (Finkelhor & Strapko, 1992).

American society values family privacy, and children are viewed as the property of their parents (Cohn, Finkelhor, & Holmes, 1985). Thus, although specific information about sexuality and specific, concrete rules and steps may be important in sexual abuse prevention efforts, many sexual abuse prevention programs exclude sexual material to appease parents and school systems (Finkelhor & Strapko, 1992; Haugaard & Reppucci, 1988; Melton, 1992). Instead, general discussions of good and bad touching and of bullies and people, usually other than parents, who attempt to coercively kiss a child are offered.

Sexual-abuse programs have tended to be ineffective in communicating that sexual abuse could be perpetrated by known adults (Finkelhor & Strapko, 1992; Melton, 1992). Moreover, prevention programs directed toward potential victims of sexual abuse have occasionally had *negative* effects, such as fostering a generalized fear of adults or of sexuality, or at best weakly positive effects (Melton, 1992). Sexual abuse prevention programs may also negatively affect children's positive relationships with adults and may cause at least temporary undue worry or fear (Haugaard & Reppucci, 1988). Also, if it is assumed that children are protected as a result of the programs, needed vigilance may decrease (Haugaard & Reppucci, 1988). Even children who are skilled at sexual abuse prevention techniques may be unable to stop some perpetrators, particularly adults who are physically and psychologically more powerful, from sexually abusing them (Reppucci & Haugaard, 1989). Simply telling children that they have control over their bodies does little to change abusive circumstances in which adults have power over children (Melton, 1992).

Unlike child physical abuse programs that have been targeted toward potential perpetrators, most child sexual abuse prevention efforts have been directed toward potential victims (Daro, 1991; Kaufman & Zigler, 1992; Melton, 1992). A sole emphasis on prevention strategies initiated by potential victims may imply that victims, rather than perpetrators, are responsible for preventing sexual aggression (see chapter 1). The sexual abuse prevention programs that are directed toward nonvictims tend to be for parents or teachers to protect children rather than toward potential perpetrators (Berrick, 1988; Borkin & Frank, 1986; Kleemeier, Webb, Hazzard, & Pohl, 1988; Kolko, Moser, & Hughes, 1989; Kolko, Moser, Litz, & Hughes, 1987; Swan, Press, & Briggs, 1985).

Whereas child physical abuse prevention programs often directly address the possibility of parents as abusers (e.g., Wolfe, 1987), child sexual abuse prevention programs rarely do so (Daro, 1988). Sexual abuse prevention programs that involve fathers may serve the dual purpose of helping fathers protect their children from sexual abuse outside the home and of discouraging fathers from becoming sexually abusive themselves because of the increased likelihood of children in sexual abuse prevention programs reporting their sexual approaches by their fathers (Finkelhor, 1986). However, rates of parental participation in child sexual abuse prevention programs are generally low (Berrick, 1988).

The identified potential perpetrators in sexual abuse prevention programs typically are adults rather than peer children. However, school-based interventions with child perpetrators can be effective. Olweus (1992) has described a program in which schools are encouraged to develop a positive and cooperative atmosphere and to take a clear stance against bullying behavior, including firm limits on unacceptable behavior and consistently applied nonhostile, nonphysical sanctions. Self-reports of bullying and of being victimized both significantly decreased over the one- to two-year period during which the program was implemented among approximately 2,500 fifth- through seventh-grade students. Presumably, a similar or modified approach would also be effective in preventing the perpetration of sexual aggression by children.

In summary, an emphasis in child sexual abuse prevention programs on young males as potential perpetrators may reduce the possibilities that young males develop cognitive distortions about sexually aggressive behavior or associate sexual arousal with sexually aggressive behavior. To the extent the child sexual abuse prevention programs reduce the likelihood of a child being sexually abused, they may prevent a child from experiencing developmentally related personality problems associated with sexually aggressive behavior. However, the emphasis on preventive strategies initiated by children—who, even when they appropriately implement prevention strategies, are often powerless to resist sexual advances by adults—underscores the importance of the responsibility of potential perpetrators in preventing sexual aggression.

Media Education

Whether or not there exists societal and community support for sex education, young males are already receiving sex education from the media. The media frequently transmit misogynous messages and propagate rape myths by portraying aggression as sexually arousing for perpetrators and victims. Thus, media violence may create less sympathy for victims of violence (Donnerstein, 1994). Such misogynous messages are not transmitted exclusively in pornography. Network television is replete with such messages. Moreover, the film ratings system is more tolerant of the presentation of sex combined with violence (i.e., R ratings) than the presentation of sex alone (i.e., X ratings; Donnerstein et al., 1987). Thus, repression of sexual information may make persons more susceptible to distorted information via the media.

Some have recommended that access to violent media, particularly that which glorifies violence or depicts violent pornography, be restricted (Herman, 1990; Lore & Schultz, 1993). However, the availability of pornography is not associated with increased sexual aggression (Kutchinsky, 1991). Moreover, it is unlikely that violent themes or violence combined with sex will ever be completely excised from the conventional media because of the public's huge appetite for violent media (see chapter 1). Even the elimination of the most extremely violent materials would probably have a negligible impact on the more conventional, mainstream portrayals of violence in the media.

Others have advocated public education concerning violent media and pornography (Donnerstein, 1994; Linz et al., 1987). Children can be taught "critical viewing skills" by parents and schools to interpret television content (American Psychological Association Commission on Violence and Youth, 1993). For example, educational programs could include information on how the mass media portray women (Donnerstein, 1994). One method of reducing the negative effects of aggressive media is debriefing that emphasizes the impact of sexual aggression on victims (Check & Malamuth, 1984). Such debriefing might be conducted in family settings or in schools. These interventions could prevent the development of physiological sexual arousal associated with sexual aggression in the media and could also prevent the development of cognitive distortions about sexually aggressive behavior.

The effects of media violence appear to be mediated by gender socialization. Media violence is associated with a long-term increase in the aggressive behavior of boys but not of girls (Turner, Hesse, & Peterson-Lewis, 1986), which suggests that it is the reinforcement of aggressive behaviors among boys, rather than the direct effects of violent media per se, that makes violent messages so influential (Lott & Maluso, 1993). Thus, it appears that gender socialization must radically change if males are to become less generally and sexually aggressive.

Feminist Socialization

Being female is a protective factor against sexually aggressive behavior insofar as the vast majority of sexual aggression is perpetrated by males (Koss et al., 1994). Although it is difficult to change biological factors associated with maleness, other than with antiandrogen hormonal treatments (see chapter 6), it may be possible to modify the manner in which males are socialized. A potentially effective alternative to traditional socialization, in which males are reinforced for aggressive behavior, is feminist socialization. There is evidence that men who possess feminine gender attributes hold fewer rape-supportive attitudes than do men who lack feminine gender attributes (Quackenbush, 1989).

Gender-based (and biased) socialization begins relatively early during a child's development. Between about ages 3 and 11 across cultures, children tend to choose same-gender playmates (Maccoby, 1988). Such gender segregation may occur because girls may find the aggressive play of boys aversive and because girls find it difficult to influence boys, who are often unresponsive (Maccoby, 1988). Thus, approximately eight influential years of a child's development are spent without much interaction with opposite-gender peers. This period of gender segregation seems to be a breeding ground for the development of sexist attitudes and behaviors.

It has been advocated that elementary schools should stop gender segregation in play and work groups (Enke & Sudderth, 1991; Parrot, 1991b). Children need opportunities to interact in nonsexual and nonromantic settings. Mutual interests and activities, rather than gender, could become the basis of friendships. Such nonsexual friendships could better prepare young men and women for sexual relationships as a deeper way of interacting (Enke & Sudderth, 1991; Wyatt et al., 1993). Males need to learn that not having sex is acceptable in a relationship and that they need not comply with peer or societal expectations to engage in sex (Enke & Sudderth, 1991; Parrot, 1991a).

One method of early prevention of sexist behaviors, and ultimately of sexual aggression, is cooperative education (Johnson & Johnson, 1989). Cooperative education rewards cooperation rather than competition. Thus, boys and girls need to be interdependent to succeed. Possible effects of combined gender cooperative education are the prevention of males' tendency to oversexualize relationships (Abbey, 1987) and the development of cross-gender empathy that may prevent the development of cognitive distortions about the effects of sexually aggressive behavior.

Interventions in Colleges

Much sexually aggressive behavior occurs on college campuses (Koss et al., 1987). As with child sexual abuse prevention programs, most college campus prevention programs typically have been directed toward potential victims (Roark, 1989). Perhaps this emphasis on potential victims has been a function of the difficulty in attracting potential perpetrators to programs on the prevention of sexual aggression. Perpetrators of acquaintance rapes on college campuses are unlikely to be apprehended for their crimes and are thus even less likely to be treated for sexually aggressive behavior in clinical settings (Hall, Shondrick, et al., 1993a). Therefore, attempts at primary preventive interventions with potential perpetrators may hold more promise than tertiary preventive interventions, which may be virtually nonexistent for perpetrators of acquaintance rapes.

What could serve as the hook for potential perpetrators on college campuses to voluntarily become involved in prevention programs? Offering voluntary seminars or classes on sexual aggression will most likely attract men who are already sufficiently sensitive to recognize the importance of such information. Another suggested approach has been to make sexual-aggression prevention a mandatory component of orientations for campus organizations that may foster sexist attitudes, including fraternities, sports teams, or campus military organizations (Herman, 1990; Koss & Gaines, 1993; Parrot, 1991a). However, mandatory prevention programs, particularly those that are confrontive, may actually result in *increased* rape myth acceptance (Fischer, 1986; Jaffe et al., 1992) when men experience psychological reactance and generate counterarguments to the information that is presented. Moreover, interventions that target specific groups may reach few of the potential perpetrators of sexual aggression on campus.

An innovative program to help college students learn to control their drinking behavior has been described by (Kivlahan, Marlatt, Fromme, Coppel, & Williams, 1990). An eight-week course on alcohol use offered students an opportunity to learn more about, or to change, their drinking behavior. Subjects were paid for their participation. A skill-training condition implemented concepts from relapse prevention (Marlatt & George, 1984) and emphasized interaction among instructors and participants. An alcohol-information condition was based on a disease model of alcoholism and consisted of lectures and films, with limited class discussion on the hazards of alcohol consumption (Kivlahan et al., 1990). Subjects in both conditions significantly reduced their self-reported alcohol consumption at a one-year follow-up, with the results favoring the skill-training approach. In a replication of the Kivlahan et al. (1990) approach, subjects who participated in a skills-training approach reduced their drinking rates by approximately 40% and maintained this reduction over a two-year follow-up (Baer et al., 1992).

The effectiveness of the Kivlahan et al. (1990) approach with college students suggests that a similar approach might be possible with the prevention of sexual aggression. However, unlike alcohol consumption, sexual aggression is a socially undesirable behavior. Thus, a venue other than a class on sexual aggression would be required. One of the most popular undergraduate courses on most college campuses is the human sexuality course. The topic of sexual aggression is appropriate in the context of this course, and many potential perpetrators could be reached because of the popularity of the course.

Similar to the Kivlahan et al. (1990) results, it appears that didactic approaches to sexual-aggression prevention may be less effective than approaches that are more personally engaging. A didactic program did not change undergraduate men's attitudes about rape or increase empathy for rape victims (Borden, Karr, & Caldwell-Colbert, 1988). However, a psychoeducational approach in which presenters role-played vignettes on rape myths significantly reduced the rape-supportive attitudes of college men at a one-month follow-up relative to men who did not receive the psychoeducational intervention (Gilbert et al., 1991). Moreover, a videotape of a rape-education workshop was as effective as a live workshop in reducing college men's and women's rape myths (Fonow, Richardson, & Wemmerus, 1992). The prevention program helped men and women learn that rapes are more likely to take place in a familiar setting, to be perpetrated by someone known to the victim, and to be a form of social control over women. A videotape of victims of sexual aggression discussing their victimization combined with instructions to imagine how the victims would feel was more effective than an informational videotape on rape myths and facts in reducing acceptance of interpersonal violence, adversarial sexual beliefs, and self-reported likelihood of sexual abuse of children and rape of women (Schewe & O'Donohue, 1993b). Thus, personal participation is not necessarily associated with prevention-program effectiveness for men, although programs that are personally engaging apparently are. Effective prevention programs for college men appear to reduce cognitive distortions concerning sexually aggressive behavior, which may be the primary motivational precursor of sexual aggression among college men (Hall & Hirschman, 1991). Combining training on controlled drinking (e.g., Kivlahan et al., 1990) and training on prevention of sexual aggression appears appropriate in that much campus sexual aggression occurs in the context of alcohol consumption (Koss & Gaines, 1993).

Interventions in Society

In the Newbery Award-winning children's book, *The Giver* (Lowry, 1993), a futuristic society is described in which there is no conflict, poverty, unemployment, divorce, injustice, inequality, or sexual aggression. As might be expected, there are also costs to this attempt at utopia. There is no color, no variety in the terrain, no experience of emotional extremes, and a strict language protocol. A committee dictates the rules of this society, and citizens are reminded of these rules via an intercom system. All sexual behavior is exclusively utilized for purposes of procreation, and procreative duties are assigned to a few individuals as a low-status job. Sexual behavior is curbed immediately following adolescents' first "stirrings" (i.e., sexual dreams or fantasies). From adolescence until death, persons in this society take pills to control their sexual desires (cf. antiandrogen hormones). Ironically, any person who violates the society's rules three times (cf. "three strikes, you're out") is "released" to an unknown "real world." However, it is later revealed that release actually means death.

The goal of preventive efforts is prevention with a minimum of unintended side effects, such as the extreme social control exercised in the society described in *The Giver*. It could be argued that preventive interventions interfere with people's right to privacy (Daro, 1991), and any of the proposed interventions described in this book could be misused. For example, antiandrogen drugs could be administered to adolescents considered "at risk" for sexually aggressive behavior. However, those who are considered at risk are likely to differ from those who are not considered at risk on a variety of sociocultural dimensions that would render the at-risk group relatively powerless. Nevertheless, some society-wide interventions may be necessary for our society to become less sexually aggressive.

Perhaps if sexually aggressive behavior and other forms of aggression carried more serious societal sanctions, potential perpetrators might be better deterred from aggression (Lore & Schultz, 1993). Rather than having negative effects, aggressive behavior, particularly that between acquaintances or family members, often has positive effects (e.g., increased control of victim; Straus, 1973). Conviction rates for sexually aggressive acts are low, and when sexual aggressors are convicted, their sentences are often limited (Allison & Wrightsman, 1993; Fitzgerald, 1993; Koss, 1993a). Caps on damage awards by the legal system imply that sexual harassment and other forms of sexual aggression are not as serious as other legal violations (Fitzgerald, 1993). If society viewed sexual aggression more seriously, perhaps potential sexual aggressors would do so, as well. However, increased societal sanctions against sexually aggressive behavior in the absence of concomitant prevention efforts, such as those described in this book, are unlikely to be effective deterrents against sexual aggression.

Poverty, poor housing, school failure, unemployment, and inadequate family life are all potential foci for societal interventions against antisocial behavior (Moffitt, 1994). Effective prevention efforts must occur at multiple levels, including with individuals, families, schools, peers, and community environments (Coie et al., 1993; Haugaard & Reppucci, 1988). Such coordinated efforts require cooperative efforts among educational, governmental, health, and human service systems (Coie et al., 1993). Coie et al. (1993) have suggested that

> it should not be difficult . . . to persuade parents, teachers, legislators, or the general public of the intrinsic merits of training children or adults in social skill development, problem solving, or family communication and conflict management, even if these skills cannot be justified as preventing a specific form of disorder (p. 1019).

Insofar as preventive interventions that may reduce the risk for sexually aggressive behavior may also reduce the risk for other disorders (e.g., nonsexual aggression), sexual aggression researchers may be able to combine their efforts with those of other prevention researchers. Ultimately, change must occur at the societal level by reducing sexism and racism, and the economic disparity between white males and others (Gottfried, 1991; Koss, 1990).

Alexander (1992) has recommended that greater support for families is a preventive measure against child sexual abuse. Such support may include maternity and paternity leave, flexible work schedules, improved day-care options, parent education, and the routine use of mediation in divorce proceedings and custody disputes (Alexander, 1992; Fitzgerald, 1993). Family support may also serve to elevate women's status in society, which may serve as a deterrent against sexually aggressive behavior (Fitzgerald, 1993). Opportunities for well-paid employment for males provide rewards for nonviolent behavior (Scott, 1992).

Conclusion

Most interventions involving potential perpetrators of sexual aggression have constituted secondary or tertiary prevention with known sexual aggressors. Primary prevention involves the identification of risk factors before a person engages in sexually aggressive behavior. Family- and school-based interventions may serve to reduce risk factors for sexually aggressive behavior among males, although there are no prevention programs specifically designed for potential child perpetrators of sexual aggression and extremely few programs specifically designed to prevent sexually aggressive behavior among men. Although certain aspects of various prevention programs address each of the four motivational precursors of sexually aggressive behavior, few directly address the affective dyscontrol motivational precursor.

Sexual aggression is intricately woven into the fabric of society. Unfortunately, sexual aggression is considered by some men as simply an assertion of the traditional masculine gender role (Herman, 1990; Koss et al., 1994). Disentangling sexual aggression from "normal" male development first requires its recognition as a problem. Victims have effectively emphasized sexual aggression as a societal problem, but society's response has typically been to create interventions for victims rather than for the perpetrators, who are responsible for sexually aggressive behavior. However, such victim-oriented prevention restricts the freedom and mobility of potential victims (Koss, 1990; Schewe & O'Donohue, 1993a). Existing perpetrator-oriented interventions have touched only the tip of the iceberg by dealing primarily with the minority of sexual aggressors who are apprehended and convicted. Perhaps this focus on these atypical sexual aggressors allows society to relegate sexual aggression to an extreme behavior engaged in only by abnormal individuals. However, a much broader focus on males at all developmental levels may be much more effective in preventing sexually aggressive behavior. Thus, society's acceptance of responsibility for sexual aggression may be the first step in effectively attempting to reduce it. And we must prevent sexual aggression if society is to become safer for future generations.

Appendix A: Clinical Interview

I. Offense Data
    A. What led up to your being here?
        (Does offender admit offense?)
    B. What happened in the offense that led to your being here?
        (How does this correspond with victim/police statements? If offender's version does not correspond, ask him about discrepancies.)
    C. Sex of victim(s)   Age of victim(s)
        1. Did you know the person (victim)?
            a. How did you know her/him?
            b. How long did you know her/him?
    D. When did you first think of having sexual contact with her/him?
        1. What led up to the sexual contact?
        2. What did you think about before the sexual contact?
            a. Did you plan the sexual contact in advance?
        3. Were you sexually excited during the sexual contact?
            a. Did you have an orgasm during the sexual contact?
    E. How did your victim react to the sexual contact?
        a. Was she/he scared of you?
        b. Was she/he hurt?
        c. Did you use physical force on your victim(s)?
        d. Did you use a weapon in your offense(s)?
    F. How many times did you have sexual contact with your victim(s)?
        1. Over what time period? (years, months).
        2. Where did the sexual contact occur?
        3. Were others present?
    G. Did you worry about getting caught?
        1. Did you do anything to prevent getting caught?
        2. Did you tell your victim(s) not to tell?
        3. Did you bribe your victim(s)?
        4. Did you threaten your victim(s)?
    H. Were drugs or alcohol involved in any of your offense(s)?
        1. How?
    I. Was there anything unusual going on in your life during the time of your offense(s)?

J. What kind of effect do you think your offense(s) had on your victim(s)?
    1. What kind of effect did your offense(s) have on you?

K. Did you ever try to stop yourself from sexual activity with your victim(s)?
    1. What did you try?
    2. How did it work?

L. How did you get caught for these offense(s)?
    1. What effect did getting caught have on you?
    2. What was wrong about what you did to your victim(s)?

M. How would you prevent yourself from sexually reoffending in the future?

II. Early Developmental History
    A. I'd like to find out a little bit about how things were when you were growing up. Where were you born?
    B. Is your father living?
        (If not) When did he die and of what?
        1. What kind of person was your father?
            (If patient has difficulty, ask how he was regarded in the community.)
        2. What did your father do for a living?
        3. How well off was your family financially?
        4. What is the longest amount of time your family spent at one location?
        5. How many times did your family move?
        6. How did you get along with your father?
        7. Was your father affectionate?
        8. How did he discipline you?
            a. Was this form of discipline fair?
        9. Did he ever do anything that was physically or sexually abusive to you or your brothers and sisters?
        10. Did you ever have any physical fights with your father?
        11. Did your father have any alcohol or drug problems?
        12. Was your father ever arrested for anything?
        13. Was your father ever absent from the home for any length of time?
        14. Was he ever in counseling or in a psychiatric hospital?
    C. Were your parents happily married?
        1. Who decided how the money was spent?
        2. Who was in charge of disciplining the children?
        3. Which of your parents were you closest to?

4. Which of your parents does your personality resemble?
5. Did your parents have any physical fights that you knew of?
6. Did either of your parents have sex outside the marriage?

D. Is your mother living? (If not) When did she die and of what?
   1. Describe your mother.
   2. Did your mother work? What kind of job?
   3. How did you get along with her?
   4. Was your mother affectionate?
   5. How did she discipline you?
      Was this form of discipline fair?
   6. Did she ever do anything that was physically or sexually abusive to you or your brothers and sisters?
   7. Did you ever have any physical fights with your mother?
   8. Did your mother have any alcohol or drug problems?
   9. Was your mother ever arrested for anything?
   10. Was your mother ever absent from the home for any length of time?
   11. Was she ever in counseling or in a psychiatric hospital?

E. Did your family go to church?
   1. What kind of church?
   2. Were your parents of the same faith?
   3. How much effect did religion have on your family?

F. Did you ever live away from home as a child?
G. Who besides your parents were frequently in the home? (e.g., grandparents, relatives, etc. Look for possible perpetrators of sexual abuse.)
H. Were your parents ever divorced?
   1. Did you ever have any stepparents?
      (If so, ask above parent questions for each stepparent.)

I. How many brothers and sisters do you have? (number older, younger)
   1. Did your position in the family (e.g., oldest, youngest, middle) have any significance in your family?
   2. How did you get along with your brothers and sisters?
   3. Did you ever have any physical fights with any of them?
   4. Did you ever have any type of sexual contact with your brothers or sisters?

5. Were your brothers or sisters arrested for anything before the age of 18?

J. How did you do in school?
   1. What kind of grades did you get?
   2. Did you ever have to repeat a grade?
   3. Were you ever in special classes? When and for what?

K. Were you ever truant from school?
   1. Were you ever suspended or expelled from school?

M. Did you have any trouble making friends?
   1. Were you a "loner?"
   2. Were you involved in any extracurricular activities,
      such as Boy Scouts or sports teams?
   3. Did you have any fights with your peers?

N. Did you have any serious medical problems growing up?
   1. Did you ever have to take any type of medicine before
      you were 18?

O. Did you ever have a job when you were growing up?
   1. (if yes) How long was the longest job?

P. Did you ever see a counselor before age 18?
   1. Were you ever in a psychiatric hospital before age 18?

III. Juvenile Sexual History
   A. How did you find out about sex?
      1. Did your parents allow you to ask questions about
         sex?
      2. How did your parents usually respond to questions
         about sex?
      3. How old were you when you had your first "wet
         dream" (nocturnal emission)?
         a. Had you been told about these in advance? How
            and by whom?
         b. How did you react?
      4. When did you begin to masturbate?
         a. What did you think about when you mastur-
            bated?
         b. Did you ever think that masturbation would
            harm you in any way?
         c. Did you ever feel guilty about masturbating?
         d. How often did you masturbate from ages 11 to
            14?
         e. Were you ever discovered while masturbating?
   B. Did you ever peep on anyone while she or he was undressing
      or having sex?
      1. Did you ever expose yourself to anyone?

C. Did you have any sexual contact with other children when you were growing up?
  1. (If yes) How old were you?
  2. How old was the other child?
  3. What did this involve?
  4. How many times did this happen?
  5. Did you have sexual contact with any other children while you were growing up?
  6. Did you ever force anyone to have sex before you were 18?

D. Do you remember any upsetting sexual experiences that occurred during childhood?
  1. Were you ever sexually abused during childhood?

E. When did you become sexually interested in girls your own age?
  1. Any difficulty making friends with girls?
  2. When did you start dating?
    a. In groups?
    b. On single dates?
  3. Did you date many different people or did you usually have a steady relationship with one person at a time?
    a. Were you involved in any type of sexual contact on these dates? (If yes, describe)
  4. Did you form any lasting relationships with girls?
  5. Did you have any sexual interest in boys?

F. When was your first sexual intercourse?
  1. How old was your partner?
  2. How did you respond sexually? (Did you have an orgasm?)
    a. Were there problems with erection or premature ejaculation?
    b. How did you feel about this?
  3. Was this in a lasting relationship?
  4. What did you think of the girls who would have sex with you?
    a. What about those who refused?

G. How many different sexual partners have you had in your life?
  1. How many of your partners were older than you?
    a. How many of your partners were younger than you?
    b. How old was your youngest partner?
      (1) How old were you?
  2. How long was your longest sexual relationship?

     3. How many of your partners have you gotten pregnant?
       a. How do you feel about this?

  H. Have any of your sexual partners been male?
     1. (If yes) Have you ever gotten into trouble for having sex with males?
     2. How many of your partners were older than you?
       a. How many of your partners were younger than you?
       b. How old was your youngest partner?
         (1) How old were you?

IV. Juvenile Delinquency
  A. Did you ever run away from home?
  B. Did you ever get into trouble for lying?
  C. Were you ever involved in any vandalism, stealing, or shoplifting?
  D. Were you ever arrested before the age of 18 for anything?
     1. If yes, were you ever in a juvenile detention center?

  E. How old were you when you began to drink?
     1. How often did you get drunk?

  F. Did you use any type of drugs before age 18?
     1. What kinds and when?
     2. How often?
     3. Were you addicted to any of these drugs?
       a. Did you inject any of these drugs?
     4. How did you get the drugs?
       a. How did you get the money for the drugs?
     5. Did you sell drugs to other people?
       a. What did you sell?

V. Military/College
  A. How far did you go in school?
     1. (if not graduated from high school) Did you complete a GED? When?
  B. How old were you when you moved away from home to live on your own?
  C. Were you ever in the military? (If no, go to D.)
     1. Branch?
     2. How long? (less than 2 years may mean problems)
     3. Did you enlist or were you drafted?
     4. What was your highest rank?
     5. What was your MOS (Military Occupational Specialty)?
     6. Where were you stationed?

7. Were you involved in combat?
8. What kinds of sexual experiences did you have in the service?
9. Did you have alcohol or drug problems during the service?
10. Did you have any disciplinary problems? (e.g., Article 15s, AWOLs, court-martials).
11. Did you ever see a counselor or a psychiatrist during the service?
12. Did you receive any honors or awards?
13. What kind of discharge did you receive?
14. Did you notice any changes in yourself before and after the service?
    a. Did anyone else notice any changes in you?

D. Did you ever attend school beyond high school?
1. (if yes) What kind of school was it?
2. What kinds of sexual experiences did you have while attending this school?
3. Did you have any problems at this school?

VI. Marital/Family History
A. Have you ever lived with a person without being married?
1. (If yes) How many different women have you lived with?
    a. How long was the longest of these relationships?
    b. How long was the shortest of these relationships?
2. Have you ever had a sexual relationship with a male that you lived with?
    a. (If yes) How long was the longest of these relationships?
    b. How long was the shortest of these relationships?

B. Are you married? (include lasting live-in relationships)
1. Happily?
2. How long have you been married?
3. How did you meet your wife?
4. What made you decide to marry her?
5. What did she like about you?
6. How old were you when you got married?
    a. How old was she?
7. How has your sexual relationship been?
    a. How often do you have sexual intercourse?
    b. Do you use any type of birth control?
    c. Have you ever forced your wife to have sex?

8. Who decides how the money is spent?
9. Does you wife work?
10. Have you had any problems in your marriage?
11. How do you handle disagreements with your wife?
12. Have you ever been separated?
13. Have you ever hit or hurt your wife for any reason?
14. Have you or your wife ever had sex with anyone else during the time you have been married?
    a. (if yes) Did your wife know about this?
    b. (or) how did you find out about this?
15. Have you ever had any type of marriage counseling?
16. How does your wife feel about your offense?

C. Have you ever been married before?
   1. When? (If so, ask above wife questions on each wife)
   2. What was the reason for your divorce(s)?

D. Do you have any children?
   1. How old are they?
   2. Who is in charge of disciplining the children?
   3. How do you discipline them? (Look for physical abuse.)
   4. How do you feel your children affect your relationship with your partner?
      a. Do you feel they affect your sexual relationship in any way?
         (1) For example, do you feel concerned about a lack of privacy with the children around?
   5. How have the children done in school?
   6. Have they had any problems?
   7. Have your children had any sexual problems?
   8. Have you fantasized about sexual contact with any of your children?
      a. Have you masturbated to fantasies about sexual contact with any of your children?
      b. Have you had sexual contact with any of your children?
   9. How do your children feel about your offense(s)?
   10. Have they had any drug or alcohol problems?
   11. Have they ever had to see a counselor or been in a psychiatric hospital?
   12. Have they ever been arrested for anything?

E. Has religion been important to your family?
   1. (If so) What church do you attend?
   2. How often?

VII. Adult Sexuality
    A. What is your attitude about sex?
        1. What specific sexual activities are enjoyable?
        2. Do you ever feel dirty or guilty about sexual thoughts or about sex?

    B. On a scale of 1 to 10, with 10 being high and 1 being low, rate how much you like the following persons sexually:

	Females	*Males*
Older		
Same age		
14–17 years		
10–13		
6–9		
2–5		
below 2		

    C. Do you feel that men and women should have distinct and different roles in nonsexual activities?
        1. In sexual activities?

    D. How do you see the place of sex in marriage?
    E. What do you think about two males having a sexual relationship?
        1. Have you had any sexual contact with other adult males since you have been an adult?

    F. Have you ever experienced any problems in having sex with your partners?
    G. Have you ever had gonorrhea or any other venereal disease?
    H. What kind of pornography have you used?
        1. Have you used pornography that depicted rape?
        2. Have you used pornography that depicted bondage, force, or violence?
        3. Have you used child pornography?
        4. Do you masturbate while using pornography?

    I. Have you peeped on anyone?
    J. Have you had any sexual contact with animals?
    K. Have you been sexually attracted to articles of clothing?
        1. Have you cross-dressed?

    L. Have you made obscene phone calls?
    M. Have you exposed yourself to anyone?
    N. Have you had any fantasies about sexual contact with anyone under the age of 18 whom you haven't already mentioned?
        1. Have you masturbated to fantasies about sexual con-

        tact with anyone under the age of 18 whom you haven't already mentioned?

    2. Have you sexual contact with anyone under the age of 18 that you haven't already mentioned?
(If yes, use the questions in Part I)

O. Have you used a prostitute?
    1. How old was the prostitute you used?
    2. What is the total number of prostitutes you have used?
    3. Were any of the prostitutes male?

P. Have you had fantasies of forcing someone to have sex?
    1. Have you masturbated to fantasies of forcing someone to have sex?
    2. Have you forced anyone to have sex with you, other than the persons you have already mentioned?
(If yes, use the questions in Part I)

VIII. Employment/Peer Relationships
  A. What kinds of jobs have you had since leaving school (or the service)?
    1. What is the longest job you have held?
    2. Have you ever had any problems with other workers or your employers?
    3. Were you ever fired from a job?
    4. Have you ever been on unemployment compensation or welfare?
    5. Are you working now?
      a. What is your job?
      b. How long have your worked there?
      c. Does your employer know about your offense history?
    6. What kind of job would you hope to have in the future?

  B. What is the longest amount of time you have lived in one location as an adult?
  C. Is there any friend or group of friends you usually spend time with?
    1. What activities do you do with them? (Elicit unspoken problem areas, probe for significance of "close" relationships.)
    2. Have they been supportive of you?
    3. Do you usually get into trouble with them?
    4. Have you had any fights with your friends about anything?

  D. What do you do in your free time?

E. Do you go to church?
    1. If yes, which church?
    2. How does your religion affect the way you live?

IX. Alcohol/Drugs
  A. Have you ever had any drinking problems?
    1. How often do you drink?
      a. How much?
    2. Have you ever missed work because of drinking?
    3. Has your drinking ever interfered with your relationships with others?
    4. How does alcohol affect you sexually?
    5. Are you able to stop drinking when you want to?
    6. Have you ever gotten sick after you stopped drinking, having a feeling that you had to have another drink?
    7. Have you ever gone to anyone for help about your drinking (e.g., counselor, Alcoholics Anonymous)?
      a. How did this treatment work?

  B. What kinds of drugs have you used as an adult?
    1. When did you use these drugs?
    2. How often?
      a. How much?
      b. Did you inject any of these drugs?
    3. How did you get the money to buy the drugs?
    4. Have you ever had problems stopping drug use?
    5. Have drugs interfered with your life in any way?
    6. How have drugs affected you sexually?
    7. Have you ever had any type of drug treatment?
      a. What type?
      b. How did it work out?

  C. Do you have any alcohol or drug related arrests? (DWIs, drunk in public, drug possession/dealing)

X. Psychiatric/Medical History
  A. How do you handle being alone?
  B. Do you find yourself being bored much of the time?
  C. Describe your general moods.
  D. Have you had any problems sleeping lately?
  E. Have you gained or lost weight recently?
  F. Have you ever thought about killing yourself without actually doing anything about it?
  G. Have you ever actually tried to hurt, harm, or kill yourself?
  H. Have you ever received any counseling or mental health treatment as an adult?
    1. Did a psychiatrist ever prescribe medication for you?

      2. Have you ever been in a psychiatric hospital as an adult?

      3. Have any of your brothers or sisters been in a psychiatric hospital as an adult?

I. Have you had any major medical problems as an adult?

J. Have you ever had any serious head injuries?

      1. Have you ever had seizures?

K. Have you ever seen or heard anything that other people might not see or hear?

      1. (If yes to heard) Did the sounds come from inside or outside of your head (inside may mean obsessional thoughts, outside may mean hallucinations)?

L. Have you ever felt afraid of germs or that you had to wash your hands several times a day?

M. Is there anything you feel afraid of?

N. Have you ever felt that things were unreal or that part of your body was paralyzed without physical reason?

O. Have you ever felt that you could magically read other people's minds?

      1. Have you ever felt that other people could read your mind or that they were plotting against you?

XI. Adult Criminal History/Impulse Control

  A. Have you committed any crimes as an adult that you have not been arrested for?

      1. Do you have any arrests as an adult for crimes other than sex offenses?

  B. Have any of your brothers or sisters been arrested as adults for anything?

  C. What kinds of situations make you angry?

      1. How do you usually express your anger?

      2. Do you have any ways of controlling your anger?

      3. Has anyone ever told you that you have an anger problem?

          a. Do you think you have an anger problem?

      4. Do you ever worry that you might physically hurt somebody?

      5. What is the most violent thing you have ever done? (Or what is the closest you have ever come to being violent?)

          a. Have you ever tried to or actually killed someone?

      6. Have you ever been in jail?

          a. Did you have any problems there?

          b. Were you ever in prison?

          (1) Did you have any problems in prison?

       7. Have you ever been on probation?
          a. Did you ever violate any of the conditions of your probation?
          b. Have you ever had your probation revoked?

XII. Outcome
    A. Do you want to receive treatment for your problems?
       1. (If not) What do you want?

References

Abbey, A. (1987). Misperceptions of friendly behavior as sexual interest: A survey of naturally occurring incidents. *Psychology of Women Quarterly, 11,* 173–194.

Abbey, A. (1991). Acquaintance rape and alcohol consumption on college campuses: How are they linked? *Journal of American College Health, 39,* 165–169.

Abel, G. G., Becker, J. V., Mittelman, M. S., Cunningham-Rathner, J., Rouleau, J. L., & Murphy, W. D. (1987). Self-reported sex crimes of nonincarcerated paraphiliacs. *Journal of Interpersonal Violence, 2,* 3–25.

Abel, G. G., Blanchard, E. B., & Barlow, D. H. (1981). Measurement of sexual arousal in several paraphilias: The effects of stimulus modality, instructional set and stimulus content on the objective. *Behaviour Research and Therapy, 19,* 25–33.

Abel, G. G., Blanchard, E. B., Murphy, W. D., Becker, J. V., & Djenderedjian, A. (1981). Two methods of measuring penile response. *Behavior Therapy, 12,* 320–328.

Abel, G. G., Gore, D. K., Holland, C., Camp, N., Becker, J., & Rathner, J. (1989). The measurement of the cognitive distortions of child molesters. *Annals of Sex Research, 2,* 135–152.

Abel, G. G., Lawry, S. S., Karlstrom, E., Osborn, C.A., & Gillespie, C. F. (1994). Screening tests for pedophilia. *Criminal Justice and Behavior, 21,* 115–131.

Abel, G. G., Mittleman, M. S., & Becker, J. V. (1985). Sex offenders: Results of assessment and recommendations for treatment. In M. H. Ben-Aron, S. J. Hucker, & C. D. Webster (Eds.), *Clinical criminology: The assessment and treatment of criminal behavior* (pp. 207–220). Toronto: M & M Graphics.

Abel, G. G., Mittleman, M., Becker, J. V., Rathner, & Rouleau, J. (1988). Predicting child molesters' response to treatment. In R. A. Prentky & V. L. Quinsey (Eds.), *Human sexual aggression: Current perspectives* (pp. 223–234). New York: New York Academy of Sciences.

Ageton, S. (1983). *Sexual assault among adolescents.* Lexington, MA: Lexington Books.

Alexander, P. C. (1992). Application of attachment theory to the study of sexual abuse. *Journal of Consulting and Clinical Psychology, 60,* 185–195.

Allison, J. A., & Wrightsman, L. S. (1993). *Rape: The misunderstood crime.* Newbury Park, CA: Sage.

American Psychiatric Association. (1980). *A psychiatric glossary* (5th ed.). Boston: Little, Brown.

American Psychiatric Association. (1994). *Diagnostic and statistical manual of mental disorders* (4th ed., revised). Washington, DC: Author.

American Psychological Association Commission on Violence and Youth. (1993). *Violence and youth: Psychology's response.* Washington, DC: American Psychological Association.

Anastasi, A. (1988). *Psychological testing* (6th ed.). New York: MacMillan.

Archer, J. (1991). The influence of testosterone on human aggression. *British Journal of Psychology, 82,* 1–28.

Associated Press (1994, May 25). Caning spurs on American plans. *Kent-Ravenna Record Courier,* A3.

Averill, J. R. (1993). Illusions of anger. In R. B. Felson & J. T. Tedeschi (Eds.), *Aggression and violence: Social interactionist perspectives* (pp. 171–192). Washington, DC: American Psychological Association.

Awad, G. A., & Saunders, E. B. (1989). Adolescent child molesters: Clinical observations. *Child Psychiatry and Human Development, 19,* 195–206.

Babcock, J. C., Waltz, J., Jacobson, N. S., & Gottman, J. M. (1993). Power and violence: The relation between communication patterns, power discrepancies, and domestic violence. Special section: Couples and couple therapy. *Journal of Consulting and Clinical Psychology, 61,* 40–50.

Bachman, R., Paternoster, R., & Ward, S. (1992). The rationality of sexual offending: Testing a deterrence/rational choice model of sexual assault. *Law and Society Review, 26,* 343–372.

Baer, J. S., Marlatt, G., Kivlahan, D. R., Fromme, K., Larimer, M. E., & Williams, E. (1992). An experimental test of three methods of alcohol risk reduction with young adults. *Journal of Consulting and Clinical Psychology, 60,* 974–979.

Barbaree, H. E. (1990). Stimulus control of sexual arousal: Its role in sexual assault. In W. L. Marshall, D. R. Laws, & H. E. Barbaree (Eds.), *Handbook of sexual assault: Issues, theories, and treatment of the offender* (pp. 115–142). New York: Plenum.

Barbaree, H. E. (1991). Denial and minimization among sex offenders: Assessment and treatment outcome. *Forum on Corrections Research, 3,* 30–33.

Barbaree, H. E., Baxter, D. J., & Marshall, W. L. (1989). Brief research report: The reliability of the rape index in a sample of rapists and nonrapists. *Violence and Victims, 4,* 299–306.

Barbaree, H. E., & Cortoni, F. A. (1993). Treatment of the juvenile sex offender within the criminal justice and mental health systems. In H. E. Barbaree, W. L. Marshall, & S. M. Hudson (Eds.), *The juvenile sex offender* (pp. 243–263). New York: Guilford.

Barbaree, H. E., & Marshall, W. L. (1989). Erectile responses among heterosexual child molesters, father-daughter incest offenders, and matched nonoffenders: Five distinct age preference profiles. *Canadian Journal of Behavioural Science, 21,* 70–82.

Barbaree, H. E., & Marshall, W. L. (1991). The role of male sexual arousal in rape: Six models. *Journal of Consulting and Clinical Psychology, 59,* 621–630.

Barbaree, H. E., Seto, M. C., Serin, R. C., Amos, N. L., & Preston, D. L. (1994). Comparisons between sexual and nonsexual rapist subtypes: Sexual arousal to rape, offense precursors, and offense characteristics. *Criminal Justice and Behavior, 21*, 95–114.

Barlow, D. (1981). On the relation of clinical research to clinical practice: Current issues. *Journal of Consulting and Clinical Psychology, 49*, 147–155.

Barlow, D. H. (1986). Causes of sexual dysfunction: The role of anxiety and cognitive interference. *Journal of Consulting and Clinical Psychology, 54*, 140–148.

Barnett, M. A., Feierstein, M. D., Jaet, B. P., Saunders, L. C., Quackenbush, S. W., & Sinisi, C. S. (1992). The effect of knowing a rape victim on reactions to other victims. *Journal of Interpersonal Violence, 7*, 44–56.

Baron, J., Beattie, J., & Hershey, J. D. (1988). Heuristics and biases in diagnostic reasoning: Congruence, information, and certainty. *Organizational Behavior and Human Decision Processes, 42*, 88–110.

Baron, R. A. (1977). *Human aggression.* New York: Plenum.

Barongan, C., & Hall, G. C. N. (1995). The influence of misogynous rap music on sexual aggression against women. *Psychology of Women Quarterly, 19*, 195–207.

Barrett, M. J., Trepper, T. S., & Fish, L. S. (1990). Feminist-informed family therapy for the treatment of intrafamily child sexual abuse. *Journal of Family Psychology, 4*, 151–166.

Barrios, B. A. (1988). On the changing nature of behavioral assessment. In A. S. Bellack & M. Hersen (Eds.), *Behavioral assessment: A practical handbook* (3rd. ed., pp. 3–41). New York: Pergamon.

Batson, C. D., Schoenrade, P., & Ventis, W. L. (1993). *Religion and the individual: A social psychological perspective.* New York: Oxford University Press.

Baxter, D. J., Barbaree, H. E., & Marshall, W. L. (1986). Sexual responses to consenting and forced sex in a large sample of rapists and nonrapists. *Behaviour Research and Therapy, 24*, 513–520.

Beck, A. T., & Freeman, A. (1990). *Cognitive therapy of emotional disorders.* New York: Guilford.

Becker, J. V., Harris, C. D., & Sales, B. D. (1993). Juveniles who commit sexual offenses: A critical review of research. In G. C. N. Hall, R. Hirschman, J. R. Graham, & M. S. Zaragoza (Eds.), *Sexual aggression: Issues in etiology, assessment, and treatment* (pp. 215–228). Washington, DC: Taylor & Francis.

Becker, R. E., & Heimberg, R. G. (1988). Assessment of social skills. In A. S. Bellack & M. Hersen (Eds.), *Behavioral assessment: A practical handbook* (3rd ed., pp. 365–395). New York: Pergamon.

Belsky, J., Steinberg, L., & Draper, P. (1991). Further reflections on an evolutionary theory. *Child Development, 62*, 682–685.

Bem, S. L. (1993). *The lenses of gender: An essay on the social reproduction of male power.* New Haven, CT: Yale University Press.

Berkowitz, L. (1983). Aversively stimulated aggression: Some parallels and differences in research with animals and humans. *American Psychologist, 38,* 1135–1144.

Berkowitz, L. (1989). Frustration-aggression hypothesis: Examination and reformulation. *Psychological Bulletin, 106,* 59–73.

Berkowitz, L. (1990). On the formation and regulation of anger and aggression: A cognitive-neoassociationistic analysis. *American Psychologist, 45,* 494–503.

Berkowitz, L. & Donnerstein, E. (1982). External validity is more than skin deep: Some answers to criticisms of laboratory experiments. *American Psychologist, 37,* 245–257.

Berrick, J. D. (1988). Parental involvement in child abuse prevention training: What do they learn? *Child Abuse and Neglect, 12,* 543–553.

Beutler, L. E. (1993). Designing outcome studies: Treatment of adult victims of childhood sexual abuse. *Journal of Interpersonal Violence, 8,* 402–414.

Biden, J. R., Jr. (1993). Violence against women: The congressional response. *American Psychologist, 48,* 1059–1061.

Billy, J. O., & Udry, J. (1985a). The influence of male and female best friends on adolescent sexual behavior. *Adolescence, 20,* 21–32.

Billy, J. O., & Udry, J. (1985b). Patterns of adolescent friendship and effects on sexual behavior. *Social Psychology Quarterly, 48,* 27–41.

Blader, J. C., & Marshall, W. L. (1989). Is assessment of sexual arousal in rapists worthwhile? A critique of current methods and the development of a response compatibility approach. *Clinical Psychology Review, 9,* 569–587.

Blaske, D. M., Borduin, C. M., Henggeler, S. W., & Mann, B. J. (1989). Individual, family, and peer characteristics of adolescent sex offenders and assaultive offenders. *Developmental Psychology, 25,* 846–855.

Blau, T. (1984). *The psychologist as expert witness.* New York: Wiley.

Boat, B. W., & Everson, M. D. (1988). Research and issues in using anatomical dolls. *Annals of Sex Research, 1,* 191–204.

Booth, C. L., Spieker, S. J., Barnard, K. E., & Morisset, C. E. (1992). Infants at risk: The role of preventive intervention in deflecting a maladaptive developmental trajectory. In J. McCord & T. E. Tremblay (Eds.), *Preventing antisocial behavior: Interventions from birth through adolescence* (pp. 21–42). New York: Guilford.

Borden, L. A., Karr, S. K., & Caldwell-Colbert, A. (1988). Effects of a university rape prevention program on attitudes and empathy toward rape. *Journal of College Student Development, 29,* 132–136.

Borduin, C. M., Henggeler, S. W., Blaske, D. M., & Stein, R. J. (1990). Multisystemic treatment of adolescent sexual offenders. *International Journal of Offender Therapy and Comparative Criminology, 34,* 105–113.

Borkin, J., & Frank, L. (1986). Sexual abuse prevention for pre-schoolers: A pilot program. *Child Welfare, 45,* 75–82.

Bozman, A. W., & Beck, J. (1991). Covariation of sexual desire and sexual arousal: The effects of anger and anxiety. *Archives of Sexual Behavior*, *20*, 47–60.

Bradford, J. M. W. (1990). The antiandrogen and hormonal treatments of sex offenders. In W. L. Marshall, D. R. Laws, & H. E. Barbaree, (Eds.), *Handbook of sexual assault: Issues, theories, and treatment of the offender* (pp. 297–310). New York: Plenum.

Bradford, J. M. W. (1993). The pharmacological treatment of the adolescent sex offender. In H. E. Barbaree, W. L. Marshall, & S. M. Hudson (Eds.), *The juvenile sex offender* (pp. 278–288). New York: Guilford.

Bradmiller, L. L., & Walters, W. S. (1985). Seriousness of sexual assault charges: Influencing factors. *Criminal Justice and Behavior*, *12*, 463–484.

Brantingham, P. J., & Faust, F. L. (1976). A conceptual model of crime prevention. *Crime and Delinquency*, *22*, 284–296.

Bresee, P. B., Stearns, G. B., Bess, B. H., & Packer, L. S. (1986). Allegations of child sexual abuse in child custody disputes: A therapeutic assessment model. *American Journal of Orthopsychiatry*, *56*, 560–569.

Brehm, S., & Brehm, J. W. (1981). *Psychological reactance: A theory of freedom and control*. New York: Academic Press.

Briere, J. (1988). The long-term clinical correlates of childhood sexual victimization. In R. A. Prentky & V. L. Quinsey (Eds.), *Human sexual aggression: Current perspectives* (pp. 327–334). New York: New York Academy of Sciences.

Browne, A. (1993). Violence against women by male partners: Prevalence, outcomes, and policy implications. *American Psychologist*, *48*, 1077–1087.

Browne, A., & Finkelhor, D. (1986). Impact of child sexual abuse: A review of the research. *Psychological Bulletin*, *99*, 66–77.

Brownell, K. D., Hayes, S. C., & Barlow, D. H. (1977). Patterns of appropriate and deviant sexual arousal: The behavioural treatment of multiple sexual deviations. *Journal of Consulting and Clinical Psychology*, *45*, 1144–1155.

Brownmiller, S. (1975). *Against our will: Men, women, and rape*. New York: Simon and Schuster.

Burman, B., Margolin, G., & John, R. S. (1993). America's angriest home videos: Behavioral contingencies observed in home reenactments of marital conflict. *Journal of Consulting and Clinical Psychology*, *61*, 28–39.

Burt, M. R. (1980). Cultural myths and supports for rape. *Journal of Personality and Social Psychology*, *38*, 217–230.

Bushman, B. J., & Cooper, H. M. (1990). Effects of alcohol on human aggression: An integrative research review. *Psychological Bulletin*, *107*, 341–354.

Buss, A. (1961). *The psychology of aggression*. New York: Wiley.

Buss, A. H., & Perry, M. (1992). The aggression questionnaire. *Journal of Personality and Social Psychology*, *63*, 452–459.

Buss, D. M., & Schmitt, D. P. (1993). Sexual strategies theory: A contextual evolutionary analysis of human mating. *Psychological Review*, *100*, 204–232.

Bussey, K., & Bandura, A. (1984). Influence of gender constancy and social power on sex-linked modeling. *Journal of Personality and Social Psychology*, 47, 1292–1302.

Butler, D., & Geis, F. L. (1990). Nonverbal affect responses to male and female leaders: Implications for leadership evaluation. *Journal of Personality and Social Psychology*, 58, 48–59.

Campbell, D. T. (1960). Recommendations of the APA test standards regarding construct, trait, and discriminant validity. *American Psychologist*, 15, 546–553.

Campbell, D., & Stanley, J. (1963). *Experimental and quasi-experimental designs for research*. Chicago: Rand-McNally.

Caplan, G. (1964). *Principles of preventive psychiatry*. New York: Basic Books.

Carlson, M., Marcus-Newhall, A., & Miller, M. (1989). Evidence for a general construct of aggression. *Personality and Social Psychology Bulletin*, 15, 377–389.

Carlson, M., Marcus-Newhall, A., & Miller, N. (1990). Effects of situational aggression cues: A quantitative review. *Journal of Personality and Social Psychology*, 58, 622–633.

Carnes, P. (1983). *Out of the shadows: Understanding sexual addiction*. Minneapolis: CompCare Publications.

Carter, D. L., Prentky, R. A., Knight, R. A., Vanderveer, P. L., & Boucher, R. (1987). Use of pornography in the criminal and developmental histories of sexual offenders. *Journal of Interpersonal Violence*, 2, 196–211.

Carver, C. S., & Scheier, M. F. (1992). *Perspectives on personality* (2nd ed.). Boston: Allyn & Bacon.

Catalano, R. F., Hawkins, J. D., Krenz, C., Gillmore, M., Morrison, D., Wells, E., & Abbott, R. (1993). Using research to guide culturally appropriate drug abuse prevention. *Journal of Consulting and Clinical Psychology*, 61, 804–811.

Cauce, A. M., Hannan, K., & Sargeant, M. (1992). Life stress, social support, and locus of control during early adolescence: Interactive effects. *American Journal of Community Psychology*, 20, 787–798.

Centers for Disease Control. (1992). Cigarette smoking among adults. *Morbidity and Mortality Weekly Report*, 41, 354–362.

Chaffin, M. (1992). Factors associated with treatment completion and progress among intrafamilial sexual abusers. *Child Abuse and Neglect*, 16, 251–264.

Charney, D. A., & Russell, R. C. (1994). An overview of sexual harassment. *American Journal of Psychiatry*, 151, 10–17.

Check, J. V. P., & Malamuth, N. M. (1984). Can there be positive effects of participation in pornography experiments? *Journal of Sex Research*, 20, 14–31.

Clark, L., & Lewis, D. (1977). *Rape: The price of coercive sexuality*. Toronto: Women's Press.

Clark, R. D., & Hatfield, E. (1989). Gender differences in receptivity to sexual offers. *Journal of Psychology and Human Sexuality*, 2, 39–55.

Clarke, J. C., & Hayes, K. (1984). Covert sensitization, stimulus relevance and the equipotentiality premise. *Behaviour Research and Therapy, 22,* 451–454.

Cloitre, M. (1993). An interview with Martin Seligman. *Behavior Therapist, 16,* 261–263.

Cohen, J., & Cohen, P. (1983). *Applied multiple regression/correlation analysis for the behavioral sciences* (2nd ed.). Hillsdale, NJ: Erlbaum.

Cohen, L. H., Sargent, M. M., & Sechrest, L. B. (1986). Use of psychotherapy research by professional psychologists. *American Psychologist, 41,* 198–206.

Cohn, A., Finkelhor, D., & Holmes, C. (1985). *Preventing adults from becoming child sexual molesters.* Chicago: National Committee for Prevention of Child Abuse.

Coie, J. D., Belding, M., & Underwood, M. (1988). Aggression and peer rejection in childhood. In B. Lahey & A. Kazdin (Eds.), *Advances in clinical child psychology* (Vol. 2, pp. 125–158). New York: Plenum.

Coie, J. D., Watt, N. F., West, S. G., Hawkins, J. D., Asarnow, J. R., Markman, H. J., Ramey, S. L., Shure, M. B., & Long, B. (1993). The science of prevention: A conceptual framework and some directions for a national research program. *American Psychologist, 48,* 1013–1022.

Condy, S. R., Templer, D. I., Brown, R., & Veaco, L. (1987). Parameters of sexual contact of boys with women. *Archives of Sexual Behavior, 16,* 379–394.

Cowen, E. L. (1983). Social and community interventions. *Annual Review of Psychology, 24,* 423–472.

Craig, M. E. (1990). Coercive sexuality in dating relationships: A situational model. *Clinical Psychology Review, 10,* 395–423.

Cronbach, L. J., & Meehl, P. E. (1955). Construct validity in psychological tests. *Psychological Bulletin, 52,* 281–302.

Cummings, C., Gordon, J. R., & Marlatt, G. A. (1980). Relapse: Strategies of prevention and prediction. In W. R. Miller (Ed.), *The addictive behaviors* (pp. 291–321). Oxford, England: Pergamon.

Darke, J. L. (1990). Sexual aggression: Achieving power through humiliation. In W. L. Marshall, D. R. Laws, & H. E. Barbaree (Eds.), *Handbook of sexual assault: Issues, theories, and treatment of the offender* (pp. 55–72). New York: Plenum.

Daro, D. (1988). *Confronting child abuse: Research for effective program design.* New York: Free Press.

Daro, D. (1991). Prevention programs. In C. R. Hollin & K. Howells (Eds.), *Clinical approaches to sex offenders and their victims* (pp. 285–305). Chichester, England: Wiley.

Davidson, P. R., & Malcolm, P. B. (1985). The reliability of the rape index: A rapist sample. *Behavioral Assessment, 7,* 283–292.

Davis, G. E., & Leitenberg, H. (1987). Adolescent sex offenders. *Psychological Bulletin, 101,* 417–427.

Dawes, R. M., Faust, D., & Meehl, P. E. (1989). Clinical versus actuarial judgment. *Science, 243,* 1668–1674.

Deffenbacher, J. L., Demm, P. M., & Brandon, A. D. (1986). High general anger: Correlates and treatment. *Behaviour Research and Therapy, 24*, 481–489.

Deffenbacher, J. L., Story, D. A., Stark, R. S., Hogg, J. A., & Brandon, A. D. (1987). Cognitive-relaxation and social skills interventions in the treatment of general anger. *Journal of Counseling Psychology, 34*, 171–176.

Demare, D., Briere, J., & Lips, H. M. (1988). Violent pornography and self-reported likelihood of sexual aggression. *Journal of Research in Personality, 22*, 140–153.

Dembo, R., Williams, L., Schmeidler, J., Getreu, A., Berry, E., Genung, L., Wish, E.D., & Christensen, C. (1991). Recidivism among high risk youths: A 2½-year follow-up of a cohort of juvenile detainees. *International Journal of the Addictions, 26*, 1197–1221.

Dent, D. Z., & Arias, I. (1990). Effects of alcohol, gender, and role of spouses on attributions and evaluations of marital violence scenarios. *Violence and Victims, 5*, 185–193.

DiGiuseppe, R., Tafrate, R., & Eckhardt, C. (1994). Critical issues in the treatment of anger. *Cognitive and Behavioral Practice, 1*, 111–132.

Dishion, T. J., Patterson, G. R., & Kavanagh, K. A. (1992). An experimental test of the coercion model: Linking theory, measurement, and intervention. In J. McCord & R. E. Tremblay (Eds.), *Preventing antisocial behavior: Interventions from birth through adolescence* (pp. 253–282). New York: Guilford.

Dixon, J. (1991). Feminist reforms of sexual coercion laws. In E. Grauerholz & M. A. Koralewski (Eds.), *Sexual coercion: A sourcebook on its nature, causes, and prevention* (pp. 161–171). Lexington, MA: Lexington Books.

Dodge, K. A. (1993). Social cognitive mechanisms in the development of conduct disorder and depression. *Annual Review of Psychology, 44*, 559–584.

Dodge, K.A., Bates, J.E., & Pettit, G.S. (1990). Mechanisms in the cycle of violence. *Science, 250*, 1678–1683.

Dodge, K. A., Coie, J. D., & Brakke, N. P. (1982). Behavior patterns of socially rejected and neglected preadolescents: The roles of social approach and aggression. *Journal of Abnormal Child Psychology, 10*, 389–410.

Dodge, K. A., Pettit, G. S., McClaskey, C. L., & Brown, M. M. (1986). Social competence in children. *Monographs of the Society for Research in Child Development, 51* (2, Serial No. 213).

Donat, P. L. N., & D'Emilio, J. (1992). A feminist redefinition of rape and sexual assault: Historical foundations and change. *Journal of Social Issues, 48*, 9–22.

Donnerstein, E. (1980). Aggressive erotica and violence against women. *Journal of Personality and Social Psychology, 39*, 269–277.

Donnerstein, E. I. (1994, August). Mass media sexual violence—Findings, solutions, and policy implications. Paper presented at the 102nd Convention of the American Psychological Association, Los Angeles.

Donnerstein, E., & Berkowitz, L. (1981). Victim reactions in aggressive erotic films as a factor in violence against women. *Journal of Personality and Social Psychology, 41*, 710–724.

Donnerstein, E., & Hallam, J. (1978). Facilitating effects of erotica on aggression against women. *Journal of Personality and Social Psychology, 36*, 1270–1277.

Donnerstein, E., Linz, D., & Penrod, S. (1987). *The question of pornography: Research findings and policy implications.* New York: Free Press.

Driver, E. (1989). Introduction. In E. Driver & A. Droisen (Eds.), *Child sexual abuse: A feminist reader* (pp. 1–68). New York: New York University Press.

Dull, R., & Giacopassi, D. J. (1987). Demographic correlates of sexual and dating attitudes: A study of date rape. *Criminal Justice and Behavior, 14*, 175–193.

Eagly, A. H., & Steffen, V. J. (1986). Gender and aggressive behavior: A meta-analytic review of the social psychological literature. *Psychological Bulletin, 100*, 309–330.

Earls, C. M., & Castonguay, L. G. (1989). The evaluation of olfactory aversion for a bisexual pedophile with a single-case multiple baseline design. *Behavior Therapy, 20*, 137–146.

Ebert, R. (1988). *Roger Ebert's movie home companion.* New York: Andrews and McMeel.

Edmonds, E. M., & Cahoon, D. D. (1986). Attitudes concerning crimes related to clothing worn by female victims. *Bulletin of the Psychonomic Society, 24*, 444–446.

Elliott, A. N., O'Donohue, W. T., & Nickerson, M. A. (1993). The use of sexually anatomically detailed dolls in the assessment of sexual abuse. *Clinical Psychology Review, 13*, 207–221.

Elliott, D. M. (1994). The impact of Christian faith on the prevalence and sequelae of sexual abuse. *Journal of Interpersonal Violence, 9*, 95–108.

Elliott, D. S., & Morse, B. J. (1987). Drug use, delinquency, and sexual activity. In C. Jones & E. McAnarney (Eds.), *Drug abuse and adolescent sexual activity, pregnancy, and parenthood* (pp. 32–60). Washington, DC: U.S. Government Printing Office.

Ellis, A. L., O'Sullivan, C. S., & Sowards, B. A. (1992). The impact of contemplated exposure to a survivor of rape on attitudes toward rape. *Journal of Applied Social Psychology, 22*, 889–895.

Ellis, B. J., & Symons, D. (1990). Sex differences in sexual fantasy: An evolutionary psychological approach. *Journal of Sex Research, 27*, 527–556.

Ellis, L. (1989). *Theories of rape: Inquiries into the causes of sexual aggression.* New York: Hemisphere.

Ellis, L. (1991). A synthesized (biosocial) theory of rape. *Journal of Consulting and Clinical Psychology, 59*, 631–642.

Endicott, J., & Spitzer, R. L. (1978). A diagnostic interview: The schedule for affective disorders and schizophrenia. *Archives of General Psychiatry, 35*, 837–844.

Enke, J. L., & Sudderth, L. K. (1991). Educational reforms. In E. Grauerholz

& M. A. Koralewski (Eds.), *Sexual coercion: A sourcebook on its nature, causes, and prevention* (pp. 149–159). Lexington, MA: Lexington Books.

Enright, S. J. (1989). Paedophilia: A cognitive/behavioural treatment approach in a single case. *British Journal of Psychiatry, 155,* 399–401.

Eron, L. D. (1987). The development of aggressive behavior from the perspective of a developing behaviorism. *American Psychologist, 42,* 435–442.

Estrich, S. (1987). *Real rape.* Cambridge, MA: Harvard University Press.

Etzioni, A. (1988). The moral dimension: Toward a new economics. New York: Free Press.

Everson, M.D., & Boat, B.W. (1989). False allegations of sexual abuse by children and adolescents. *Journal of the American Academy of Child and Adolescent Psychiatry, 28,* 230–235.

Everson, M. D., & Boat, B. W. (1990). Sexualized doll play among young children: Implications for the use of anatomical dolls in sexual abuse evaluations. *Journal of the American Academy of Child and Adolescent Psychiatry, 29,* 736–742.

FBI Uniform Crime Reports. (1991). *Crime in the United States.* Washington, DC: U.S. Department of Justice.

Fagan, J., & Wexler, S. (1988). Explanations of sexual assault among violent delinquents special issue: Adolescent sexual behavior. *Journal of Adolescent Research, 3,* 363–385.

Fairchild, H. H. (1991). Scientific racism: The cloak of objectivity. *Journal of Social Issues, 47,* 101–115.

Faller, K. C. (1991). Possible explanations for child sexual abuse allegations in divorce. *American Journal of Orthopsychiatry, 61,* 86–91.

Farrington, D. P., Ohlin, L., & Wilson, J. Q. (1986). *Understanding and controlling crime.* New York: Springer-Verlag.

Faust, D. (1986). Research on human judgment and its application to clinical practice. *Professional Psychology: Research and Practice, 17,* 420–430.

Fedoroff, J. P., Wisner-Carlson, R., Dean, S., & Berlin, F. S. (1992). *Journal of Offender Rehabilitation, 18,* 109–123.

Feran, T. (1994, February 27). TV changing its tunes. *The Plain Dealer,* pp 4-I, 10-I.

Fingerhut, L., Ingram, D., & Feldman, J. (1992). Firearm and nonfirearm homicide among persons 15 through 19 years of age. *Journal of the American Medical Association, 267,* 3048–3053.

Finkelhor, D. (1984). *Child sexual abuse: New theory and research.* New York: Free Press.

Finkelhor, D. (1986). Prevention: A review of programs and research. In D. Finkelhor, S. Araji, L. Baron, A. Browne, S. D. Peters, & G. E. Wyatt (Eds.), *A sourcebook on child sexual abuse* (pp. 224–254). Beverly Hills, CA: Sage.

Finkelhor, D. (1988). The trauma of sexual abuse: Two models. In G. Wyatt & G. J. Powell (Eds.), *Lasting effects of child sexual abuse* (pp. 61–82). Newbury Park, CA: Sage.

Finkelhor, D., & Strapko, N. (1992). Sexual abuse prevention education: A review of evaluation studies. In D. J. Willis, E. W. Holden, & M. Rosenberg (Eds.), *Prevention of child maltreatment: Developmental and ecological perspectives* (pp. 150–1167). New York: Wiley.

Finkelhor, D., & Yllo, K. (1985). *License to rape: Sexual abuse of wives.* New York: Holt, Rinehart, & Winston.

Fischer, G. J. (1986). College student attitudes toward forcible date rape: I. Cognitive predictors. *Archives of Sexual Behavior, 15,* 457–466.

Fitzgerald, L. F. (1993). Sexual harassment: Violence against women in the workplace. *American Psychologist, 48,* 1070–1076.

Fonow, M. M., Richardson, L., & Wemmerus, V. A. (1992). Feminist rape education: Does it work? *Gender and Society, 6,* 108–121.

Forehand, R. (1993). Twenty years of research on parenting: Does it have practical implications for clinicians working with parents and children? *Clinical Psychologist, 46,* 169–176.

Freedman, J. L. (1988). Keeping pornography in perspective. *Contemporary Psychology, 33,* 858–860.

Freund, K. (1990). Courtship disorder. In W. L. Marshall, D. R. Laws, & H. E. Barbaree (Eds.), *Handbook of sexual assault: Issues, theories, and treatment of the offender* (pp. 195–207). New York: Plenum.

Freund, K., & Blanchard, R. (1989). Phallometric diagnosis of pedophilia. *Journal of Consulting and Clinical Psychology, 57,* 100–105.

Friedrich, W. N. (1990). *Psychotherapy of sexually abused children and their families.* New York: Norton.

Friedrich, W. N., Grambsch, P., Damon, L., Hewitt, S. K., Koverola, C., Lang, R. A., Wolfe, V., & Broughton, D. (1992). Child Sexual Behavior Inventory: Normative and clinical comparisons. *Psychological Assessment, 4,* 303–311.

Furby, L., Weinrott, M. R., & Blackshaw, L. (1989). Sex offender recidivism: A review. *Psychological Bulletin, 105,* 3–30.

Garcia, J., & Koelling, R. A. (1966). Relation of cue to consequence in avoidance learning. *Psychonomic Science, 4,* 123–124.

Garland, R. J., & Dougher, M. J. (1991). Motivational intervention in the treatment of sex offenders. In W. R. Miller & S. Rollnick (Eds.), *Motivational interviewing: Preparing people to change addictive behavior* (pp. 303–313). New York: Guilford.

Geen, R. G., & Donnerstein, E. I. (1983). *Aggression: Theoretical and empirical reviews: Vol. 2. Issues in research.* New York: Academic Press.

Geen, R. G., Stonner, C., & Shope, G. L. (1975). The facilitation of aggression by aggression: Evidence against the catharsis hypothesis. *Journal of Personality and Social Psychology, 31,* 721–726.)

Gelles, R. J. (1993). Family unification/family preservation: Are children really being protected? *Journal of Interpersonal Violence, 8,* 557–562.

George, W. H., & Marlatt, G. A. (1989). Introduction. In D. R. Laws (Ed.), *Relapse prevention with sex offenders* (pp. 1–31). New York: Guilford.

Gilbert, B. J., Heesacker, M., & Gannon, L. J. (1991). Changing the sexual aggression-supportive attitudes of men: A psychoeducational intervention. *Journal of Counseling Psychology, 38,* 197–203.

Gillmore, M. R., Catalano, R. F., Morrison, D. M., Wells, E. A., Iritani, B., & Hawkins, J. D. (1990). Racial differences in acceptability and availability of drugs and early initiation of substance abuse. *American Journal of Drug and Alcohol Abuse, 16,* 185–206.

Gillmore, M. R., Hawkins, J. D., Catalano, R. F., Day, L. E., Moore, M., & Abbott, R. (1991). Structure of problem behaviors in preadolescence. *Journal of Consulting and Clinical Psychology, 59,* 499–506.

Goldberg-Ambrose, C. (1992). Unfinished business in rape law reform. *Journal of Social Issues, 48,* 173–186.

Goodman, G. S., & Helgeson, V. S. (1988). Children as witnesses: What do they remember. In L. E. A. Walker (Ed.), *Handbook on sexual abuse of children* (pp. 109–136). New York: Springer.

Gottfredson, M. R., & Hirschi, T. (1993). A control theory interpretation of psychological research on aggression. In R. B. Felson & J. T. Tedeschi (Eds.), *Aggression and violence: Social interactionist perspectives* (pp. 47–68). Washington, DC: American Psychological Association.

Gottfried, H. (1991). Preventing sexual coercion: A feminist agenda for economic change. In E. Grauerholz & M. A. Koralewski (Eds.), *Sexual coercion: A sourcebook on its nature, causes, and prevention* (pp. 173–183). Lexington, MA: Lexington Books.

Graham, J. R. (1987). *The MMPI: A practical guide* (2nd ed.). New York: Oxford University Press.

Grasmick, H. G., Bursik, R. J., & Kimpel, M. (1991). Protestant fundamentalism and attitudes toward corporal punishment of children. *Violence and Victims, 6,* 283–298.

Gray, A., Jackson, D. N., & McKinlay, J. B. (1991). The relation between dominance, anger, and hormones in normally aging men: Results from the Massachusetts Male Aging Study. *Psychosomatic Medicine, 53,* 375–385.

Greenberg, L. S. (1991). *Emotion, psychotherapy, and change.* New York: Guilford.

Groth, A. N. (1979). *Men who rape: The psychology of the offender.* New York: Plenum.

Haapasalo, J., & Tremblay, R. E. (1994). Physically aggressive boys from ages 6 to 12: Family background, parenting behavior, and prediction of delinquency. *Journal of Consulting and Clinical Psychology, 62,* 1044–1052.

Hall, E. R., & Flannery, P. J. (1984). Prevalence and correlates of sexual assault experiences in adolescents. *Victimology, 9,* 398–406.

Hall, G. C. N. (1980). An integration of science and theology in a Piagetian epistemology. *Journal of Psychology and Theology, 8,* 293–302.

Hall, G. C. N. (1988). Criminal behavior as a function of clinical and actuarial variables in a sexual offender population. *Journal of Consulting and Clinical Psychology, 56,* 773–775.

Hall, G. C. N. (1989a). Self-reported hostility as a function of offense characteristics and response style in a sexual offender population. *Journal of Consulting and Clinical Psychology, 57*, 306–308.

Hall, G. C. N. (1989b). Sexual arousal and arousability in a sexual offender population. *Journal of Abnormal Psychology, 98*, 145–149.

Hall, G. C. N. (1990a). Prediction of sexual aggression. *Clinical Psychology Review, 10*, 229–245.

Hall, G. C. N. (1990b). The role of sexual arousal in the forensic assessment of sexual offenders. *The Expert Witness, The Trial Attorney and The Trial Judge, 4*, 31–36.

Hall, G. C. N. (1990c). Validity of physiological measures of pedophilic sexual arousal in a sexual offender population: Reply to Quinsey and Laws. *Journal of Consulting and Clinical Psychology, 58*, 889–891.

Hall, G. C. N. (1995, August). *Prevention of sexual aggression: Lessons from ethnic minority communities*. Division 45 Presidential Address at the 103rd Annual Convention of the American Psychological Association, New York.

Hall, G. C. N. (1995a). The preliminary development of theory-based community treatment for sexual offenders. *Professional Psychology: Research and Practice, 26*, 478–483.

Hall, G. C. N. (1995b). Sexual offender recidivism revisited: A meta-analysis of recent treatment studies. *Journal of Consulting and Clinical Psychology, 63*, 802–809.

Hall, G. C. N., & Andersen, B. L. (1993). Sexual dysfunction and deviation. In A. S. Bellack & M. Hersen (Eds.), *Psychopathology in adulthood* (pp. 295–318). Boston: Allyn and Bacon.

Hall, G. C. N., & Crowther, J. H. (1991). Psychologists' involvement in cases of child maltreatment: Additional limits of assessment methods. *American Psychologist, 46*, 79–80.

Hall, G. C. N., Graham, J. R., & Shepherd, J. B. (1991). Three methods of developing MMPI taxonomies of sexual offenders. *Journal of Personality Assessment, 56*, 2–13.

Hall, G. C. N., & Hirschman, R. (1991). Toward a theory of sexual aggression: A quadripartite model. *Journal of Consulting and Clinical Psychology, 59*, 662–669.

Hall, G. C. N., & Hirschman, R. (1992). Sexual aggression against children: A conceptual perspective of etiology. *Criminal Justice and Behavior, 19*, 8–23.

Hall, G. C. N., & Hirschman, R. (1993). Use of a new laboratory methodology to conceptualize sexual aggression. In G. C. N. Hall, R. Hirschman, J. R. Graham, & M. S. Zaragoza (Eds.), *Sexual aggression: Issues in etiology, assessment, and treatment* (pp. 115–132). Washington, DC: Taylor & Francis.

Hall, G. C. N., & Hirschman, R. (1994). The relationship between men's sexual aggression inside and outside the laboratory. *Journal of Consulting and Clinical Psychology, 62*, 375–380.

Hall, G. C. N., Hirschman, R., & Beutler, L. E. (1991). Introduction to the Special Section. *Journal of Consulting and Clinical Psychology, 59*, 619–620.

Hall, G. C. N., Hirschman, R., Boardman, A. F., Shondrick, D. D., Stafford, K. P., Codispoti, V., Heinbaugh, G., Neuhaus, S., & Krenrick, D. (1993). Conclusion: Complementary approaches to sexual aggression. In G. C. N. Hall, R. Hirschman, J. R. Graham, & M. S. Zaragoza (Eds.), *Sexual aggression: Issues in etiology, assessment, and treatment* (pp. 229–233). Washington, DC: Taylor & Francis.

Hall, G. C. N., Hirschman, R., & Oliver, L. L. (1994). Ignoring a woman's dislike of sexual material: Sexually impositional behavior in the laboratory. *Journal of Sex Research, 31,* 3–10.

Hall, G. C. N., Hirschman, R., & Oliver, L. L. (in press). Sexual arousal and arousability to pedophilic stimuli in a community sample of "normal" men. *Behavior Therapy.*

Hall, G. C. N., Maiuro, R. D., Vitaliano, P. P., & Proctor, W. C. (1986). The utility of the MMPI with men who have sexually assaulted children. *Journal of Consulting and Clinical Psychology, 54,* 493–496.

Hall, G. C. N., & Proctor, W. C. (1987). Criminological predictors of recidivism in a sexual offender population. *Journal of Consulting and Clinical Psychology, 55,* 111–112.

Hall, G. C. N., Proctor, W. C., & Nelson, G. M. (1988). Validity of physiological measures of pedophilic sexual arousal in a sexual offender population. *Journal of Consulting and Clinical Psychology, 56,* 118–122.

Hall, G. C. N., Shepherd, J. B., & Mudrak, P. (1992). MMPI taxonomies of child sexual and nonsexual offenders: A cross-validation and extension. *Journal of Personality Assessment, 58,* 127–137.

Hall, G. C. N., Shondrick, D. D., & Hirschman, R. (1993a). Conceptually-derived treatments for sexual aggressors. *Professional Psychology: Research and Practice, 24,* 62–69.

Hall, G. C. N., Shondrick, D. D., & Hirschman, R. (1993b). The role of sexual arousal in sexually aggressive behavior: A meta-analysis. *Journal of Consulting and Clinical Psychology, 61,* 1091–1095.

Hall, R. L. (1989). Relapse rehearsal. In D. R. Laws (Ed.), *Relapse prevention with sex offenders* (pp. 197–206). New York: Guilford.

Hall, S. (1980). Self-management and therapeutic maintenance: Theory and research. In P. Karoly & J. J. Steffen (Eds.), *Toward a psychology of therapeutic maintenance: Widening perspectives* (pp. 263–300). New York: Gardner.

Hamilton, J. A. (1989). Emotional consequences of victimization and discrimination in "special populations" of women. *Psychiatric Clinics of North America, 12,* 35–51.

Hammock, G. S., Rosen, S., Richardson, D. R., & Bernstein, S. (1989). Aggression as equity restoration. *Journal of Research in Personality, 23,* 398–409.

Hanson, K. A., & Gidycz, C. A. (1993). Evaluation of a sexual assault prevention program. *Journal of Consulting and Clinical Psychology, 61,* 1046–1052.

Hanson, R. (1990). The psychological impact of sexual assault on women and children: A review. *Annals of Sex Research, 3,* 187–232.

Hanson, R., Cox, B.J., & Woszczyna, C. (1991). Assessing treatment outcome for sexual offenders. *Annals of Sex Research, 4,* 177–208.

Hanson, R. K., Gizzarelli, R., & Scott, H. (1994). The attitudes of incest offenders: Sexual entitlement and acceptance of sex with children. *Criminal Justice and Behavior, 21,* 187–202.

Hanson, R. K., Steffy, R. A., & Gauthier, R. (1993). Long-term recidivism of child molesters. *Journal of Consulting and Clinical Psychology, 61,* 646–652.

Harris, G. T., Rice, M. E., Quinsey, V. L., Chaplin, T. C., & Earls, C. (1992). Maximizing the discriminant validity of phallometric assessment data. *Psychological Assessment, 4,* 502–511.

Hart, S. D., Webster, C. D., & Menzies, R. J. (1993). A note on portraying the accuracy of violence predictions. *Law and Human Behavior, 17,* 695–700.

Hathaway, S. R., & McKinley, J. C. (1940). A multiphasic personality schedule (Minnesota): I. Construction of the schedule. *Journal of Psychology, 10,* 249–254.

Hatfield, E., Sprecher, S., Pillemer, J.T., Greenberger, D., & Wexler, P. (1988). Gender differences in what is desired in the sexual relationship. *Journal of Psychology and Human Sexuality, 1,* 39–52.

Haugaard, J. J., & Reppucci, N. D. (1988). *The sexual abuse of children.* San Francisco: Jossey-Bass.

Hawkins, J. D., Catalano, R. F., Morrison, D. M., O'Donnell, J., Abbott, R. D., & Day, L. E. (1992). The Seattle Social Development Project: Effects of the first four years on protective factors and problem behaviors. In J. McCord & R. E. Tremblay (Eds.), *Preventing antisocial behavior: Interventions from birth through adolescence* (pp. 139–161). New York: Guilford.

Hayes, S. C., Brownell, K. D., & Barlow, D. H. (1978). The use of self-administered covert sensitization in the treatment of exhibitionism and sadism. *Behavior Therapy, 9,* 283–289.

Haynes, S. N. (1990). Behavioral assessment of adults. In G. Goldstein & M. Hersen (Eds.), *Handbook of psychological assessment* (2nd ed., pp. 423–463). New York: Pergamon.

Haywood, T. W., Grossman, L. S., & Cavanaugh, J. L. (1990). Subjective versus objective measurements of deviant sexual arousal in clinical evaluations of alleged child molesters. *Psychological Assessment, 2,* 269–275.

Hazan, C., & Shaver, P. (1987). Romantic love conceptualized as an attachment process. *Journal of Personality and Social Psychology, 52,* 511–524.

Hazan, C., & Shaver, P. R. (1990). Love and work: An attachment-theoretical perspective. *Journal of Personality and Social Psychology, 59,* 270–280.

Helms, J. E. (1990). *Black and White racial identity: Theory, research, and practice.* Westport, CT: Greenwood.

Herman, J. L. (1981). *Father-daughter incest.* Cambridge, MA: Harvard University Press.

Herman, J. L. (1990). Sex offenders: A feminist perspective. In W. L. Marshall, D. R. Laws & H. E. Barbaree (Eds.), *Handbook of sexual assault: Issues, theories, and treatment of the offender* (pp. 177–193). New York: Plenum.

Herman, J. L. (1992). *Trauma and recovery.* New York: Basic Books.

Hershorn, M., & Rosenbaum, A. (1991). Over- vs. undercontrolled hostility: Application of the construct to the classification of maritally violent men. *Violence and Victims, 6,* 151–158.

Hildebran, D., & Pithers, W. D. (1989). Enhancing offender empathy for sexual-abuse victims. In D. R. Laws (Ed.), *Relapse prevention with sex offenders* (pp. 236–246). New York: Guilford.

Hildebran, D. D., & Pithers, W. D. (1992). Relapse prevention: Application and outcome. In W. O'Donohue & J. H. Geer (Eds.), *The sexual abuse of children: Clinical issues* (Vol. 2, pp. 365–393). Hillsdale, NJ: Erlbaum.

Hill, H. M., Soriano, F. I., Chen, S. A., & LaFromboise, T. D. (1994). Sociocultural factors in the etiology and prevention of violence among ethnic minority youth. In L. D. Eron, J. H. Gentry, & P. Schegel (Eds.), Reason to hope: A psychosocial perspective on violence and youth (pp. 59–97). Washington, DC: American Psychological Association.

Hinshaw, S. P. (1993). Externalizing behavior problems and academic underachievement in childhood and adolescence: Causal relationships and underlying mechanisms. *Psychological Bulletin, 111,* 127–155.

Hlady, L., & Gunter, E. (1990). Alleged child abuse in custody access disputes. *Child Abuse and Neglect, 14,* 591–593.

Ho, C. K. (1990). An analysis of domestic violence in Asian American communities: A multicultural approach to counseling. Special issue: Diversity and complexity in feminist therapy: I. *Women and Therapy, 9,* 129–150.

Hogarth, R. M. (1987). *Judgment and choice: The psychology of decision* (2nd ed.). Chichester, England: Wiley.

Holland, T. R., Holt, N., & Beckett, G. E. (1982). Prediction of violent versus nonviolent recidivism from prior violent and nonviolent criminality. *Journal of Abnormal Psychology, 91,* 178–182.

Hollon, S. D., & Kriss, M. R. (1984). Cognitive factors in clinical research and practice. *Clinical Psychology Review, 4,* 35–76.

Hollon, S. D., Shelton, R. C., & Loosen, P. T. (1991). Cognitive therapy and pharmacotherapy for depression. *Journal of Consulting and Clinical Psychology, 59,* 88–99.

Holtzworth-Munroe, A. (1992). Social skill deficits in maritally violent men: Interpreting the data using a social information processing model. *Clinical Psychology Review, 12,* 605–617.

Holtzworth-Munroe, A., & Hutchinson, G. (1993). Attributing negative intent to wife behavior: The attributions of maritally violent versus nonviolent men. *Journal of Abnormal Psychology, 102,* 206–211.

Hotaling, G. T., & Sugarman, D. B. (1986). An analysis of risk markers in husband to wife violence: The current state of knowledge. *Violence and Victims, 1,* 101–124.

Howard, G. S. (1990). On the construct validity of self-reports: What do the data say? *American Psychologist*, *45*, 292–294.

Howland, E. W., Kosson, D. S., Patterson, C. M., & Newman, J. P. (1993). Altering a dominant response: Performance of psychopaths and low-socialization college students on a cued reaction time task. *Journal of Abnormal Psychology*, *102*, 379–387.

Huang, K., & Uba, L. (1992). Premarital sexual behavior among Chinese college students in the United States. *Archives of Sexual Behavior*, *21*, 227–240.

Hudson, S. M., Ward, T., & Marshall, W. L. (1992). The abstinence violation effect in sex offenders: A reformulation. *Behaviour Research and Therapy*, *30*, 435–441.

Hughes, R. C. (1977). Covert sensitization treatment of exhibitionism. *Journal of Behavior Therapy and Experimental Psychiatry*, *8*, 177–179.

Hucker, S. J., & Bain, J. (1990). Androgenic hormones and sexual assault. In W. L. Marshall, D. R. Laws, & H. E. Barbaree (Eds.), *Handbook of sexual assault: Issues, theories, and treatment of the offender* (pp. 93–102). New York: Plenum.

Hunter, J. A., & Goodwin, D. W. (1992). The clinical utility of satiation therapy with juvenile sexual offenders: Variations and efficacy. *Annals of Sex Research*, *5*, 71–80.

Huston, T. L., & Ashmore, R. D. (1986). Women and men in personal relationships. In R. D. Ashmore & F. K. Del Boca (Eds.), *The social psychology of female-male relations* (pp. 167–210). Orlando, FL: Academic Press.

Hyde, J. S. (1984). How large are gender differences in aggression? A developmental meta-analysis. *Developmental Psychology*, *20*, 722–736.

Ima, K., & Hohm, C. F. (1991). Child maltreatment among Asian and Pacific Islander refugees and immigrants. *Journal of Interpersonal Violence*, *6*, 267–285.

Intons-Peterson, M. J., Roskos-Ewoldsen, B., Thomas, L., Shirley, M., & Blut, D. (1989). Will educational materials reduce negative effects of exposure to sexual violence? *Journal of Social and Clinical Psychology*, *8*, 256–275.

Jacobson, N. S., Follette, W. C., & Revenstorf, D. (1984). Psychotherapy outcome research: Methods for reporting variability and evaluating clinical significance. *Behavior Therapy*, *15*, 336–352.

Jacobson, N. S., & Truax, P. (1991). Clinical significance: A statistical approach to defining meaningful change in psychotherapy research. *Journal of Consulting and Clinical Psychology*, *59*, 12–19.

Jaffe, P. G., Suderman, M., Reitzel, D., & Killip, S. M. (1992). An evaluation of a secondary school primary prevention program on violence in intimate relationships. *Violence and Victims*, *7*, 129–146.

Jaudes, P. K., & Morris, M. (1990). Child sexual abuse: Who goes home? *Child Abuse and Neglect*, *14*, 61–68.

Jeffords, C. R. (1984). The impact of sex-role and religious attitudes upon forced marital intercourse norms. *Sex Roles*, *11*, 543–552.

Jessor, R., Costa, F., Jessor, L., & Donovan, J. E. (1983). Time of first intercourse: A prospective study. *Journal of Personality and Social Psychology*, 44, 608–626.

Johnson, D. W., & Johnson, R. T. (1989). *Cooperation and competition: Theory and research*. Edina, MN: Interaction Book Co.

Johnson, J. D., & Jackson, L. A. (1988). Assessing the effects of factors that might underlie the differential perception of acquaintance and stranger rape. *Sex Roles*, 19, 37–44.

Johnson, T. C. (1988). Child perpetrators—Children who molest other children: Preliminary findings. *Child Abuse and Neglect*, 12, 219–229.

Johnston, P., Hudson, S. M., & Marshall, W. L. (1992). The effects of masturbatory reconditioning with nonfamilial child molesters. *Behaviour Research and Therapy*, 39, 559–561.

Julien, E., & Over, R. (1984). Male sexual arousal with repeated exposure to erotic stimuli. *Archives of Sexual Behavior*, 13, 211–222.

Kahn, A. S., Mathie, V. A., & Torgler, C. (1994). Rape scripts and rape acknowledgement. *Psychology of Women Quarterly*, 18, 53–66.

Kanin, E. J. (1983). Rape as a function of relative sexual frustration. *Psychological Reports*, 52, 133–134.

Kanin, E. J. (1984). Date rape: Unofficial criminals and victims. *Victimology*, 9, 95–108.

Kanin, E. J. (1985). Date rapists: Differential sexual socialization and relative deprivation. *Archives of Sexual Behavior*, 14, 218–232.

Kanin, E. J., & Parcell, S. R. (1977). Sexual aggression: A second look at the offended female. *Archives of Sexual Behavior*, 6, 67–76.

Katz, R. C. (1990). Psychosocial adjustment in adolescent child molesters. *Child Abuse and Neglect*, 14, 567–575.

Kaufman, J., & Zigler, E. (1992). The prevention of child maltreatment: Programming, research, and policy. In D. J. Willis, E. W. Holden, & M. Rosenberg (Eds.), *Prevention of child maltreatment: Developmental and ecological perspectives* (pp. 269–295). New York: Wiley.

Kazdin, A. E. (1987a). *Conduct disorders in childhood and adolescence*. Newbury Park, CA: Sage.

Kazdin, A. E. (1987b). Treatment of antisocial behavior in children: Current status and future directions. *Psychological Bulletin*, 102, 187–203.

Keating, J., & Over, R. (1990). Sexual fantasies of heterosexual and homosexual men. *Archives of Sexual Behavior*, 19, 461–475.

Keisatsucho [National Police Agency]. (1992, August). *Heisei 4 nen keisatsu hakusho* [Criminal statistics in 1991]. Tokyo: Author.

Kelly, R. J. (1982). Behavioral reorientation of pedophiliacs: Can it be done? *Clinical Psychology Review*, 2, 387–408.

Kendall-Tackett, K. A., & Simon, A. F. (1987). Perpetrators and their acts: Data from 365 adults molested as children. *Child Abuse and Neglect*, 11, 237–245.

Kendall-Tackett, K. A., Williams, L. M., & Finkelhor, D. (1993). Impact of sexual abuse on children: A review and synthesis of recent empirical studies. *Psychological Bulletin, 113*, 164–180.

Kivlahan, D. R., Marlatt, G. A., Fromme, K., Coppel, D. B., & Williams, E. (1990). Secondary prevention with college drinkers: Evaluation of an alcohol skills training program. *Journal of Consulting and Clinical Psychology, 58*, 805–810.

Kleemeier, C., Webb, C., Hazzard, A., & Pohl, J. (1988). Child sexual abuse prevention: Evaluation of a teacher training model. *Child Abuse and Neglect, 12*, 555–561.

Knight, R. A., & Prentky, R. A. (1990). Classifying sexual offenders: The development and corroboration of taxonomic models. In W. L. Marshall, D. R. Laws, & H. E. Barbaree (Eds.), *Handbook of sexual assault: Issues, theories, and treatment of the offender* (pp. 23–52). New York: Plenum.

Knight, R. A., Prentky, R. A., & Cerce, D. D. (1994). The development, reliability, and validity of an inventory for the multidimensional assessment of sex and aggression. *Criminal Justice and Behavior, 21*, 72–94.

Knopp, F. H., Freeman-Longo, R., & Stevenson, W. F. (1992). *National survey of juvenile and adult sex-offender treatment programs & models*. Orwell, VT: Safer Society Press.

Kolko, D. J., Moser, J. T., & Hughes, J. (1989). Classroom training in sexual victimization awareness and prevention skills: An extension of the Red Flag/ Green Flag People program. *Journal of Family Violence, 4*, 25–45.

Kolko, D. J., Moser, J., Litz, J., & Hughes, J. (1987). Promoting awareness and prevention of child sexual victimization using red flag/green flag program: An evaluation with follow-up. *Journal of Family Violence, 2*, 11–35.

Koss, M. P. (1985). The hidden rape victim: Personality, attitudinal, and situational characteristics. *Psychology of Women Quarterly, 9*, 193–212.

Koss, M. P. (1990). The women's mental health research agenda: Violence against women. *American Psychologist, 45*, 374–380.

Koss, M. P. (1992). The underdetection of rape: Methodological choices influence incidence estimates. *Journal of Social Issues, 48*, 61–75.

Koss, M. P. (1993a). Rape: Scope, impact, interventions, and public policy responses. *American Psychologist, 48*, 1062–1069.

Koss, M. P. (1993b, August). *Sex gone wrong: Current perspectives on rape and sexual harassment*. Paper presented at the 101st Convention of the American Psychological Association, Toronto.

Koss, M. P., & Dinero, T. E. (1988). Predictors of sexual aggression among a national sample of male college students. *Annals of the New York Academy of Sciences, 528*, 133–147.

Koss, M. P., & Gaines, J. A. (1993). The prediction of sexual aggression by alcohol use, athletic participation, and fraternity affiliation. *Journal of Interpersonal Violence, 8*, 94–108.

Koss, M. P., Gidycz, C. A., & Wisniewski, N. (1987). The scope of rape: Incidence and prevalence of sexual aggression and victimization in a national sample of higher education students. *Journal of Consulting and Clinical Psychology, 55,* 162–170.

Koss, M. P., Goodman, L. A., Browne, A., Fitzgerald, L. F., Keita, G. P., & Russo, N. F. (1994). *Male violence against women at home, at work, and in the community.* Washington, DC: American Psychological Association.

Koss, M. P., Leonard, K. E., Beezly, D. A., & Oros, C. J. (1985). Non-stranger sexual aggression: A discriminant analysis of the psychological characteristics of undetected offenders. *Sex Roles, 12,* 981–992.

Koukounas, E., & Over, R. (1993). Habituation and dishabituation of male sexual arousal. *Behaviour Research and Therapy, 31,* 575–585.

Kratochwill, T. R., & Mace, F. C. (1983). In M. Hersen, A. E. Kazdin, & A. S. Bellack (Eds.), *The clinical psychology handbook* (pp. 197–221). New York: Pergamon.

Kreitman, N. (1986). Alcohol consumption and the preventive paradox. *British Journal of Addiction, 81,* 353–363.

Krueger, R. F., Schmutte, P. S., Caspi, A., Moffitt, T. E., Campbell, K., & Silva, P. A. (1994). Personality traits are linked to crime among men and women: Evidence from a birth cohort. *Journal of Abnormal Psychology, 103,* 328–338.

Kuhn, T. S. (1970). *The structure of scientific revolutions* (2nd ed.). Chicago: University of Chicago Press.

Kutchinsky, B. (1991). Pornography and rape: Theory and practice? Evidence from crime data in four countries where pornography is easily available. *International Journal of Law and Psychiatry, 14,* 47–64.

Lai, T. A. (1986). Asian women: Resisting the violence. In M. C. Burns (Ed.), *The speaking profits us: Violence in the lives of women of color* (pp. 8–11). Seattle: Center for the Prevention of Sexual and Domestic Violence.

Lalumiere, M. L., & Quinsey, V. L. (1994). The discriminability of rapists from non-sex offenders using phallometric measures: A meta-analysis. *Criminal Justice and Behavior, 21,* 150–175.

Landy, S., & Peters, R. D. (1992). Toward an understanding of a developmental paradigm for aggressive conduct problems during the preschool years. In R. D. Peters, R. J. McMahon, & V. L. Quinsey (Eds.), *Aggression and violence throughout the life span* (pp. 1–30). Newbury Park, CA: Sage.

Lang, R. A., Flor-Henry, P., & Frenzel, R. R. (1990). Sex hormone profiles in pedophilic and incestuous men. *Annals of Sex Research, 3,* 59–74.

Langevin, R., Lang, R. A., Wright, P., Handy, L., & Majpruz, V. (1989). Identifying violence-proneness in sex offenders. *Annals of Sex Research, 2,* 49–66.

Langevin, R., Paitich, D., Hucker, S. J., Newman, S., Ramsay, G., Pope, S., Geller, G., & Anderson, C. (1979). The effect of assertiveness training, Provera, and sex of therapist in the treatment of genital exhibitionism. *Journal of Behavior Therapy and Experimental Psychiatry, 10,* 275–282.

Langevin, R., Wright, P., & Handy, L. (1988). What treatment do sex offenders want? *Annals of Sex Research, 1,* 363–385.

Lanyon, R. I. (1986). Psychological assessment procedures in court-related settings. *Professional Psychology: Research and Practice, 17,* 260–268.

Lanyon, R. I. (1993). Validity of MMPI sex offender scales with admitters and nonadmitters. *Psychological Assessment, 5,* 302–306.

Lanyon, R. I., Dannenbaum, S. E., & Brown, A. R. (1991). Detection of deliberate denial in child abusers. *Journal of Interpersonal Violence, 6,* 301–309.

Lanyon, R. I., & Lutz, R. W. (1984). MMPI discrimination of defensive and nondefensive felony sex offenders. *Journal of Consulting and Clinical Psychology, 52,* 841–843.

Laws, D. R. (1989). *Relapse prevention with sex offenders.* New York: Guilford.

Laws, D. R., & Marshall, W. L. (1990). A conditioning theory of the etiology and maintenance of deviant sexual preference and behavior. In W. L. Marshall, D. R. Laws, & H. E. Barbaree (Eds.), *Handbook of sexual assault: Issues, theories, and treatment of the offender* (pp. 209–229). New York: Plenum.

Laws, D. R., Meyer, J., & Holmen, M. L. (1978). Reduction of sadistic sexual arousal by olfactory aversion: A case study. *Behaviour Research and Therapy, 16,* 281–285.

Laws, D. R., & Osborn, C. A. (1983). How to build and operate a behavioral laboratory to evaluate and treat sexual deviance. In J. G. Greer & I. R. Stuart (Eds.), *The sexual aggressor: Current perspectives on treatment* New York: Van Nostrand Reinhold.

Lazarus, R. S., & Folkman, S. (1984). *Stress, appraisal, and coping.* New York: Springer.

Leitenberg, H., Greenwald, E., & Tarran, M. J. (1989). The relation between sexual activity among children during preadolescence and/or early adolescence and sexual behavior and sexual adjustment in young adulthood. *Archives of Sexual Behavior, 18,* 299–313.

Levenstein, P. (1992). The Mother-Child Home Program: Research methodology and the real world. In J. McCord & R. E. Tremblay (Eds.), *Preventing antisocial behavior: Interventions from birth through adolescence* (pp. 43–66). New York: Guilford.

Levine, M., & Battistoni, L. (1991). The corroboration requirement in child sex abuse cases. *Behavioral Sciences and the Law, 9,* 3–20.

Levine, M., & Perkins, D. V. (1987). *Principles of community psychology: Perspectives and applications.* New York: Oxford University Press.

Linz, D., Donnerstein, E., & Penrod, S. (1987). The findings and recommendations of the Attorney General's Commission on Pornography: Do the psychological "facts" fit the political fury? *American Psychologist, 42,* 946–953.

Lipton, D. N., McDonel, E. C., & McFall, R. M. (1987). Heterosocial perception in rapists. *Journal of Consulting and Clinical Psychology, 55,* 17–21.

Lochman, J. E., & Dodge, K. A. (1994). Social-cognitive processes of severely violent, moderately aggressive, and nonaggressive boys. *Journal of Consulting and Clinical Psychology, 62,* 366–374.

Lochman, J. E., & Lenhart, L. A. (1993). Anger coping intervention for aggressive children: Conceptual models and outcome effects. *Clinical Psychology Review*, *13*, 785–805.

Lockhart, L. (1985). Methodological issues in comparative racial analyses: The case of wife abuse. *Social Work Research and Abstracts*, *21*, 35–41.

Loeber, R. (1982). The stability of antisocial and delinquent child behavior: A review. *Child Development*, *53*, 1431–1446.

Loeber, R. (1985). Patterns and development of antisocial child behavior. *Annals of Child Development*, *2*, 77–116.

Loftus, E. F. (1993). The reality of repressed memories. *American Psychologist*, *48*, 518–537.

Lonsway, K. A., & Fitzgerald, L. F. (1994). Rape myths: In review. *Psychology of Women Quarterly*, *18*, 133–164.

Lore, R. K., & Schultz, L. A. (1993). Control of human aggression: A comparative perspective. *American Psychologist*, *48*, 16–25.

Lott, B., & Maluso, D. (1993). The social learning of gender. In A. E. Beall & R. J. Sternberg (Eds.), *The psychology of gender* (pp. 99–123). New York: Guilford.

Lowry, L. (1993). *The giver*. Boston: Houghton Mifflin.

Maccoby, E. E. (1988). Gender as a social category. *Developmental Psychology*, *24*, 755–765.

Maccoby, E. E. (1991). Different reproductive strategies in males and females. *Child Development*, *62*, 676–681.

MacDonald, G. J., & DiFuria, G. (1971). A guided self-help approach to the treatment of the habitual sex offender. *Hospital and Community Psychiatry*, *22*, 310–313.

Maddahian, E., Newcomb, M. D., & Bentler, P. M. (1988). Adolescent drug abuse and intention to use drugs: Concurrent and longitudinal analyses of four ethnic groups. *Addictive Behaviors*, *13*, 191–195.

Maiuro, R. D., Cahn, T. S., Vitaliano, P. P., Wagner, B. C., & Zegree, J. B. (1988). Anger, hostility, and depression in domestically violent versus generally assaultive men and nonviolent control subjects. *Journal of Consulting and Clinical Psychology*, *56*, 17–23.

Malamuth, N. M. (1983). Factors associated with rape as predictors of laboratory aggression against women. *Journal of Personality and Social Psychology*, *45*, 432–442.

Malamuth, N. M. (1986). Predictors of naturalistic sexual aggression. *Journal of Personality and Social Psychology*, *50*, 953–962.

Malamuth, N. M. (1988a). A multidimensional approach to sexual aggression: Combining measures of past behavior and present likelihood. In R. A. Prentky & V. L. Quinsey (Eds.), *Human sexual aggression: Current perspectives* (pp. 123–132). New York: New York Academy of Sciences.

Malamuth, N. M. (1988b). Predicting laboratory aggression against female and male targets: Implications for sexual aggression. *Journal of Research in Personality*, *22*, 474–495.

Malamuth, N. M., & Check, J. V. P. (1983). Sexual arousal to rape depictions: Individual differences. *Journal of Abnormal Psychology, 92,* 55–67.

Malamuth, N. M., Heavey, C. L., & Linz, D. (1993). Predicting men's antisocial behavior against women: The interaction model of sexual aggression. In G. C. N. Hall, R. Hirschman, J. R. Graham, & M. S. Zaragoza (Eds.), *Sexual aggression: Issues in etiology, assessment, and treatment* (pp. 63–97). Washington, DC: Taylor & Francis.

Malamuth, N. M., Sockloskie, R. J., Koss, M. P., & Tanaka, J. S. (1991). Characteristics of aggressors against women: Testing a model using a national sample of college students. Special Section: Theories of sexual aggression. *Journal of Consulting and Clinical Psychology, 59,* 670–681.

Maletzky, B. M. (1974). "Assisted" covert sensitization in the treatment of exhibitionism. *Journal of Consulting and Clinical Psychology, 42,* 34–40.

Maloney, M. P. (1985). *A clinician's guide to forensic psychological assessment.* New York: Free Press.

Maloney, M. P., & Ward, M. P. (1976). *Psychological assessment: A conceptual approach.* New York: Oxford University Press.

Margolin, G., & Burman, B. (1993). Wife abuse versus marital violence: Different terminologies, explanations, and solutions. *Clinical Psychology Review, 13,* 59–73.

Marlatt, G. A. (1983). The controlled-drinking controversy: A commentary. *American Psychologist, 38,* 1097–1110.

Marlatt, G. A. (1985). Cognitive factors in the relapse process. In G. A. Marlatt & J. R. Gordon (Eds.), *Relapse prevention: Maintenance strategies in the treatment of addictive behaviors* (pp. 128–200). New York: Guilford.

Marlatt, G. A. (1989). Feeding the PIG: The problems of immediate gratification. In D. R. Laws (Ed.), *Relapse prevention with sex offenders* (pp. 56–62). New York: Guilford.

Marlatt, G. A. (1990). Cue exposure and relapse prevention in the treatment of addictive behaviors. *Addictive Behaviors, 15,* 395–399.

Marlatt, G. A., & George, W. (1984). Relapse prevention: Introduction and overview of the model. *British Journal of Addiction, 79,* 261–273.

Marlatt, G. A., & Gordon, J. R. (1985). *Relapse prevention: Maintenance strategies in the treatment of addictive behaviors.* New York: Guilford.

Marlatt, G. A., Larimer, M. E., Baer, J. S., & Quigley, L. A. (1993). Harm reduction for alcohol problems: Moving beyond the controlled drinking controversy. *Behavior Therapy, 24,* 461–504.

Marques, J. K., Day, D. M., Nelson, C., & West, M. A. (1994). Effects of cognitive-behavioral treatment on sex offender recidivism: Preliminary results of a longitudinal study. *Criminal Justice and Behavior, 21,* 28–54.

Marques, J. K., & Nelson, C. (1992). The relapse prevention model: Can it work with sex offenders? In R. D. Peters, R. J. McMahon, & V. L. Quinsey (Eds.), *Aggression and violence throughout the life span* (pp. 222–243). Newbury Park, CA: Sage.

Marques, J., Nelson, C., West, M. A., & Day, D. M. (1994). The relationship between treatment goals and recidivism among child molesters. *Behaviour Research and Therapy, 32,* 577–588.

Marshall, W. L. (1979). Satiation therapy: A procedure for reducing deviant sexual arousal. *Journal of Applied Behavior Analysis, 12,* 377–389.

Marshall, W. L. (1989). Intimacy, loneliness and sexual offenders. *Behaviour Research and Therapy, 27,* 491–503.

Marshall, W. L. (1993). A revised approach to the treatment of men who sexually assault adult females. In G. C. N. Hall, R. Hirschman, J. R. Graham, & M. S. Zaragoza (Eds.), *Sexual aggression: Issues in etiology, assessment, and treatment* (pp. 143–165). Washington, DC: Taylor & Francis.

Marshall, W. L. (1994). Treatment effects on denial and minimization in incarcerated sex offenders. *Behaviour Research and Therapy, 32,* 559–564.

Marshall, W. L., & Barbaree, H. E. (1978). The reduction of deviant arousal: Satiation treatment for sexual aggressors. *Criminal Justice and Behavior, 5,* 294–304.

Marshall, W. L., & Barbaree, H. E. (1984). A behavioral view of rape. Special issue: Empirical approaches to law and psychiatry. *International Journal of Law and Psychiatry, 7,* 51–77.

Marshall, W. L., & Barbaree, H. E. (1988). The long-term evaluation of a behavioral treatment program for child molesters. *Behaviour Research and Therapy, 26,* 499–511.

Marshall, W. L., & Barbaree, H. E. (1990a). An integrated theory of the etiology of sexual offending. In W. L. Marshall, D. R. Laws, & H. E. Barbaree (Eds.), *Handbook of sexual assault* (pp. 257–275). New York: Plenum.

Marshall, W. L., & Barbaree, H. E. (1990b). Outcome of comprehensive cognitive-behavioral treatment programs. In W. L. Marshall, D. R. Laws, & H. E. Barbaree (Eds.), *Handbook of sexual assault* (pp. 363–385). New York: Plenum.

Marshall, W. L., & Eccles, A. (1993). Pavlovian conditioning processes in adolescent sex offenders. In H. E. Barbaree, W. L. Marshall, & S. M. Hudson (Eds.), *The juvenile sex offender* (pp. 118–142). New York: Guilford.

Marshall, W. L., Eccles, A., & Barbaree, H. E. (1991). The treatment of exhibitionists: A focus on sexual deviance versus cognitive and relationship features. *Behaviour Research and Therapy, 29,* 129–135.

Marshall, W. L., Hudson, S. M., & Hodkinson, S. (1993). The importance of attachment bonds in the development of juvenile sex offending. In H. E. Barbaree, W. L. Marshall, & S. M. Hudson (Eds.), *The juvenile sex offender* (pp. 164–181). New York: Guilford.

Marshall, W. L., Jones, R., Ward, T., Johnston, P., & Barbaree, H. E. (1991). Treatment outcome with sex offenders. *Clinical Psychology Review, 11,* 465–485.

Marshall, W. L., & Pithers, W. D. (1994). A reconsideration of treatment outcome with sex offenders. *Criminal Justice and Behavior, 21,* 10–27.

Matarazzo, J. D. (1972). *Wechsler's measurement and appraisal of adult intelligence* (5th ed., enlarged). New York: Oxford University Press.

McCall, G. J. (1993). Risk factors and sexual assault prevention. *Journal of Interpersonal Violence, 8,* 277–295.

McConaghy, N. (1989). Validity and ethics of penile circumference measures of sexual arousal: A critical review. *Archives of Sexual Behavior, 18,* 357–370.

McConaghy, N. (1993). *Sexual behavior: Problems and management.* New York: Plenum.

McConaghy, N., Blaszczynski, A., & Kidson, W. (1988). Treatment of sex offenders with imaginal desensitization and/or medroxyprogesterone. *Acta Psychiatrica Scandinavica, 77,* 199–206.

McFall, R. M. (1990). The enhancement of social skills. In W. L. Marshall, D. R. Laws, & H. E. Barbaree (Eds.), *Handbook of sexual assault: Issues, theories, and treatment of the offender* (pp. 311–330). New York: Plenum.

McGovern, F. J., & Nevid, J. S. (1986). Evaluation apprehension on psychological inventories in a prison-based setting. *Journal of Consulting and Clinical Psychology, 54,* 576–578.

McKibben, A., Proulx, J., & Lusignan, R. (1994). Relationships between conflict, affect and deviant sexual behaviors in rapists and pedophiles. *Behaviour Research and Therapy, 32,* 571–575.

McMahon, R. J. (1994). Diagnosis, assessment, and treatment of externalizing problems in children: The role of longitudinal data. *Journal of Consulting and Clinical Psychology, 62,* 901–917.

McNeil, D. E., & Binder, R. L. (1991). Clinical assessment of risk of violence among psychiatric inpatients. *American Journal of Psychiatry, 148,* 1317–1321.

Mednick, S. A., Gabrielli, W. F., & Hutchings, B. (1984). Genetic influences in criminal convictions: Evidence from an adoption court. *Science, 224,* 891–894.

Megargee, E. I. (1966). Undercontrolled and overcontrolled personality types in extreme antisocial aggression. *Psychological Monographs, 80,* (3, Whole No. 611).

Megargee, E. I. (1984). Aggression and violence. In H. E. Adams & P. B. Sutker (Eds.), *Comprehensive handbook of psychopathology* (pp. 523–545). New York: Plenum.

Meichenbaum, D. (1985). *Stress inoculation training.* New York: Pergamon.

Melton, G. B. (1992). The improbability of prevention of sexual abuse. In D. J. Willis, E. W. Holden, & M. Rosenberg (Eds.), *Prevention of child maltreatment: Developmental and ecological perspectives* (pp. 168–189). New York: Wiley.

Melton, G. B., Petrila, J., Poythress, N. G., & Slobogin, C. (1987). *Psychological evaluations for the courts: A handbook for mental health professionals and lawyers.* New York: Guilford.

Mercy, J. A., Rosenberg, M. L., Powell, K. E., Broome, C. V., & Roper, W. L. (1993, Winter). Public health policy for preventing violence. *Health Affairs,* 7–29.

Meyer, W. J., Cole, C., & Emory, E. (1992). Depo provera treatment for sex offending behavior: An evaluation of outcome. *Bulletin of the American Academy of Psychiatry and the Law*, *20*, 249–259.

Mikkelsen, E. J., Gutheil, T. G., & Emens, M. (1992). False sexual-abuse allegations by children and adolescents: Contextual factors and clinical subtypes. *American Journal of Psychotherapy*, *46*, 556–570.

Miller, S. L., & Simpson, S. S. (1991). Courtship violence and social control: Does gender matter? Special issue: Gender and sociolegal studies. *Law and Society Review*, *25*, 335–365.

Miller, W. R., Benefield, R. G., & Tonigan, J. S. (1993). Enhancing motivation for change in problem drinking: A controlled comparison of two therapist styles. *Journal of Consulting and Clinical Psychology*, *61*, 455–461.

Milner, J. S., & Robertson, K. R. (1990). Comparison of physical child abusers, intrafamilial sexual child abusers, and child neglecters. *Journal of Interpersonal Violence*, *5*, 37–48.

Miner, M. H., Day, D. M., & Nafpaktitus, M. K. (1989). Assessment of coping skills: Development of a situational competency test. In D. R. Laws (Ed.), *Relapse prevention with sex offenders* (pp. 127–136). New York: Guilford.

Mischel, W. (1966). A social-learning view of sex differences in behavior. In E. E. Maccoby (Ed.), *The development of sex differences* (pp. 56–81). Stanford, CA: Stanford University Press.

Moffitt, T. E. (1993). "Life-course-persistent" and "adolescence-limited" antisocial behavior: A developmental taxonomy. *Psychological Review*, *100*, 674–701.

Moffitt, T. E. (1994, August). *Antisocial behavior from childhood to adulthood*. Paper presented at the 102nd Convention of the American Psychological Association, Los Angeles.

Monahan, J. (1981). *Predicting violent behavior: An assessment of clinical techniques*. Beverly Hills, CA: Sage.

Money, J. (1988). *Gay, straight, and in-between: The sexology of erotic orientation*. New York: Oxford University Press.

Morgan, C. L. (1894). *An introduction to comparative psychology*. London: Scott.

Mosher, D. L. (1991). Macho men, machismo, and sexuality. *Annual Review of Sex Research*, *2*, 199–247.

Mosher, D. L., & Anderson, R. D. (1986). Macho personality, sexual aggression, and reactions to guided imagery of realistic rape. *Journal of Research in Personality*, *20*, 77–94.

Mosher, D. L., & Sirkin, M. (1984). Measuring a macho personality constellation. *Journal of Research in Personality*, *18*, 150–163.

Mosher, D. L., & Tomkins, S. S. (1988). Scripting the macho man: Hypermasculine socialization and enculturation. *Journal of Sex Research*, *25*, 60–84.

Mossman, D. (1994). Assessing predictions of violence: Being accurate about accuracy. *Journal of Consulting and Clinical Psychology*, *62*, 783–792.

Muehlenhard, C. L. (1988). Misinterpreted dating behaviors and the risk of date rape. *Journal of Social and Clinical Psychology*, *6*, 20–37.

Muehlenhard, C. L., & Falcon, P. L. (1990). Men's heterosocial skill and attitudes toward women as predictors of verbal sexual coercion and forceful rape. *Sex Roles, 23,* 241–259.

Muehlenhard, C. L., & Hollabaugh, L. C. (1988). Do women sometimes say no when they mean yes? The prevalence and correlates of women's token resistance to sex. *Journal of Personality and Social Psychology, 54,* 872–879.

Muehlenhard, C. L., & Linton, M. A. (1987). Date rape and sexual aggression in dating situations: Incidence and risk factors. *Journal of Counseling Psychology, 34,* 186–196.

Murphy, W. D. (1990). Assessment and treatment of cognitive distortions in sex offenders. In W. L. Marshall, D. R. Laws, & H. E. Barbaree (Eds.), *Handbook of sexual assault: Issues, theories, and treatment of the offender* (pp. 331–342). New York: Plenum.

Murphy, W. D., Haynes, M. R., Coleman, E. M., & Flanagan, B. (1985). Sexual responding of "nonrapists" to aggressive sexual themes: Normative data. *Journal of Psychopathology and Behavioral Assessment, 7,* 37–47.

Murphy, W. D., & Peters, J. M. (1992). Profiling child sexual abusers: Psychological considerations. *Criminal Justice and Behavior, 19,* 24–37.

Murray, D. M., Perry, C. L., O'Connell, C., & Schmid, L. (1987). Seventh-grade cigarette, alcohol, and marijuana use: Distribution in a north central U. S. metropolitan population. *International Journal of the Addictions, 22,* 357–376.

National Adolescent Perpetrator Network. (1988). Preliminary report from the National Task Force on Juvenile Sexual Offending. *Juvenile and Family Court Journal, 39,* 1–67.

Newcomb, M. D., & Bentler, P. M. (1988). *Consequences of adolescent drug use: Impact on psychosocial development and young adult role responsibility.* Beverly Hills, CA: Sage.

Newcomb, A. F., Bukowski, W. M., & Pattee, L. (1993). Children's peer relations: A meta-analytic review of popular, rejected, neglected, controversial, and average sociometric status. *Psychological Bulletin, 113,* 99–128.

Newcomb, M. D., Maddahian, E., Skager, R., & Bentler, P. M. (1987). Substance abuse and psychosocial risk factors among teenagers: Associations with sex, age, ethnicity, and type of school. *American Journal of Drug and Alcohol Abuse, 13,* 413–433.

Newcomer, S., & Udry, J. (1987). Parental marital status effects on adolescent sexual behavior. *Journal of Marriage and the Family, 49,* 235–240.

Newman, J. P., & Wallace, J. F. (1993). Diverse pathways to deficient self-regulation: Implications for disinhibitory psychopathology in children. *Clinical Psychology Review, 13,* 699–720.

Nichols, H. R., & Molinder, I. (1984). *Multiphasic Sex Inventory Manual.* Tacoma, WA: Authors.

Novaco, R. W. (1976). Treatment of chronic anger through cognitive and relaxation controls. *Journal of Consulting and Clinical Psychology, 44,* 681.

Novaco, R. W. (1977). Stress inoculation: A cognitive therapy for anger and its application to a case of depression. *Journal of Consulting and Clinical Psychology, 45*, 600–608.

O'Brien, R. M. (1987). The interracial nature of violent crimes: A reexamination. *American Journal of Sociology, 92*, 817–835.

O'Connell, M. A., Leberg, E., & Donaldson, C. R. (1990). *Working with sex offenders: Guidelines for therapist selection.* Newbury Park, CA: Sage.

Oliver, L. L., Hall, G. C. N., & Neuhaus, S. M. (1993). A comparison of the personality and background characteristics of adolescent sex offenders and other adolescent offenders. *Criminal Justice and Behavior, 20*, 359–370.

Oliver, M. B. & Hyde, J. S. (1993). Gender differences in sexuality: A meta-analysis. *Psychological Bulletin, 114*, 29–51.

Olweus, D. (1979). Stability of aggressive behavior patterns in males: A review. *Psychological Bulletin, 86*, 852–875.

Olweus, D. (1992). Bullying among schoolchildren: Intervention and prevention. In R. D. Peters, R. J. McMahon, & V. L. Quinsey (Eds.), *Aggression and violence throughout the lifespan* (pp. 100–125). Newbury Park, CA: Sage.

Orford, J., & Keddie, A. (1986). Abstinence of controlled drinking in clinical practice: A test of the dependence and persuasion hypotheses. *British Journal of Addiction, 81*, 495–504.

Parrot, A. (1991a). Institutional response: How can acquaintance rape be prevented? In A. Parrot & L. Bechhofer (Eds.), *Acquaintance rape: The hidden crime* (pp. 355–367). New York: Wiley.

Parrot, A. (1991b). Vital childhood lessons: The role of parenting in preventing sexual coercion. In E. Grauerholz & M. A. Koralewski (Eds.), *Sexual coercion: A sourcebook on its nature, causes, and prevention* (pp. 123–132). Lexington, MA: Lexington Books.

Patterson, G. R., DeBaryshe, B. D., & Ramsey, E. (1989). A developmental perspective on antisocial behavior. *American Psychologist, 44*, 329–335.

Patterson, G. R., Reid, J. B., & Dishion, T. J. (1992). *Antisocial boys.* Eugene, OR: Castalia.

Perry, D. G., Perry, L. C., & Weiss, R. J. (1989). Sex differences in the consequences that children anticipate for aggression. *Developmental Psychology, 25*, 312–319.

Peters, S. D., Wyatt, G. E., & Finkelhor, D. (1986). Prevalence. In D. Finkelhor (Ed.), *A sourcebook on child sexual abuse* (pp. 15–59). Beverly Hills: Sage.

Petersen, L., & Brown, D. (1994). Integrating child injury and abuse-neglect research: Common histories, etiologies, and solutions. *Psychological Bulletin, 116*, 293–315.

Peterson, C., Maier, S. F., & Seligman, M. E. P. (1993). *Learned helplessness: A theory for the age of personal control.* New York: Oxford University Press.

Pithers, W. D. (1990). Relapse prevention with sexual aggressors: A method for maintaining therapeutic gain and enhancing external supervision. In W. L.

Marshall, D. R. Laws, & H. E. Barbaree (Eds.), *Handbook of sexual assault: Issues, theories, and treatment of the offender* (pp. 343–361). New York: Plenum.

Pithers, W. D. (1993). Treatment of rapists: Reinterpretation of early outcome data and exploratory constructs to enhance therapeutic efficacy. In G. C. N. Hall, R. Hirschman, J. R. Graham, & M. S. Zaragoza (Eds.), *Sexual aggression: Issues in etiology, assessment, and treatment* (pp. 167–196). Washington, DC: Taylor & Francis.

Pithers, W. D. (1994). Process evaluation of a group therapy component designed to enhance sex offenders' empathy for sexual abuse survivors. *Behaviour Research and Therapy, 32,* 565–570.

Pithers, W. D., Kashima, K. M., Cumming, G. F., & Beal, L. S. (1988). Relapse prevention: A method of enhancing maintenance of change in sex offenders. In A.C. Salter (Ed.), *Treating child sex offenders and victims: A practical guide* (pp. 131–170). Newbury Park, CA: Sage.

Pithers, W. D., Marques, J. K., Gibat, C. C., & Marlatt, G. A. (1983). Relapse prevention with sexual aggressives: A self-control model of treatment and maintenance of change. In J. G. Greer & I. R. Stuart (Eds.)., *The sexual aggressor: Current perspectives on treatment* (pp. 214–239). New York: Van Nostrand Reinhold.

Pollock, N. L., & Hashmall, J. M. (1991). The excuses of child molesters. *Behavioral Sciences and the Law, 9,* 53–59.

Popper, K. R. (1972). *The logic of scientific discovery.* London: Hutchinson.

Prentky, R., & Burgess, A. W. (1990). Rehabilitation of child molesters: A cost-benefit analysis. *American Journal of Orthopsychiatry, 60,* 108–117.

Prentky, R. A., Burgess, A. W., & Carter, D. L. (1986). Victim responses by rapist type: An empirical and clinical analysis. *Journal of Interpersonal Violence, 1,* 73–98.

Prentky, R. A., & Knight, R. A. (1991). Identifying critical dimensions for discriminating among rapists. *Journal of Consulting and Clinical Psychology, 59,* 643–661.

Prentky, R. A., & Knight, R. A. (1993). Age of onset of sexual assault: Criminal and life history correlates. In G. C. N. Hall, R. Hirschman, J. R. Graham, & M. S. Zaragoza (Eds.), *Sexual aggression: Issues in etiology, assessment, and treatment* (pp. 43–62). Washington, DC: Taylor & Francis.

Pribor, E. F., & Dinwiddie, S. H. (1992). Psychiatric correlates of incest in childhood. *American Journal of Psychiatry, 149,* 52–56.

Prochaska, J. O., & DiClemente, C. C. (1983). Stages and processes of self-change of smoking: Toward an integrative model of change. *Journal of Consulting and Clinical Psychology, 51,* 390–395.

Quackenbush, R. L. (1989). A comparison of androgynous, masculine sex-typed, and undifferentiated males on dimensions of attitudes toward rape. *Journal of Research in Personality, 23,* 318–342.

Quinsey, V. L. (1984). Sexual aggression: Studies of offenders against women.

In D. Weisstub (Ed.), *Law and mental health: International perspectives* (Vol.1). New York: Pergamon.

Quinsey, V. L. (1986). Men who have sex with children. In D. N. Weisstub (Ed.). *Law and mental health: International perspectives* (Vol. 2). New York: Pergamon.

Quinsey, V. L., & Earls, C. M. (1990). The modification of sexual preferences. In W. L. Marshall, D. R. Laws, & H. E. Barbaree (Eds.), *Handbook of sexual assault: Issues, theories, and treatment of the offender* (pp. 279–295). New York: Plenum.

Quinsey, V. L., Harris, G. T., Rice, M. E., & Lalumiere, M. L. (1993). Assessing treatment efficacy in outcome studies of sex offenders. *Journal of Interpersonal Violence, 8,* 512–523.

Quinsey, V. L., & Marshall, W. L. (1983). Procedures for reducing inappropriate sexual arousal: An evaluative review. In J. G. Greer & I. R. Stuart (Eds.), *The sexual aggressor: Current perspectives on treatment* (pp. 267–289). New York: Van Nostrand Reinhold.

Raine, A. (1993). *The psychopathology of crime: Criminal behavior as a clinical disorder.* San Diego: Academic Press.

Reed, D., & Weinberg, M. S. (1984). Premarital coitus: Developing and established sexual scripts. *Social Psychology Quarterly, 47,* 129–138.

Reppucci, N., & Haugaard, J. J. (1989). Prevention of child sexual abuse: Myth or reality. *American Psychologist, 44,* 1266–1275.

Rice, M. E., Quinsey, V. L., & Harris, G. T. (1991). Sexual recidivism among child molesters released from a maximum security psychiatric institution. *Journal of Consulting and Clinical Psychology, 59,* 381–386.

Riger, S. (1993). What's wrong with empowerment? *American Journal of Community Psychology, 21,* 279–292.

Riveland, C. (1994). Baseball or public policy. *Journal of Interpersonal Violence, 9,* 424–425.

Rivera, B., & Widom, C.S. (1990). Childhood victimization and violent offending. *Violence and Victims, 5,* 19–35.

Roark, M. (1989). Sexual violence. *New Directions for Student Services, 47,* 41–52.

Roberts, R. E., Abrams, L., & Finch, J. R. (1973). Delinquent sexual behavior among adolescents. *Medical Aspects of Human Sexuality, 7,* 162–183.

Robins, L. N., Helzer, J. E., Croughan, J., & Ratcliff, K. S. (1981). National Institute of Mental Health Diagnostic Interview Schedule. Its history, characteristics, and validity. *Archives of General Psychiatry, 10,* 41–61.

Rodgers, J. L., & Rowe, D. C. (1993). Social contagion and adolescent sexual behavior: A developmental EMOSA model. *Psychological Review, 100,* 479–510.

Rogers, R., & Cavanaugh, J. L. (1983). "Nothing but the truth" . . . A reexamination of malingering. *Journal of Psychiatry and Law, 11,* 443–460.

Rogers, R., & Dickey, R. (1991). Denial and minimization among sex offenders:

A review of competing models of deception. *Annals of Sex Research*, 4, 49–63.

Rohsenow, D. J., & Marlatt, G. A. (1981). The balanced placebo design: Methodological considerations. *Addictive Behaviors*, 6, 107–122.

Rozee, P. D. (1993). Forbidden or forgiven? Rape in cross-cultural perspective. *Psychology of Women Quarterly*, 17, 499–514.

Rubinstein, M., Yeager, C.A., Goodstein, C., & Lewis, D. O. (1993). Sexually assaultive male juveniles: A follow-up. *American Journal of Psychiatry*, 150, 262–265.

Rushton, J. P. (1988). Race differences in behaviour: A review and evolutionary analysis. *Personality and Individual Differences*, 9, 1009–1024.

Russell, D. E. H. (1982). *Rape in marriage*. New York: Macmillan.

Russell, D. E. H. (1988a). The incidence and prevalence of intrafamilial and extrafamilial sexual abuse of female children. In L. E. A. Walker (Ed.), *Handbook on sexual abuse of children* (pp. 19–36). New York: Springer.

Russell, D. E. (1988b). Pornography and rape: A causal model. *Political Psychology*, 9, 41–73.

Ryan, G. (1989). Victim to victimizer: Rethinking victim treatment. *Journal of Interpersonal Violence*, 4, 325–341.

Saunders, E. B., & Awad, G. A. (1988). Assessment, management, and treatment planning for male adolescent sexual offenders. *American Journal of Orthopsychiatry*, 58, 571–579.

Saywitz, K. J., Goodman, G. S., Nicholas, E., & Moan, S. F. (1993). Children's memories of a physical examination involving genital touch: Implications for reports of child sexual abuse. *Journal of Consulting and Clinical Psychology*, 59, 682–691.

Saxe, L. (1994). Detection of deception: Polygraph and integrity tests. *Current Directions in Psychological Science*, 3, 69–73.

Schewe, P., & O'Donohue, W. (1993a). Rape prevention: Methodological problems and new directions. *Clinical Psychology Review*, 13, 667–682.

Schewe, P. A., & O'Donohue, W. (1993b). Sexual abuse prevention with high-risk males: The roles of victim empathy and rape myths. *Violence and Victims*, 8, 339–351.

Scott, D. A. (1992). Early identification of maternal depression as a strategy in the prevention of child abuse. *Child Abuse and Neglect*, 16, 345–358.

Scully, D., & Marolla, J. (1984). Convicted rapists' vocabulary of motive: Excuses and justifications. *Social Problems*, 31, 530–544.

Sears, D. O. (1986). College sophomores in the laboratory: Influences of a narrow data base on social psychology's view of human nature. *Journal of Personality and Social Psychology*, 51, 515–530.

Segal, Z. V., & Marshall, W. L. (1985). Heterosexual social skills in a population of rapists and child molesters. *Journal of Consulting and Clinical Psychology*, 53, 55–63.

Segal, Z. V., & Marshall, W. L. (1986). Discrepancies between self-efficacy predictions and actual performance in a population of rapists and child molesters. *Cognitive Therapy and Research, 10,* 363–375.

Seghorn, T. K., Prentky, R. A., & Boucher, R. J. (1987). Childhood sexual abuse in the lives of sexually aggressive offenders. *Journal of the American Academy of Child and Adolescent Psychiatry, 26,* 262–267.

Serin, R. C., Malcolm, P. B., Khanna, A., & Barbaree, H. E. (1994). Psychopathy and deviant sexual arousal in incarcerated sexual offenders. *Journal of Interpersonal Violence, 9,* 3–11.

Shedler, J., & Block, J. (1990). Adolescent drug use and psychological health: A longitudinal inquiry. *American Psychologist, 45,* 612–630.

Shondrick, D. D., Hall, G. C. N., & Hirschman, R. (1992, August). Laboratory sexual aggression as a function of perceived provocation. In G. C. N. Hall (Chair), *Laboratory approaches to sexual aggression.* Symposium conducted at the 100th Annual Convention of the American Psychological Association, Washington, D.C.

Shoor, M., Speed, M. H., & Bertelt, C. (1966). Syndrome of the adolescent child molester. *American Journal of Psychiatry, 122,* 783–789.

Shotland, R. L. (1989). A model of the causes of date rape in developing and close relationships. In C. Hendrick (Ed.), *Close relationships* (pp. 247–270). Newbury Park, CA: Sage.

Shotland, R. L. (1992). A theory of the causes of courtship rape: Part 2. *Journal of Social Issues, 48,* 127–143.

Siegel, J. M., Sorenson, S. B., Golding, J. M., Burnam, M. A., & Stein, J.A. (1987). The prevalence of childhood sexual assault. *American Journal of Epidemiology, 126,* 1141–1153.

Simon, W. T., & Schouten, P. G. (1991). Plethysmography in the assessment and treatment of sexual deviance: An overview. *Archives of Sexual Behavior, 20,* 75–91.

Slaby, R. G., & Guerra, N. G. (1988). Cognitive mediators of aggression in adolescent offenders: 1. Assessment. *Developmental Psychology, 24,* 580–588.

Sloane, D. M., & Potvin, R. H. (1986). Religion and delinquency: Cutting through the maze. *Social Forces, 65,* 87–105.

Small, M. A. (1992). The legal context of mentally disordered sex offender (MDSO) treatment programs. *Criminal Justice and Behavior, 19,* 127–142.

Smith, E. A. (1989). A biosocial model of adolescent sexual behavior. In G. R. Adams, R. Montemayor, & T. P. Gullotta (Eds.), *Biology of adolescent behavior and development* (pp. 143–167). Newbury Park: Sage.

Smith, E. A., Udry, J., & Morris, N. M. (1985). Pubertal development and friends: A biosocial explanation of adolescent sexual behavior. *Journal of Health and Social Behavior, 26,* 183–192.

Sorenson, S. B., & Siegel, J. M. (1992). Gender, ethnicity, and sexual assault: Findings from a Los Angeles study. *Journal of Social Issues, 48,* 93–104.

Sorenson, S. B., Stein, J. A., Siegel, J. M., Golding, J. M., & Burnam, M. A. (1987). The prevalence of adult sexual assault: The Los Angeles Epidemiologic Catchment Area Project. *American Journal of Epidemiology, 126,* 1154–1164.

Spielberger, C. D., Gorsuch, R. L., & Lushene, R. E. (1970). *Manual for the State-Trait Anxiety Inventory.* Palo Alto, CA: Consulting Psychologists Press.

Spouse battering: The crime wave too often forgotten. (1994, June 21). *Los Angeles Times,* p. 6.

Sprecher, S., McKinney, K., & Orbuch, T. L. (1987). Has the double standard disappeared? An experimental test. *Social Psychology Quarterly, 50,* 24–31.

Steinberg, L., Dornbusch, S. M., & Brown, B. B. (1992). Ethnic differences in adolescent achievement: An ecological perspective. *American Psychologist, 47,* 723–729.

Stermac, L., & Segal, Z. V. (1989). Adult sexual contact with children: An examination of cognitive factors. *Behavior Therapy, 20,* 573–584.

Stevenson, H. C., & Renard, G. (1993). Trusting ole' wise owls: Therapeutic use of cultural strengths in African-American families. *Professional Psychology: Research and Practice, 24,* 433–442.

Straus, M. (1973). A general systems theory approach to a theory of violence between family members. *Social Science Information, 12,* 105–125.

Straus, M. A., & Gelles, R. J. (1986). Societal change and change in family violence from 1975 to 1985 as revealed by two national surveys. *Journal of Marriage and the Family, 48,* 465–479.

Studd, M. V., & Gattiker, U. E. (1991). The evolutionary psychology of sexual harassment in organizations. *Ethology and Sociobiology, 12,* 249–290.

Sue, D. W., & Sue, D. (1990). *Counseling the culturally different: Theory and practice* (2nd ed.). New York: Wiley.

Sue, S., & Okazaki, S. (1990). Asian-American educational achievements: A phenomenon in search of an explanation. *American Psychologist, 45,* 913–920.

Sue, S., & Sue, D. W. (1973). Chinese-American personality and mental health. In S. Sue & N. Wagner (Eds.), *Asian Americans: Psychological perspectives* (pp. 111–124). Palo Alto, CA: Science and Behavior Books.

Swan, H. L., Press, A. N., & Briggs, S. L. (1985). Child sexual abuse prevention: Does it work? *Child Welfare, 44,* 395–405.

Swift, C. (1979). The prevention of sexual child abuse: Focus on the perpetrator. *Journal of Clinical Child Psychology, 8,* 133–136.

Taylor, S. P. (1986). The regulation of aggressive behavior. In R. Blanchard & C. Blanchard (Eds.), *Advances in the study of aggression* (Vol. 2, pp. 91–119). New York: Academic Press.

Thoennes, N., & Tjaden, P. G. (1990). The extent, nature, and validity of sexual abuse allegations in custody/visitation disputes. *Child Abuse and Neglect, 14,* 151–163.

Thornhill, R., & Thornhill, N.W. (1991). Coercive sexuality of men: Is there psychological adaptation to rape? In E. Grauerholz & M. A. Koralewski (Eds.), *Sexual coercion: A sourcebook on its nature, causes, and prevention* (pp. 91–107). Lexington, MA: Lexington Books.

Torres, S. (1987). Hispanic-American battered women: Why consider cultural differences? *Response to the Victimization of Women and Children, 10,* 20–21.

Tracy, F., Donnelly, H., Morgenbesser, L., & MacDonald, D. (1983). Program evaluation: Recidivism research involving sex offenders. In J. G. Greer & I. R. Stuart (Eds.), *The sexual aggressor: Current perspectives on treatment* (pp. 198–213). New York: Van Nostrand Reinhold.

Travis, C. B., & Yeager, C. P. (1991). Sexual selection, parental investment, and sexism. *Journal of Social Issues, 47,* 117–130.

Trepper, T. S., & Barrett, M. (1986). Vulnerability to incest: A framework for assessment. *Journal of Psychotherapy and the Family, 2,* 13–25.

Triandis, H. C., Bontempo, R., Villareal, M. J., Asai, M., & Lucca, N. (1988). Individualism and collectivism: Cross-cultural perspectives on self-ingroup relationships. *Journal of Personality and Social Psychology, 54,* 323–338.

Turk, D. C., & Salovey, P. (1988). *Reasoning, inference, and judgment in clinical psychology.* New York: Free Press.

Turner, C. W., Hesse, B. W., & Peterson-Lewis, S. (1986). Naturalistic studies of the long-term effects of television violence. *Journal of Social Issues, 42,* 51–73.

Tutty, L. M. (1992). The ability of elementary school children to learn child sexual abuse prevention concepts. *Child Abuse and Neglect, 16,* 369–384.

Uba, L. (1994). *Asian Americans: Personality patterns, identity, and mental health.* New York: Guilford.

Udry, J., & Billy, J. O. (1987). Initiation of coitus in early adolescence. *American Sociological Review, 52,* 841–855.

U.S. Commission on Civil Rights. (1992). The plight of battered Asian women. *In Civil rights issues facing Asian Americans in the 1990s* (pp. 174–180). Washington, DC: Author.

U.S. Department of Health. (1964). *Smoking and health: Report of the advisory committee to the surgeon general of the Public Health Service* (PHS Report No. 1103). Bethesda, MD: U.S. Public Health Service.

Vredenburg, K., Flett, G. L., & Krames, L. (1993). Analogue versus clinical depression: A critical reappraisal. *Psychological Bulletin, 113,* 327–344.

Walker, W. D., Rowe, R. C., & Quinsey, V. L. (1993). Authoritarianism and sexual aggression. *Journal of Personality and Social Psychology, 65,* 1036–1045.

Warr, M. (1985). Fear of rape among urban women. *Social Problems, 32,* 239–250.

Weikart, D. P., & Schweinhart, L. J. (1992). High/Scope preschool program outcomes. In J. McCord & R. E. Tremblay (Eds.), *Preventing antisocial behavior: Interventions from birth through adolescence* (pp. 67–86). New York: Guilford.

Welham, C. V. (1990). Incest: An evolutionary model. *Ethology and Sociobiology, 11,* 97–111.

Wells, E. A., Morrison, D. M., Gillmore, M. R., Catalano, R. F., Iritani, B., &

Hawkins, J. D. (1992). Race differences in antisocial behaviors and attitudes and early initiation of substance use. *Journal of Drug Education, 22,* 115–130.

Welsh, W. N., & Gordon, A. (1991). Cognitive mediators of aggression: Test of a causal model. *Criminal Justice and Behavior, 18,* 125–145.

White, G. L., & Mullen, P. E. (1989). *Jealousy: Theory, research, and clinical strategies.* New York: Guilford.

Wille, R., & Beier, K. M. (1989). Castration in Germany. *Annals of Sex Research, 2,* 103–133.

Williams, J. E. (1985). Mexican-American and Anglo attitudes about sex roles and rape. *Free Inquiry in Creative Sociology, 13,* 15–20.

Williams, L. M., & Finkelhor, D. (1990). The characteristics of incestuous fathers: A review of recent studies. In W. L. Marshall, D. R. Laws & H. E. Barbaree (Eds.), *Handbook of sexual assault: Issues, theories, and treatment of the offender* (pp. 231–255). New York: Plenum.

Wolfe, D. A. (1987). *Child abuse: Implications for child development and psychopathology.* Newbury Park, CA: Sage.

Wolff, C. (1994, August 27). Crime trend: Rapists wear condoms. *New York Times,* reported in the *Cleveland Plain Dealer,* p. 2-F.

Wyatt, G. E. (1985). The sexual abuse of Afro-American and white American women in childhood. *Child Abuse and Neglect, 9,* 507–519.

Wyatt, G. E. (1989). Reexamining factors predicting Afro-American and White American women's age at first coitus. *Archives of Sexual Behavior, 18,* 271–298.

Wyatt, G. E. (1994). The sociocultural relevance of sex research: Challenges for the 1990s and beyond. *American Psychologist, 49,* 748–754.

Wyatt, G. E., Newcomb, M. D., & Riederle, M. H. (1993). *Sexual abuse and consensual sex: Women's developmental patterns and outcomes.* Newbury Park, CA: Sage.

Yates, E., Barbaree, H. E., & Marshall, W. L. (1984). Anger and deviant sexual arousal. *Behavior Therapy, 15,* 287–294.

Yoshihama, M. (1994, August). *Violence against Asian Pacific Women perpetrated by male intimates.* Paper presented at the 102nd Convention of the American Psychological Association, Los Angeles.

Yoshihama, M., Parekh, A. L., & Boyington, D. (1991). Dating violence in Asian/Pacific communities. In B. Levy (Ed.), *Dating violence: Young women at risk* (pp. 184–195). Seattle: Seal Press.

Yoshihama, M., & Sorenson, S.B. (1994). Physical, sexual, and emotional abuse by male intimates: Experiences of women in Japan. *Violence and Victims, 9,* 125–138.

Zaitchik, M. C., & Mosher, D. L. (1993). Criminal justice implications of the macho personality constellation. *Criminal Justice and Behavior, 20,* 227–239.

Zane, N. W. S., Sue, S., Hu, L., & Kwon, J. (1991). Asian-American assertion: A social learning analysis of cultural differences. *Journal of Counseling Psychology, 38,* 63–70.

Zillmann, D. (1984). *Connections between sex and aggression*. Hillsdale, NJ: Erlbaum.

Zillmann, D., Hoyt, J. L., & Day, K. D. (1974). Strength and duration of the effect of aggressive, violent, and erotic communications on subsequent aggressive behavior. *Communication Research*, *1*, 286–306.

Index

245